A MODERN INTRODUCTION TO PSYCHOLOGY

BY

REX KNIGHT, M.A.

LATE PROFESSOR OF PSYCHOLOGY IN THE UNIVERSITY OF ABERDEEN

AND

MARGARET KNIGHT, M.A.

LECTURER IN PSYCHOLOGY IN THE UNIVERSITY OF ABERDEEN

UNIVERSITY TUTORIAL PRESS LTD

CLIFTON HOUSE, EUSTON ROAD, LONDON, N.W.1

To

E. P. H. AND J. A. E.

Published 1948
Reprinted 1949
Second Edition 1951
Third Edition 1952
Fourth Edition 1954
Fifth Edition 1957
Sixth Edition 1959
Reprinted 1961, 1964
Seventh Edition 1966

introspection. We can introspect our sensations, and other simple cognitive processes, without much difficulty. But to introspect our emotions and motives is a different matter. If we are in the grip of a strong emotion, such as fear or rage, we are in no state to examine and record our experience. Even the paler emotions cannot really be scrutinised while we are having them, for the mere fact of examining an emotion tends to change its nature. Thus most so-called introspection of emotion is really retrospection. As for our motives, these are notoriously difficult to examine impartially; and some motives, being subconscious, cannot be inspected at all. Moreover, even in the field of cognition, where introspection is less likely to be distorted, it provides data that are at best imprecise. We may be able to state with confidence that the pain of a burn is more intense than the pain of a pinprick, or that our visual image of a rose is clearer than our olfactory image of its scent: but we cannot measure the strength of these sensations or images in ordinary quantitative terms, and say that one is x times as strong as the other. Finally, the data of introspection have the disadvantage of being "private" to the observer. Not only can we not accurately measure a sensation or an image; we cannot observe any sensations or images but our own.

Thus a "science" based mainly on introspection was doomed to failure; and the view gained ground that introspection should be supplemented, and where possible replaced, by the objective study and measurement of behaviour[1] under controlled conditions. This is, broadly speaking, the view of most modern psychologists.

The contrast between the two methods, introspection and behaviour study, is well illustrated by two pieces of research in the psychology of aesthetics which were carried out in the early 1920's. Myers[2] studied individual differences in reaction to music by playing gramophone records to a number of

---

[1] "Behaviour," as here used, is not confined to overt behaviour. It includes also "visceral" or "implicit" behaviour (such as changes in blood-pressure or in the electrical activity of the skin) which requires special instruments for its observation.

[2] "Individual Differences in Listening to Music," *Brit. J. Psychol.,* 1922, **13,** 52.

subjects,[1] and asking them to give detailed introspective reports of their experience. This experiment, though it involved no external observation or measurement, nevertheless yielded some suggestive results. Myers (following Bullough) distinguished four main types of response. (i) The *Intra-subjective Types*, where the subject describes the feelings and sensations aroused in him by the music. For example: "A beautiful thrill, localised in the diaphragm"; "That lovely feeling of depth and goodness coming out of you, like you get in church"; "Sensations of something coming up from the abdomen and surging up to the head." (ii) The *Association Type*, where the subject describes the associations (usually visual) that the music evokes. For example: "Flamboyant architecture"; "A vast procession of people slowly moving . . . with gold-coloured dresses"; "Dancing spray, with the sun on it"; "A dance of savages." (iii) The *Character Type*, where human feelings and characteristics, such as "yearning," "sinister," "jovial," "plaintive," or "vulgar," are ascribed to the music. (iv) The *Objective Type* (most common amongst trained musicians), where the subject analyses and criticises the music as such. For example: "I noticed how he gathered up his climax by syncopation"; "When the second tune came in with the 'cellos, it didn't stand out enough."

At about the same time, an American experimenter, Hyde,[2] was studying behavioural reactions to music by measuring the effect of different types of music on blood-pressure, pulse-rate and the electrical activity of the heart muscles. She made the interesting discovery that, among subjects sensitive to music, these functions tend to be depressed by "sad" music, such as Tchaikowsky's Tragic Symphony, and stimulated by "cheerful" music, such as the Toreador song from *Carmen*.

Clearly laboratory experiment, like introspection, has its weaknesses, the chief of these being a certain artificiality in the laboratory situation. A person who is attached to an electrocardiagraph and a sphygmomanometer, and who knows

[1] Persons taking part in psychological experiments are known as experimental subjects.
[2] "Effects of Music upon Electrocardiagrams and Blood Pressure," *J. Exp. Psychol.*, 1924, 7, 213.

PREFACE TO THE SIXTH EDITION

THIS book is intended primarily for first-year University students, but we hope that it will also be of interest to that growing section of the general public known collectively as "the inquiring layman". In an introductory book of this kind no topic can be treated exhaustively, and our aim has been to give the student a general view of a wide stretch of country, before he sets out to explore it in detail. Aids to more specialised study are provided in the Notes on Reading at the end of each chapter.

The present edition has been substantially revised. The chapter on Brain and Mind has been rewritten, and considerable additions and alterations have been made in other chapters—particularly in those on The Scope and Methods of Psychology, The Nervous System, Association and the Conditioned Reflex, The Ductless Glands, Animal Learning, and Instinct.

Our thanks are due to Professor F. G. Young for valuable advice and assistance in the revision of Chapter V, and to Mr J. W. Osselton for permission to reproduce the EEG records in Fig. 14.

REX KNIGHT.

Aberdeen.   MARGARET KNIGHT.

NOTE TO THE SEVENTH EDITION

The Notes on Reading have again been brought up to date, but as before, where a book has passed through more than one edition, the year of the original edition has been preserved for historical reasons, unless some later edition has contained a substantial revision.

Aberdeen.   MARGARET KNIGHT.

CONTENTS

A MODERN INTRODUCTION TO PSYCHOLOGY

CHAPTER I

THE SCOPE AND METHODS OF PSYCHOLOGY

The Subject-Matter of Psychology

Psychology may be defined as the systematic study of experience and behaviour—human and animal, normal and abnormal, individual and social. This vast field may be divided into six main areas:

(i) *Physiological Psychology*. This involves the study of those aspects of the body—such as the physiology of the brain, the nervous system, the sense organs and the ductless glands—that are most closely bound up with our mental life.

(ii) *The Psychology of Cognition*. This covers the study of those activities of the mind—such as perception, attention, learning, memory and reasoning—that are concerned with *knowledge* as distinct from emotions and desires.

(iii) *Psychometry*. Psychometry is concerned with the measurement of mental and behavioural qualities. The most highly developed branch of psychometry is intelligence testing; but many so-called "special abilities," such as mechanical ability or musical ability, can now be assessed with a fair degree of accuracy, and rapid progress is being made in the measurement of attitudes and personality traits.

(iv) *Animal Psychology*. Important psychological problems arise in connection with instinct in animals, the learning processes of animals, and the sense, if any, in which animals can be said to possess intelligence. Much of our knowledge about the functions of the brain and nervous system has also been gained by experiments with animals.

(v) *Psychology of Motivation*. This branch of psychology is concerned with the innate and acquired motives, both conscious and unconscious, that impel us to action.

(vi) *Social Psychology*.   This branch of psychology is concerned with the ways in which the thought and behaviour of individuals are influenced by the relations to other individuals, and by the structure, institutions, customs and dynamic forces of the various social groups of which they form part.

A second principle of division, which cuts across the preceding one, is the division into *pure* and *applied* psychology.   The "pure" psychologist is concerned simply to increase psychological knowledge.   The applied psychologist is concerned with the application of psychological knowledge to the prevention and cure of mental disorders and to practical problems in education, industry, the upbringing of children, the choice of an occupation, and many other fields.

In the late nineteenth century, when psychology was first recognised as an independent branch of study, psychologists were concerned almost entirely with pure psychology, more especially with the psychology of cognition.   To-day there has been a change of emphasis.   Applied psychology has come into its own; and there has been a rapid development in branches other than cognition, particularly psychometry, social psychology and the psychology of motivation.   With this change of emphasis has gone a rapid development in technique.   Broadly speaking, the last sixty or seventy years have seen the advance from introspection and anecdote to controlled observation and experiment.

Introspection and the Study of Behaviour

Psychology differs from most other sciences in that it employs not only external observation, but also internal observation or introspection.   ("Introspection," as the term is technically used, simply means the observation of one's own mental processes.)   In the early days of psychology, introspection was regarded as the chief source of information about the mind.   Since we all possess minds, it was argued, we all have access to the relevant facts, and all that is necessary is to observe these facts systematically, and to draw conclusions from them.   In pursuit of this aim, however, psychologists soon ran into difficulties, and it became clear that a scientific psychology could not be based wholly, or mainly, on that his reactions are the subject of interested observation, may not respond to the *Liebestod* from *Tristan* for example, in quite the same way as he would in the concert hall. This problem of artificiality dogs many laboratory experiments in psychology; but we shall return to this point later.

The reaction against introspection has gone so far that a school of psychologists, known as Behaviourists, urges that it should be abandoned altogether. These psychologists reject the definition of psychology as "the study of experience and behaviour." Experience, they argue, cannot, by its very nature, be the object of scientific study, and psychology should therefore devote itself to the study of behaviour alone— preferably those aspects of behaviour that can be accurately observed and measured. In the words of John B. Watson (1878-1958), the founder of the Behaviourist school:

> "Psychology, as the Behaviourist views it, is a purely objective, experimental branch of natural science, which needs introspection as little as do the sciences of chemistry and physics. It is granted that the behaviour of animals can be investigated without appeal to consciousness. The position is taken here that the behaviour of man and the behaviour of animals must be considered on the same plane." "It is possible to define [psychology] as 'the science of behaviour' and never to go back upon the definition: never to use the terms consciousness, mental states, mind, content, will, imagery, and the like . . . It can be done in terms of stimulus and response, in terms of habit formation, habit integration, and the like." [1]

In practice, however, Behaviourists have been obliged to "go back on the definition" to some extent, in that they cannot entirely dispense with concepts like "wanting," "attending," "fearing," etc.—concepts which they disparagingly term "mentalistic." But they insist that no use must be made of introspection in identifying or defining these concepts. In the words of E. C. Tolman, one of the leading members of this school, "wanting," "fearing," etc., are "naught but inferred

[1] *Behaviour: an Introduction to Comparative Psychology* (1914), pp. 9, 27.

determinants of behaviour, which ultimately are deducible from behaviour," and if these terms are used at all they must be "identified and defined in terms of the behaviours to which they lead." [1] [2] The non-Behaviourist agrees that when we say that a person "wants" or "fears" something, it is often because we have inferred the fact from his behaviour. But he points out (i) that we should not make the inference if we did not already know by introspection what "wanting" and "fearing" mean, and (ii) that it is seldom possible to infer from a person's behaviour what (for example) he is imagining, dreaming or thinking about: so that if we want to investigate these facts, which are by no means without psychological importance, we can do so only by taking account of what the subject tells us.

Psychologists, after all, are not the only people who employ introspection. Introspective data are constantly used in medicine. The veterinary surgeon knows how much he is handicapped by not being able to ask his patient where the pain is, or whether he feels sick; and no doctor would hesitate to make use of such information from a human patient, even though the pain is "private" to the sufferer, and he cannot express its intensity in mathematical terms. The doctor, of course, does not rely wholly on the subject's account of his symptoms: most of his information is gained by such objective techniques as taking the patient's temperature. But in medicine, introspection and objective measurement go hand in hand, and the same is true in psychology.

The point may be illustrated from one of the most familiar experiments in psychology, the reaction-time experiment. This measures the time that it takes to react to a stimulus. The subject is told to make a certain response (such as depressing a key), when he receives a certain signal (such as a sound or a light). An electric circuit is closed by the occurrence of

---

[1] *Purposive Behaviour in Animals and Men* (1932), p. 3.
[2] Definitions of mental concepts "in terms of the behaviours to which they lead" are known as *operational* definitions. They are by no means easy to frame. For example, we all know reasonably well by intro-spection what it means to ask whether an organism is conscious. But when Tolman tries to define consciousness operationally, the best he can do is to say that it "consists in the performance of a 'sampling' or 'running back and forth' behaviour" (*op. cit.*, p. 206).

the signal, and broken by the subject's reaction; and a chrono-
scope placed in the circuit records in thousandths of a second
the time that elapses between the stimulus and the response.
We might think that this experiment involves only the measurement of behaviour, and that introspective data are unnecessary.
But we should be wrong in this view; for the reaction time of
every subject varies within certain limits, and introspection
reveals that one of the chief factors underlying this variation
is the direction of the subject's attention while he is awaiting
the signal. If his attention is concentrated on the *response*
he is about to make, the reaction is usually quicker than if
his attention is concentrated on the *stimulus*.

But it is unnecessary to labour this point, since the limitations that Behaviourists have imposed on themselves have not,
in practice, proved as severe as might be expected. There
are two reasons for this. First, the Behaviourist's favourite
experimental subject is the laboratory rat, from whom introspections are in any case unobtainable. Second, when they
are experimenting with human subjects, most Behaviourists
to-day make an all-important concession. They say that
speech, after all, is a form of behaviour, and that, therefore,
it is legitimate for an experimenter to take account of what
a subject says—provided he is careful not to describe what
the subject says as his introspections, but to use the term
"verbal report" or "verbal behaviour." This face-saving
device has proved invaluable, since it has given the Behaviourists access to many important facts which a strict interpretation
of their theory would have ruled out of order.

The present book is written from the undramatic but
(we believe) reasonable standpoint that introspection and
behaviour-study each has its advantages and its limitations,
and that a scientific psychology must employ both—allowing
each method, where possible, to counteract the defects of the
other.

The Anecdotal Method

The advance from pure introspection has been accompanied by advance from anecdote to precise observation. In
fields where introspection is obviously impracticable, such as

animal psychology and the study of infants, the older psychologists relied largely on anecdote—that is, on casual and
unsystematic observations, which often contained a large element of unconscious interpretation, and were sometimes made
by untrained observers and reported at second or third hand.
This method has now given way to systematic observation and
measurement under controlled conditions.

For example, the fact that dogs are colour-blind has now
been established by Pavlov, by a series of brilliantly-designed
experiments that are described on p. 53. But in the early
days of psychology (and biology), the whole question was
debated at the anecdotal level. "My puppy has two play-
things, one blue and one red. He constantly prefers the
red one, which proves that he is not colour-blind." The
deficiencies of such evidence are obvious. Even if the
observation is substantially correct, and the puppy's selection
of the red plaything is too frequent to be due to chance, there
remains the possibility that the objects also differ in some
other respect, such as smell, weight or texture, and that it is
this factor, rather than colour, that determines the puppy's
preference.

A once-famous book on animal behaviour by Romanes,[1]
consists largely of anecdotes which had been reported to the
author, and which he repeats and amplifies with what now
appears an extraordinary naïveté. Some examples may be
quoted. The facts alleged are not in all cases as incredible
as the interpretations, which are freely supplied both by the
observers and by Romanes himself.

> "Mrs. Hubbard tells me of a cat . . . which was in the
> habit of poaching young rabbits to 'eat privately in the
> seclusion of a disused pigsty.' One day this cat caught
> a small black rabbit, and instead of eating it, as she
> always did the brown ones, brought it into the house
> unhurt and laid it at the feet of her mistress. 'She
> clearly recognised the black rabbit as an unusual
> specimen, and apparently thought it right to show it to
> her mistress.'"

[1] *Animal Intelligence* (1882). The quotations are taken from
pp. 414-25.

"Mr. W. Brown, writing from Greenock to *Nature* gives a remarkable story of a cat . . . While a paraffin lamp was being trimmed, some of the oil fell upon the back of the cat, and was afterwards ignited by a cinder falling upon it from the fire. The cat with her back 'in a blaze, in an instant made for the door . . . and sped up the street about 100 yards' where she plunged into the village watering trough, and extinguished the flame. 'The trough had eight or nine inches of water, and puss was in the habit of seeing the fire put out with water every night.' The latter point is important, as it shows the data of observation on which the animal reasoned."

The last, and choicest, specimen is again quoted from *Nature*—Romanes remarking that, though the case may appear "almost incredible," he does not feel justified in suppressing it, since "I cannot on the one hand see much room for mal-observation, and on the other hand it is, as I shall show, to some extent corraborated by an independent observation of my friend Dr. Klein."

"Our servants have been accustomed during the late frost to throw out the crumbs remaining from the breakfast-table to the birds, and I have several times noticed that our cat used to wait there in ambush. . . . For the past few days the practice of feeding the birds has been left off. The cat, however, with an almost incredible amount of forethought, was observed by myself, together with two other members of the household, to scatter crumbs on the grass with the obvious intention of enticing the birds."

The reader will find it instructive, at a later stage, to compare these anecdotes with the accounts of experimental investigations into animal behaviour by Thorndike, Köhler, and others, which are given in Chapter XII.

The Methods of Psychology

Psychology is one of the youngest of the sciences, and it would be idle to claim that its experimental technique is as highly developed as that of chemistry or physics, or that no psychologist ever mistakes a hypothesis for an established law, or a brilliant guess for a discovery. Nevertheless, the day is long past when psychology consisted mainly of arm-chair speculation on a basis of unconfirmed data. The method of psychology, it is now realised, is fundamentally the same as that of the other sciences. Essentially, it consists of forming a hypothesis on the basis of observed facts, then trying out the hypothesis by testing its capacity to predict facts as yet unobserved. This trying-out process may take place in a laboratory, in the course of a "field" experiment, or in a psychiatric clinic or mental hospital, where research and treatment go hand in hand.

Laboratory experiments, which often involve elaborate and delicate apparatus, are of special value in physiological psychology (particularly in connection with the sensori-motor functions), and in the detailed study of learning processes. In the laboratory it is possible to isolate the factor to be investigated, to control conditions, and to measure results, with extreme precision. The weakness of the method, as already stated, is a certain artificiality. The situations and activities of the laboratory may bear little relation to those of real life. In certain types of experiment—for example, if we are measuring a subject's reaction-time, or the number of words that he can read in a momentary glance—the artificiality of the situation does not seriously affect the value of the result. But the more complex and interesting forms of human activity do not lend themselves so readily to laboratory measurement.

Consequently, in certain branches of psychology, there is a growing tendency to substitute "field" for laboratory investigations. In social psychology, in particular, field observation and experiment is often the only practicable method, and valuable work has been done on such questions as the structure of urban, rural, ethnic, family and other groups; the effect of different types of group leadership; the cause and effects of different ways of treating children in different societies; the effects of propaganda, etc. In research of this type, conditions obviously cannot be controlled, and behaviour cannot be observed, in such precise detail as in the laboratory; but against this disadvantage is the advantage that the psychologist is observing individuals in real-life situations, and not merely measuring some isolated aspect of behaviour under artificial conditions.

Field investigations are not confined to social psychology, strictly so-called. Valuable experiments have been carried out in schools, on the effects of different methods of instruction, different sizes of class, etc.; and in factories and offices, on the factors underlying morale, or on the effects of different types of incentive, different techniques of supervision and different methods of work. Vocational psychology, also, has developed largely through field work: indeed, the methods of selecting personnel that were developed for the Services during the Second World War might from one point of view be regarded as having derived from a gigantic field experiment, which was amply justified by its results.

An indispensable tool of the experimental psychologist is statistics. Most quantitative measurement in the social sciences involves the calculation of averages and dispersions, so that individual measurements can be evaluated in relation to a norm. Also, since the experimenter has usually to work with a sample drawn at random from a large group or "population," he must use special statistical techniques to estimate the degree of sampling error, and to determine whether a result obtained from a sample can be regarded as holding good for the whole population from which the sample is drawn. This is known as calculating the *significance* of a result. For example, if an experimenter finds a relation between low intelligence and delinquency, or a difference between the scores of boys and girls in a test of mechanical ability, he must use the appropriate statistical techniques to find whether this result is significant—*i.e.* whether it indicates a genuine relationship (or difference), or whether it may be merely an accidental characteristic of the particular groups investigated.

"Schools" of Psychology

Finally, a word is necessary about the various "schools" of psychology. The beginner is sometimes given the impression that psychologists are divided into different and warring factions. But it is easy to exaggerate the amount of disagreement between the different schools. A parallel with medicine may again be helpful. Doctors frequently differ about the treatment of a particular case, or about the value of a new discovery. (At the time of writing, for example, it is possible to get entirely conflicting statements from different doctors about the nature and treatment of "slipped discs.") But this does not alter the fact that there is a large and growing body of established medical knowledge; and to a lesser extent, the same holds good in psychology. There are undoubtedly certain topics on which different schools at present hold different and irreconcilable views. But in many cases the differences between the schools are differences of approach and emphasis rather than of theory. The field of psychology is now so wide that no one can take the whole of it for his province. Some specialisation is essential, and the physiological psychologist, the learning theorist and the Freudian, for example, are not antagonists; it is simply that they are interested in different aspects of the subject.

NOTES ON READING

There are many general textbooks, of a more advanced and detailed kind, to which the present book stands in the relation of a small-scale map to an Ordnance Survey. The most widely used is probably N. L. Munn, *Psychology: The Fundamentals of Human Adjustment* (Harrap: 4th revised ed., 1961.

Other recommended textbooks are D. O. Hebb, *A Textbook of Psychology* (Philadelphia and London, W. B. Saunders: 1958); D. Krech and R. C. Crutchfield, *Elements of Psychology* (New York, Knopf: 1958); R. H. Thouless, *General and Social Psychology* (Univ. Tutorial Press: 4th revised ed., 1958); C. T. Morgan, *Introduction to Psychology* (McGraw Hill: 2nd revised ed., 1961); F. A. Geldard, *Fundamentals of Psychology* (New York, John Wiley: 1962); and Howard H. Kendler, *Basic Psychology* (Methuen: 1963).

Reference must also be made to that psychological classic William James, *Principles of Psychology* (2 vols., 1890), and its one-volume abridgement *A Textbook of Psychology* (1892). Both are now available in paperback editions—the

Principles in Dover Publications (Constable) and the *Textbook* in Torchbooks (Harper). *William James,* a selection from his writings, with an Introduction by Margaret Knight, was published in the Pelican Series in 1950.

Other valuable, and often neglected, sources of information are *Chambers's Encyclopaedia* and the *Encyclopaedia Britannica.* These have the advantage of being accessible in most public libraries, and they contain first-rate articles by leading authorities on many psychological topics. Special mention may be made of the articles in both encyclopaedias on Psychology, Psychoanalysis, and Psychological Tests, in *Chambers's* on Social Psychology, and in the *Britannica* on Comparative Psychology and History of Psychology.

On the experimental side, the standard reference books for the more advanced student, are R. S. Woodworth and H. Schlosberg, *Experimental Psychology* (Methuen: 1955), and S. S. Stevens, *Handbook of Experimental Psychology* (Chapman and Hall: 1951). A valuable textbook of experimental method and design is F. J. McGuigan, *Experimental Psychology: a Methodological Approach* (New Jersey and London, Prentice-Hall: 1960).

Useful textbooks of statistics for the student of psychology are H. E. Garrett, *Statistics in Psychology and Education* (Longmans: 5th revised ed., 1958); P. E. Vernon, *The Measurement of Abilities* (Univ. of London Press: 1940); and R. S. Rodger, *Statistical Reasoning in Psychology* (Univ. Tutorial Press: 1961). Many general textbooks on psychology include chapters on statistical method; the chapter in D. O. Hebb, *A Textbook of Psychology,* will be the most helpful to the beginner. Anne Anastasi, *Psychological Testing* (New York and London, Macmillan: 2nd revised ed., 1961), contains a valuable section on statistics, and M. J. Moroney, *Facts from Figures* (Pelican Books: 3rd revised ed., 1965), can also be recommended.

On the historical side the standard works are J. C. Flugel, *A Hundred Years of Psychology* (Methuen. University Paperbacks: revised ed., 1964), Gardner Murphy, *A Historical Introduction to Modern Psychology* (Kegan Paul: 2nd revised ed., 1949), and L. S. Hearnshaw, *A Short History of British Psychology,* 1840-1940 (Methuen: 1964).

CHAPTER II

THE NERVOUS SYSTEM

The nervous system has often been likened to an elaborate telephone system, by which all parts of the body are kept in communication with the brain and with one another. The analogy is a useful one, although, like most analogies, it becomes misleading if it is pressed too far.

No diagram could give an adequate idea of the complexity of the human nervous system, but the principal nerve-paths are shown in Fig. 1.

It will be seen that nerves from the limbs and trunk run to the spinal cord, and that the spinal cord runs direct to the brain. (The spinal cord is a thick rope of nervous tissue that runs up through the bones composing the spine or backbone.) The brain and spinal cord compose, so to speak, the exchange of the telephone system, and together they form what is known as the Central Nervous System (written CNS). The outlying nerves compose the Peripheral Nervous System.

Reflex Action

The working of the nervous system can best be understood if we start with the simplest form of human behaviour, known as reflex actions. These are the simple involuntary actions that are innate in all human beings, and that we perform, automatically and sometimes quite unconsciously, in response to certain stimuli: for example, "jumping" at a pinprick or a sudden noise; blinking at a bright light; sneezing when something irritates the nose; or jerking the foot if we are tapped beneath the kneecap. These are "muscle" reflexes, but there are also reflexes involving glands. The salivary glands, for example, discharge saliva in response to the taste or smell of food, and the lachrymal, or tear, glands become active if the eye is irritated.

Let us consider a particular example of reflex action. If we flinch from a pinprick, what happens, in physiological

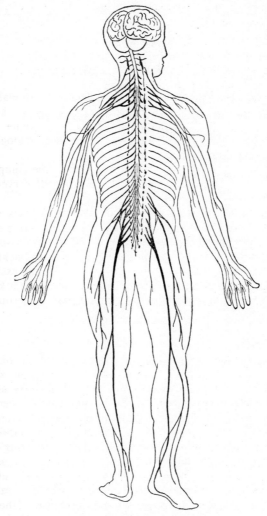

Fig. 1. THE NERVOUS SYSTEM.
The chains on either side of the spinal cord represent the autonomic
system, which is described on pp. 29-31.

terms, is that the pin stimulates the ends of the sensory nerves in its neighbourhood, and a message, or nerve-current, passes up these nerves to the spinal cord (it does not need to go all the way to the brain, as we shall see later). The message is there "put through" to the appropriate motor nerves, and, running down these nerves, produces a sharp contraction of the muscles.

The above description is a very bald one, and the terms "nerve" and "nerve-current" need further elucidation.

Neurons and Nerve-Currents

Nerves, or neurons, are of various kinds. In the peripheral nervous system, there are two main types of nerves: the afferent or sensory nerves, which conduct impulses *to* the

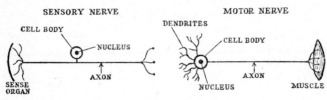

Fig. 2.

"exchange" from the sense organs, and the efferent or motor nerves, which conduct impulses *from* the "exchange" to the muscles. These two types of nerves are shown diagrammatically in Fig. 2.

The *cell-body*, with its nucleus, is the fundamental part, from which all the rest is developed. The *axon* is the nerve-fibre, which in some cases may be several feet long. The *dendrites* are thin, tendril-like growths or arborizations at the receiving end of the nerve. It will be noted that the position of the cell-body differs in the two types of nerve, and that dendrites of the sensory nerve are relatively undeveloped.

The diagram is, of course, purely schematic. Some idea of what a motor nerve actually looks like is conveyed by Fig. 3.

But even this represents only the simplest type of motor nerve. Often the axon divides into branches; or minor nerves, known as "collaterals," run out of the main axon. The complete unit or nerve-cell, consisting of the cell-body, the axon, single or branching, and the dendrites, is called a neuron. It is estimated that the human body contains some 10,000,000,000 neurons.

Besides the sensory and motor nerves, which connect outlying parts of the body with the "exchange," there are

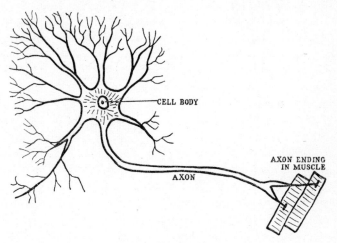

Fig. 3.   MOTOR NEURON.
The axon is relatively very much longer than is shown in the figure.
[Adapted from Woodworth, *Psychology* (Methuen).]

millions of nerves known as internuncial or association nerves, which lie wholly within the CNS. These internuncial nerves are of many different types: three types are shown in Fig. 4. They enable the CNS to fulfil its function as an exchange or central switchboard, by making possible an immense variety of connections between incoming and outgoing impulses.

Every neuron, whether sensory, motor or internuncial, is a complete, self-contained unit. No two neurons ever fuse, but the tip of one nerve makes contact with the dendrites or cell-body of another, and the nerve-current can jump across the minute gap or synapse between them, rather as a spark will jump a gap in an electric circuit.

The exact nature of the current transmitted by the nerve is still unknown. It is almost certainly electrical in nature,

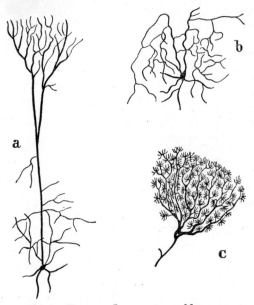

Fig. 4.   TYPES OF INTERNUNCIAL NEURONS.
a and *b* in cortex, *c* in cerebellum. [Adapted from Lovatt Evans, *Principles of Human Physiology* (Churchill), and Fulton, *Physiology of the Nervous System* (O.U.P.).]

but it differs in many ways from an ordinary electric current transmitted by wires. Nerve-current travels far more slowly than electric current, and its passage along the axon is impeded by factors like cold and pressure, which certainly do not affect such conductors as electric-light flex. The most widely accepted view is that nerve-current consists of electro-chemical waves. Stimulation, it is thought, produces a series of

chemical changes, and these in their turn give rise to waves
or pulses of electrical activity in the nerve-fibre. But there is
still much to be learned on this subject.

The mechanism of reflex action is commonly depicted as
in Fig. 5—the impulse from the sensory nerve jumping across
the synapse and activating the motor nerve.

But this is over-simplified in two respects. In the first
place, it is only in a few of the simplest types of reflex action
that sensory and motor nerves make contact directly: usually
they are linked up by internuncial neurons. In the second
place, even the simplest response involves far more than one

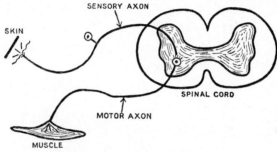

Fig. 5. REFLEX ACTION.

The shaded area, shaped approximately like a butterfly, represents the
"core" of the spinal cord. It consists of a mass of nerve cells, whose
fibres run into the surrounding tissue of the cord.

nerve of each type. Nerves do not really work singly, but
in groups and systems, but, as this fact is not conducive to
the making of tidy diagrams, it tends to be under-emphasised.
Actually, to depict reflex action by Fig. 5 is rather like
describing a tank battle in terms of the movement of one tank
on each side. But, provided its limitations are realised, even
such a description has some expository value.

Synaptic Resistance

There is always a certain resistance to the passage of
nervous impulse at the synapse, and probably an impulse
from one sensory nerve alone is seldom enough to overcome

it.   Usually, impulses must arrive from several sensory nerves simultaneously before the gap is crossed and the motor nerve activated.   An important consequence of this fact is that the effect of a number of stimuli occurring together does not necessarily equal the sum of their effects in isolation.   Fig. 6 illustrates this point.

The sensory nerve *A* activates the motor nerve *a*, and *B* activates *b*.   Neither *A* nor *B* by itself can activate *c*, but when *A* and *B* are stimulated together, *c* is activated.   This fact, as will be seen later, has an important bearing on certain aspects of sense perception.   A related point is that the same stimulus does not always produce the same response.   Synaptic resistance is constantly varying—rising in one place, falling in another—owing to the presence or absence of activity in

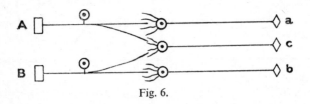

Fig. 6.

surrounding nerve-cells.   So the effect of any stimulus may depend partly on other stimuli that precede or accompany it, as well as on the general state of the organism.

Synaptic Resistance and Learning

Evidence suggests that the frequent passage of nerve-impulse along a particular path tends to reduce synaptic resistance, so that nerve-paths are worn smooth, so to speak, by constant use.   This has an important bearing on so-called "motor" or "habit" memory: it helps to explain how it is that a skilled movement (such as a golf swing or a tennis service) becomes easier and more automatic, the more often we practise it.   It was thought at one time that all learning of the physical kind, and all habit-formation, could be accounted for in this way; and even the more intellectual forms of learning were tentatively explained along similar lines, as the result of the smoothing of nerve-paths in the brain. This view has an attractive tidiness, but unfortunately, even as regards "motor" learning, it is too neat to fit the facts. Taken strictly, it would imply that acquiring a new skill involved learning a completely stereotyped sequence of movements. But when we play a set of tennis, for example, we seldom make precisely the same movement twice. Even in such a relatively unvaried performance as serving at tennis, we do not make exactly similar movements on each occasion: what we repeat is the same characteristic *pattern* or *rhythm* of movements. These facts do not completely rule out explanations in terms of lowered synaptic resistance, but they certainly mean that the explanation must be less simple than was once supposed.

Evolution of the Brain

The most primitive type of nervous system, such as is found in sea-anemones and jellyfish, is very simple, and is distributed more or less evenly over the body. These creatures have no CNS. Their afferent and efferent [1] nerves are linked directly, and not through the medium of internuncial neurons. Reactions are therefore few, and extremely stereotyped. The variety and adaptability of reaction that we find in higher animals is due to the complicated central switchboard of the CNS. Where this is absent, the creature can make only certain fixed automatic responses to stimuli.

A further result of the lack of a CNS is that different parts of the creature show a striking degree of autonomy. The creeping foot of a sea-anemone, for example, will continue, on appropriate stimulation, to creep, even when it has been severed from the body. The stimulus-response connection is made directly, and not through a distant central "exchange."

In creatures such as earthworms, slightly higher in the evolutionary scale, the nervous system is still very diffuse, but we find the rudiments of a CNS in the tendency of nerve-cells to gather together in clusters. These nerve-clusters, or

[1] These terms are better than "sensory" and "motor" when we are dealing with such forms of life as jellyfish, for creatures at this level are probably incapable of sensation.

nerve-ganglia, represent the first step towards the evolution of the brain; for the brain itself is, in essence, nothing more than a vast mass, or system, of neurons.

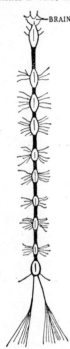

Fig. 7. CENTRAL NERVOUS SYSTEM OF AN EARWIG. [Adapted from Imms, *Social Behaviour in Insects* (Methuen).]

It is only in vertebrates that the brain is obviously the centre of the nervous system. The CNS of most non-vertebrates consists of a chain of nerve-ganglia of the type shown in Fig. 7, the title of "brain" being bestowed, as it were by courtesy, on the ganglion at the head end of the chain. In the simplest vertebrates, nerve-ganglia developed mainly in the spinal cord, and particularly in a swelling at the top known as the bulb or *medulla*. From this small outgrowth of the spinal cord the complex human brain evolved. Fig. 8 shows the brains of creatures at successive stages of development. In the lowest vertebrates, the brain consists mainly of the medulla, the cerebellum, the optic lobes and a rudimentary cerebrum. The last is the most highly-developed part of the brain, on which all the more complex mental processes depend.

The most striking change as we go up the scale is the steady growth in size of the cerebrum, which in man has completely overlaid and covered the older parts of the brain. The difference in size between human and animal brains is obvious, but it is even greater than appears at first sight, because a large part of what is really the surface of the human cerebrum is hidden from view in the deep folds and fissures that developed as its size increased.

The Old Brain

As the cerebrum increases in size, it tends to take over many of the functions of the old brain from which it

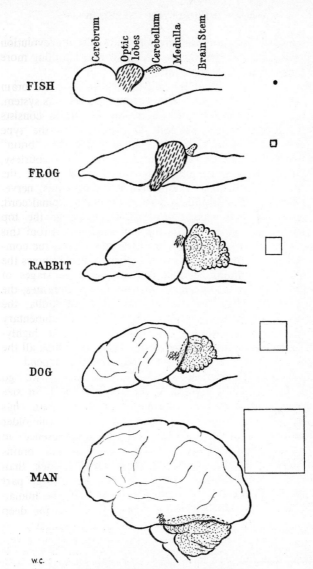

Cerebrum
Optic lobes
Cerebellum
Medulla
Brain Stem

FISH

FROG

RABBIT

DOG

MAN

w.c.

Fig. 8. EVOLUTION OF THE BRAIN.
The relative size of the smaller brains is exaggerated, but the true proportions are shown by the adjacent squares.

developed. This is illustrated by the steady diminution in the relative size of the optic lobes. All that remains of these in the human brain is a small area in front of the cerebellum (shown by cross-hatching), which controls the reflex responses to light. The other functions of vision are controlled by the cerebrum. Even in man, however, the old brain has not been wholly superseded. It still has many functions, though they are relatively humble ones, concerned with our more primitive and automatic activities.[1]

The main parts of the old brain are: the cerebellum; the medulla, or bulb, with its extension, the pons, or bridge; and the thalamus. (For simplicity's sake, the latter term is used to cover the whole thalamic region of the brain, which includes such subordinate structures as the hypothalamus.)

The *cerebellum* deals with posture, muscular adjustment, and the maintenance of balance. It enables us to walk upright without falling, and it controls those complex and delicate muscular adjustments that we make, usually quite unconsciously, when, for example, we throw a stone, kick a football, or pick something up off the floor without overbalancing.

The *medulla* controls many of our continuous and unconscious activities, such as breathing, heartbeat, and the constriction of the arteries.

The *thalamus* in the lower animals is the seat of sense-experience, but in man and the higher animals this function has largely been taken over by the new brain—as has already been illustrated in the case of the optic lobes. Primitive and generalised sensations, such as pain, may be experienced at the level of the thalamus, but sensory discrimination and the more complex forms of sense-experience are possible only through the cerebrum. All sensory nerve-impulses that go to the new brain must, however, pass through the thalamus

[1] The terms "old brain" and "new brain" are practically useful, but they must not be interpreted too strictly, since both the cerebrum and the other parts of the brain contain older and newer structures. For example, the limbic lobes (cf. Fig. 9) of the human cerebrum are biologically primitive; and the human cerebellum contains older parts which control the movements involved, *e.g.* in crawling and swimming, and newer parts which control the movements involved in walking upright.

on their way, and the thalamus probably acts as a sort of intermediate station, from which impulses are directed to the appropriate parts of the cerebrum.

But this does not exhaust the functions of the thalamic area. The hypothalamus is the primary seat of the emotions; and, in conjunction with adjacent areas known as the *basal ganglia* (shown in Fig. 12), it controls those involuntary physical

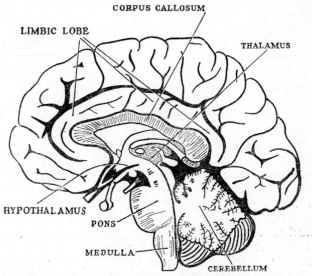

Fig. 9. MEDIAL SURFACE OF THE RIGHT HEMISPHERE.

The *corpus callosum* is a mass of nerve fibres that spans the cleft between the two hemispheres of the brain, and unites them in a single functioning organ.

reactions—trembling, sweating, increased blood-pressure, etc. —by which emotions are expressed.

The hypothalamus also transmits nerve-impulse to adjacent areas of the cerebrum known as the limbic lobes (cf. Fig. 9). These areas mediate the *experience*, as distinct from the *expression*, of emotion; their functions are further discussed on p. 35.

The old brain and the spinal cord together are often known collectively as the *lower centres*, as distinct from the *higher centres* in the cerebrum.   It remains to describe the functions of the spinal cord.

The Spinal Cord and Reflex Action

The spinal cord controls most of the simple reflex actions already described.   The principal exceptions are the "head" reflexes, such as salivation and the reflex responses to light and sound, which are controlled by the old brain.   Reflex actions, which are mere automatic responses to physical stimuli, do not require the co-operation of the cerebrum. This fact has been demonstrated by many well-known experiments.

For example, if a frog is decapitated, and the arteries ligatured, it will survive for some hours—"alive" as a plant is alive, though it can feel nothing, can make no voluntary movement, and has no consciousness or experience of any kind.   But, if we take a small piece of blotting-paper dipped in acid, and with it lightly touch the skin on the frog's right side, the headless creature will draw up its right foot and scratch the affected spot.   If we hold the right foot immovable, then, after a momentary pause, the left foot is drawn up and crossed over, and the scratching performed as accurately as before.   To the onlooker, the impression of conscious, deliberate purpose is almost irresistible; but, in fact, the frog can experience nothing, and the action is as unconscious and involuntary as the beating of its heart.

The fact that reflex action is independent of the cerebrum has been demonstrated in an even more striking way with human subjects.   There are cases on record in which a human being has survived an accident in which the spinal cord has been severed.   Now, all messages from the brain to the limbs must pass by way of the spinal cord: and so, if the cord is broken, all communication is cut between the brain and the parts of the body below the break.   (Reference to Fig. 1 on p. 15 may make this point clearer.)   Thus the patient's legs seem to be completely "dead": he has no sensation from them, and he cannot move them voluntarily.   But, though the leg muscles can no longer take orders from the brain, they are still capable, for a time, of making the simple reflex movements that are controlled by the spinal cord. If a pin is stuck into the patient's foot, he will jerk it away; and if his feet are tickled with a feather, he will squirm and wriggle like a normal person.

The Reflex Arc and Consciousness

But the alert reader will ask how the patient can react to the pinprick or tickling if he cannot feel them. The answer to this question involves an important fact about reflex action.

Some reflexes, such as the movements of the stomach in digestion, are wholly unconscious. In others, such as

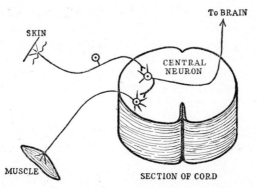

Fig. 10. DOUBLE CONNECTION MADE THROUGH CENTRAL NEURON.

flinching from a pinprick, the stimulus may be accompanied by sensation. In reflexes of the latter type, we naturally tend to think that it is the sensation that produces the response, but in fact this is not so. The sensation accompanies the response, but it plays no part in causing it.

Sensation occurs in such cases, because the sensory and motor nerves "link up" in the spinal cord through the medium of internuncial neurons that connect, along other branches, with the brain. Thus the sensory nerve makes, through the central neuron, a double connection: one with the motor nerve, producing the reflex response, and one with the brain, giving rise to sensation. Fig. 10, though, like all such diagrams, it is grossly over-simplified, gives a rough idea of the facts.

The sensation is thus a mere by-product, or in Huxley's phrase, an "epiphenomenon." If the connection with the brain is severed, so that sensation is abolished, the reflex response can still occur. It may seem hard to believe that, when we flinch from a pinprick, or wriggle in response to tickling, we are doing it automatically, and not because we dislike the sensation: but such is the fact.

The Brain in Reflex Action

A few points remain to be clarified. As we have now learned, reflex action is independent of the brain, in the sense that it can occur when the brain is removed or disconnected. Nevertheless, when the brain and spinal cord are in their normal relation, the brain does exert some indirect influence on reflex action. For reflex responses can be made with greater or less intensity; and, though this intensity depends largely on the stimulus, it also depends partly on the general condition of the cord, which in turn is affected by the brain. When we are "nervy" and "jumpy" we may start violently at a touch which normally we should hardly notice. As was emphasised on p. 20, the same stimulus does not always produce the same response; and in normal (as distinct from brainless) creatures, this applies even at the simple reflex level.

Also, the brain can, within limits, control certain reflex responses—as when we deliberately stifle a sneeze, or force ourselves to keep still when we are pricked by a surgeon's needle. In some cases this control may be achieved simply by throwing into action an antagonistic set of muscles, so that, though the original muscles receive the message from the motor nerves, they cannot act upon it. Probably, however, this is not the whole explanation. There is considerable evidence that the brain can directly inhibit the passage of nerve-current by raising synaptic resistance, though the mechanism of this control is not fully understood.

Extension of Term "Reflex"

Some comment is necessary on the modern use of the term "reflex." Throughout this discussion, the word has been used in its strict sense, to denote an innate and involuntary response that is independent of the higher centres. There is a current tendency, however, to use the term more widely, and to describe any response to a stimulus, at whatever level, as a reflex. This use has led to great confusion. The Behaviourist school, for example, has put forward, as a new and revolutionary theory, the view that all human behaviour is reducible to combinations of reflexes. In the strict sense of the word "reflex," this is obviously false; in the wider sense, it may well be true, but it is in no way revolutionary— it is simply the familiar view that all human behaviour is due ultimately to physiological causes. This view is discussed in Chapter IV.

The Autonomic Nervous System

Before turning our attention to the new brain, which dominates the central nervous system, we must refer briefly to another, biologically more primitive, system, which is partly independent of the CNS. This is the so-called autonomic or vegetative nervous system, which is shown schematically in Fig. 11. The cell-bodies of the autonomic system are collected in ganglia, most of which lie in two chains, joined at the bottom, which run on either side of the spinal cord and strongly resemble the primitive nervous systems of non-vertebrates (cf. Fig. 7 on p. 22). The middle or thoraco-lumbar section of the spinal cord (running roughly from the chest to the pelvis) is directly connected by nerve-fibres with these ganglionic chains.

The ganglia of the autonomic system are all connected with the medulla and thalamus, either directly, or indirectly through the spinal cord. Their main function is to mediate the control exerted by these parts of the old brain over the involuntary internal processes of the body. Nerves of the autonomic system connect with the heart, and with the involuntary muscles of the lungs, stomach, intestines, and other viscera; also with duct glands, such as the lachrymal, salivary and sweat glands, and with certain ductless glands, particularly the adrenals (cf. p. 65). Variations in the activity of these organs produced by emotion, by violent exertion, and by environmental conditions such as temperature change, all

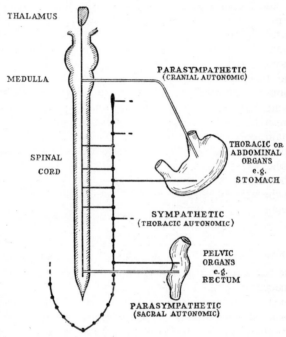

Fig. 11. SCHEMATIC DIAGRAM OF THE AUTONOMIC NERVOUS SYSTEM. Only one side of the ganglionic chain is shown. Connections of the sympathetic system are indicated by single lines, and of the parasympathetic by double lines.

depend on the transmission of impulses via the autonomic nervous system.

Functionally, the autonomic system is divided into two main parts, the sympathetic or thoraco-lumbar division, and the parasympathetic, which comprises the cranial and sacral divisions. The interrelation of the sympathetic and para-sympathetic systems is very complex: it is shown in broad outline in Fig. 11.

Both systems are dominated by the thalamus and medulla, but (i) in the sympathetic division, the medulla and thalamus operate through the thoraco-lumbar section of the spinal cord, and the ganglionic chains with which it is connected, and (ii) in the parasympathetic, they operate either through the nerve-fibres that link them directly with the organs (cranial division) or through the lower parts of the spinal cord (sacral division).

The functions of the sympathetic and parasympathetic divisions are antagonistic, or at least complementary. Broadly speaking, the former system is concerned to marshal energy for instant use in emergency or emotion, and the latter to maintain, conserve and restore the body's resources. More technically, the former is mainly katabolic, and the latter mainly anabolic, in function. Thus the sympathetic system accelerates heart-beat, increases blood-pressure and retards digestion, while the parasympathetic has the opposite effect. The close connection of the sympathetic division with the adrenal glands will be discussed more fully in Chapter V.

The New Brain

The functions of the new brain, or cerebrum, can best be approached through study of the behaviour of creatures in which it is lacking. An animal whose entire brain has been removed or disconnected is described as "spinal," since it has nothing of the CNS left but the spinal cord. A "decerebrate" creature is one from which only the cerebrum has been detached, leaving the lower centres (*i.e.* the old brain and the cord) uninjured. It is not always necessary actually to remove the cerebrum, as it can be effectively "cut off" by severing the nerves that connect it with the old brain.

The effect of decerebration varies greatly with the level of development of the animal. Decerebrate monkeys retain simple reflex responses, but they are unable to walk, are almost completely deprived of sensation, and require the

constant ministrations of human beings to keep them alive.
But in lower animals sensation and movement are still
controlled by the old brain. They are therefore far less
dependent on the cerebrum, and a decerebrate frog, for
example, seems at first sight surprisingly normal. It walks,
hops and swims like an ordinary frog, and in the breeding
season its sex activities are unaffected. But closer observation reveals a significant difference.   The decerebrate frog
reacts to external stimuli, but it shows a complete lack of
spontaneous activity. If food is put in its way, it will eat it;
but, however long it is starved, it will never go and look for
food.   It lets the experimenter manipulate it as he will,
without making any attempt at escape or resistance. It is in
fact a mere automaton, in the sense that it never makes
a spontaneous or unexpected movement.

Similar experiments, giving broadly similar results, have
been performed with other creatures, such as pigeons. The
results show the fundamental difference in function between
the higher and lower centres. The lower centres act only in
response to present stimuli; the higher centres can act from
memory and anticipation.   "Higher" activities, such as
reasoning, are possible only through the cerebrum.

Structure of the Cerebrum

Fig. 12 shows a vertical cross-section of the cerebrum, from
which we see that it is completely surrounded by a layer of
greyish material. This outer layer is known as the *cortex*
(Lat. rind or bark)—or, more popularly, as "grey matter."
Like the internal grey matter of the spinal cord (cf. Fig. 5),
it consists of millions of nerve-cells, whose fibres run down
into the white matter beneath. It is the most highly-
developed and important part of the brain.

The cerebrum as a whole is divided into two homologous
halves or *hemispheres,* of which the right half controls the left
side of the body and vice versa. The cleft between the hemispheres is spanned by the *corpus callosum* (cf. Fig. 9). The
cerebrum is also divided (though in this case somewhat
arbitrarily) into four main divisions or *lobes,* known as the

frontal, parietal, occipital, and temporal lobes. Their location is shown in Fig 13. Both the brain and the spinal cord
are surrounded by *cerebro-spinal fluid*, which also fills certain
spaces in the interior of the brain known as the *ventricles*.

It was at one time believed that different mental "faculties,"
such as memory, will, imagination and the like, were housed
in different parts of the brain. This belief is quite unfounded;
but there is some localisation of function in the cerebrum,
though of a different kind. The different types of sense-

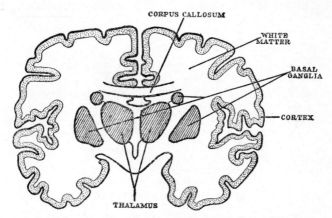

Fig. 12. VERTICAL CROSS-SECTION THROUGH THE HUMAN BRAIN.
(Adapted from Le Gros Clark, "The Anatomical Basis of Sensory
Experience," *New Biology I*.)

organs transmit their messages to different parts of the brain;
and different parts of the brain control the movements of the
different muscles.

Great advances in our knowledge of this subject were made
during the First World War, when it was observed that certain
types of brain-injury produced deafness, other types blindness,
other types paralysis, and so on, even though the ears, eyes
or muscles were undamaged. Much information was gained
in this way, and it was supplemented by other methods; for
example, by tracing nerve-fibres from various parts of the brain

to the sense-organs or muscles (an extremely difficult and delicate process), and by removing, under anaesthetic, various parts of the brains of animals[1] and observing the results. By these means, it was eventually possible to map out the main sensory and motor areas of the brain, as shown in Fig. 13.

There are cases on record in which, when the skull had been opened up by operation or injury, it was possible to stimulate different sensory or motor areas directly, by weak electric currents. We might expect that this would produce acute pain, but, paradoxically, the brain itself is quite insensitive to pain. If the auditory area is directly stimulated, the

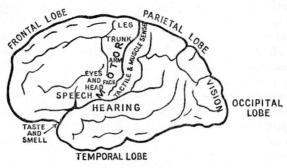

Fig. 13.

[Adapted from Bainbridge and Menzies, *Essentials of Physiology* (Longmans).]

subject "hears" sounds; if the visual area, he "sees" lights moving and flickering; if the motor area, he moves arms, legs, etc., according to the part of the area to which the stimulus is applied. (Incidentally, we know that a hard blow on the back of the head causes us to "see stars." This is direct stimulation of the visual areas by a cruder method.)

[1] It is dangerous, however, to generalise too freely from animals to men, since in animals the sensori-motor functions are still partly controlled by the old brain. Human beings deprived of the visual areas of the cerebrum are completely blind, whereas rats similarly deprived can still make simple visual discriminations, as between a black and a white circle, though they cannot distinguish between a circle and a triangle.

The Cerebrum in Emotion

Recent research has shown that the cerebrum plays an essential role in emotion, as well as in sensori-motor functioning. It was thought at one time that the only "emotion centre" in the brain was the hypothalamus. But it is now realised that, though the *expression* of emotion depends on the hypothalamus, operating through the autonomic nervous system, the *experience* of emotion depends on an area of the cerebrum which is closely connected with the hypothalamus, and which also mediates the sense of smell.

This area comprises the limbic lobes (from Latin, *limbus*, border). It lies, so to speak, on the "floor" of the cerebrum (cf. Fig. 9); its cortex is situated entirely on the inner, or medial, surface of the hemispheres, and is not visible unless they are separated. The area was formerly known as the rhinencephalon (lit. nose-brain), since it was thought to be solely concerned with the sense of smell.

In the evolution of the cerebrum, the limbic lobes were the first to develop, and biologically they are still the most primitive part of the "new brain." (Many authorities, indeed, treat them as part of the "old brain.") Study of their functions is still in its infancy, and it is possible that further knowledge will shed considerable light on the nature and cause of psychosomatic illness.

The Association Areas

The sensory, motor and emotional areas in the brains of the higher animals are very like those of human beings, though they differ in relative size. It is when we go beyond these areas that the fundamental difference between human and animal brains is evident. If we mark off the sensory, motor and emotional areas in the brain of a dog or a monkey, there is not very much left. In the human brain, on the other hand, there is a great deal left, since the areas in question are separated by large intervening areas, known as the *association areas*. It is the greater development of these areas that constitutes the most important difference between human and animal brains.

Essentially, the function of the association areas is to enable us to react to *symbols* as well as to immediate sense-impressions. To take a simple example: a young baby plays with, or reaches towards, a toy so long as he can see it, but if it is taken out of his sight he behaves as though it had ceased to exist. It is not until the age of five months or thereabouts that he turns and looks around for a toy that has been moved behind him. When he does this, he is clearly reacting, not to the *sight* of the toy, but to an *image* or *memory* of it: or, in more physiological terms, his behaviour is mediated, not by an immediate visual stimulus, but by a brain-process which represents a past stimulus. These "symbolic processes," as they are now generally called, take place in the association areas.

Symbols, of which symbolic processes are the neurological counterparts, include images, memories, expectations, and, in fact, everything which the older psychologists denoted by the somewhat vague term "idea." One of the most important differences between men and animals is man's much greater capacity for forming, and using, symbols. It is because our immediate sense-experience is enriched by symbolic functioning that the various sights, sounds, etc., that we experience do not come as separate and disconnected sensations. We regard different sensations, received at different times, as being "of" the same object: we connect something we see to-day with something we heard yesterday, and so on. In brief, we do not merely have isolated sensations, but we relate one sensation to another, we recognise objects, we impute meanings, we remember, and we understand.[1]

To take a concrete example. We hear a friend's voice in the hall, and immediately recognise it—we think to ourselves, "Why, that's John Smith." What has happened, in physiological terms, is that the sound-waves produced by

[1] These statements apply primarily to the human brain. How far, and in what sense, animals can be said to recognise, understand and remember, is a question that will be discussed later. But association areas exist in even the most primitive brains. Indeed, the tiny cerebra of creatures like frogs and fishes consist mainly of association areas, since at this level sensation and movement are still controlled by the old brain.

John Smith's voice affect the ear, and cause a stimulus to be transmitted to certain nerve-cells in the auditory area of the brain. Fibres running from these cells into the association areas rouse into activity other nerve-cells, and produce symbolic processes giving rise to images and memories of such things as the look of John Smith's face, the sound of his name, and so on. The whole combination of primary sensations and symbols called up by association, constitutes the experience that we call "recognising John Smith's voice." [1]

Thus the nerve-cells of the brain are of two main kinds— those which are stimulated directly through the sense-organs, giving rise to sensations, and those which are stimulated indirectly by activity in other cerebral nerve-cells, giving rise to symbols. Around each sensory area is an association area concerned with memories, images, etc., related to that particular sense; and similarly with the motor areas. In addition, there are large unspecialised association areas, that are concerned mainly with the more abstract thought-processes.

"Patterns" of Stimulation

There is an immense amount still to be learned, however, about what happens in the brain when we "remember" and "recognise." One would naturally suppose that, whenever we remember a particular thing or topic, a particular set of nerve-cells is being activated. But many experiments have thrown doubt on this view, and suggest that, at all events where the association areas are concerned, what is fundamental is not so much the *place* as the *pattern* of neural activity.

This conception, which revolutionised many of the accepted views about the brain, received its strongest experimental support from the work of the American psychologist, Lashley (1890-1958). Lashley removed, under anaesthesia, different parts of the cortex of rats that had learned to run a maze, and found that maze-running ability was impaired in proportion to the *amount* of cortex destroyed, irrespective of the

---

[1] This description is over-simplified, but the matter is more fully discussed in the chapter on Perception.

area of destruction. He also found that the brain-injured rats could re-learn the maze, sometimes more rapidly than they had learned it originally; showing that intact parts of the cortex were capable of taking over the functions of the parts that had been destroyed.

These facts led Lashley to formulate the principle of "equipotentiality" or "non-specificity," which asserts that all parts of the association areas are potentially equal in function. On this view, it makes no difference which particular nerve-cells are stimulated: what is important is the *pattern*[1] of stimulation. The same pattern may be set up at different times in different parts of the association areas, just as the same tune may be played in different keys.

It may be dangerous, however, to generalise too freely from rats to other mammals.[2] Experiments with monkeys did not support the view that there is *complete* equipotentiality of function between the various association areas, since damage to the frontal areas of the cortex had considerably more effect on learning capacity than damage elsewhere. Evidence of some considerable degree of specificity was also obtained from studies of human beings who had sustained accidental brain injuries, or who had had parts of the cortex removed by operation. The truth (as so often) probably lies between the two extreme theories of complete equipotentiality and complete specificity.

These findings have an important bearing on the theory of learning and memory, since they appear quite incompatible with the older view (cf. pp. 20-1), which held that all learning could be explained in terms of the smoothing of particular nerve-paths, either in the peripheral nervous system or in the brain. We may one day be able to give a complete physiological account of learning, but the day is not yet, and the account will certainly not be simple.

---

[1] One naturally tends to think of a pattern in spatial terms, but the word is here used in its widest sense to mean simply "a related system." The relations are not necessarily spatial: on Lashley's view, they must be described ultimately in terms of relations (and differences) of electric potential. But the whole theory is still extremely speculative.

[2] There is some truth in the criticism that whereas the older psychology was too anthropomorphic, present-day psychology is too rodentomorphic!

Effects of Damage to Association Areas

Much knowledge about the association areas, as about the sensory areas, has been gained by observation of what happens if they are destroyed or damaged. It is, of course, rare for the association areas to be seriously injured without some corresponding damage to the sensory or motor areas, but such cases have occurred, and they are highly instructive. If, for example, the visual association area is seriously damaged, while the visual area itself is unharmed, the patient's sight is unaffected, but his capacity to form visual images is greatly reduced. Since recognition, understanding and remembering often depend largely on such images, the patient's sensory experience may lose much of its acquired meaning; he may see objects, and hear sounds, but be unable to recognise them. Severe damage to the motor association areas may result in loss of ability to plan and carry out a connected series of movements—even such a simple series, for example, as taking out, filling and lighting a pipe. The person can make the various movements easily enough, as is shown by the fact that he can imitate them if someone else makes them. But he cannot carry them out on his own initiative, for he can no longer see their connection with the desired result.

The Frontal Association Areas

Among the largest of the unspecialised association areas, are the *pre-frontal* or *frontal association areas*, lying in the forepart of the frontal lobes. The pre-frontal areas are directly linked with the thalamus, and their main function seems to be to control and modify the impulses initiated from that region. The pre-frontal areas are involved to some extent in the higher-thought processes, but their main concern is not with purely intellectual operations but with the rational control of behaviour. It is in virtue of these areas of the brain that our behaviour is influenced by symbolic processes, as well as by immediate stimulation: that we do not live wholly in the present, but "look before and after," often resisting a momentary impulse in the light of past experience or for the sake of some distant goal. If such qualities as foresight, initiative, will-power and self-control can be assigned to any particular part of the brain, it must be to the pre-frontal areas.

Self-awareness, also, would appear to have its seat in these regions. It is the impulses initiated in the pre-frontal areas rather than the cruder instinctive strivings of the thalamus, that we tend to regard as composing our "real" selves. As James long ago pointed out in another context, we say that we controlled our fear or resisted the temptation to idleness; but, if the more primitive impulse conquers, we do not say that we controlled our courage or resisted our industry.

One might venture the statement that civilised social life depends, in the last analysis, on the high development of the pre-frontal areas of the human brain. But *corruptio optimi pessima*: lack of harmonious interaction between the pre-frontal areas and the thalamus appears to be the ultimate physiological basis of chronic anxiety, depression and melancholia.

Pre-Frontal Lobectomy in Apes

Experiments with apes have shed much light on the function of the pre-frontal areas. Jacobsen describes the case of a chimpanzee, which went into paroxysms of distress and anxiety when it failed in a delayed reaction test (cf. p. 151). The pre-frontal areas in both hemispheres were removed under anaesthetic, and, when the ape had recovered from the operation, it appeared, in the words of Jacobsen, to have "joined the happiness cult of the elder Micheaux and to have placed its burdens on the Lord." [1]   It still remained interested and co-operative in the test situation, but, when it failed (which it now did far more frequently than before), it showed no emotional disturbance whatever.

Many other experiments have confirmed this general impression. To quote Fulton, lobectomised apes can be distinguished from normal animals by their "restlessness, distractibility, and by a rather fatuous equanimity of spirit that one encounters in a good-natured drunkard." [2]   The

[1] "Influence of Motor and Pre-motor Area Lesions upon the Retention of Acquired Skilled Movements in Monkeys and Chimpanzees." *Res. Pub. of Assoc. Nerv. and Mental Diseases*, **13**, 1934.

[2] *Physiology of the Nervous System* (1943), p. 425.

purely intellectual results of the operation are difficult to assess. Probably the basic effect of leucotomy is to reduce the extent to which behaviour is affected by symbolic processes. Lobectomised apes, as has been said, are extremely distractible: they cannot concentrate on a goal that is distant in space or time, if there is any immediate sensory stimulation to divert them. This distractibility inevitably affects their performance in such tasks as the delayed reaction test. If, however, the test is carried out in semi-darkness, with every possible source of distraction removed, some lobectomised apes give a normal performance. This suggests that lobectomy does not destroy the capacity for symbolic functioning, but that it makes it difficult for such functioning to occur (or to affect behaviour) when distracting direct stimulation is coming in through the sense-organs.

Lobectomy in Human Beings

Occasionally, though rarely, a severe brain lesion has made it necessary to remove surgically the entire pre-frontal areas from the cerebrum of a human being. One of the best known of such cases, that of a New York stockbroker aged about 40, has been described by Brickner.[1] Physically, the patient made a good recovery from the operation, but his whole personality underwent profound changes, of a type similar to those observed in lobectomised apes. He lost all capacity for sustained effort, and became extremely restless and distractible, given to wild boasting, inconsiderate towards others, indecent in speech, and unrestrained in his social behaviour. The intellectual effects of the operation could not be determined, because the patient's intelligence before the operation had not been assessed. After the operation, though he would embark cheerfully on intelligence tests, he soon lost interest and was with difficulty induced to complete them. When allowance was made for this fact, however, his intelligence appeared to be only slightly below average.

[1] *The Intellectual Functions of the Frontal Lobes* (1936), and *Arch. Neurol. and Psychiat.*, 1939, **41**, 580.

Pre-Frontal Leucotomy

Clearly, lobectomy is a desperate measure, and is performed only when the alternative is death. But one of the most dramatic recent developments in human brain-surgery has been the discovery that many forms of insanity can be relieved, or completely cured, by a less radical operation, which involves severing some of the nerve-fibres between the pre-frontal areas and the thalamus. This operation, which was first performed by the Portuguese surgeon, Moniz, in 1935, is known in Great Britain as leucotomy, and in America as lobotomy. It is far less dangerous to life, and less serious in its psychological after-effects, than complete lobectomy.

In the original procedure a small hole was made in each side of the skull, and a long, fine knife, called a leucotome, was inserted through each hole and moved so as to sever some or all of the white fibres (hence "leucotomy," from Greek *leukos*, white) that connect the pre-frontal areas with the thalamus. The technique has now been improved, and the operation is often performed through burr-holes in the top of the skull, by the so-called "open method" which allows the surgeon to see which fibres he is cutting.

Leucotomy is a drastic (though not a dangerous) operation, and in Great Britain it is seldom performed except on patients who would previously have been regarded as incurably insane.[1] The results in such cases are often spectacular. Patients who had been dangerously violent, or in a permanent state of acute apprehension or terror, pass rapidly into a state of carefree happiness. Delusions and hallucinations may persist after the operation, but they cease to be emotionally disturbing, and often fade away gradually with the passage of time.

"Follow-up" of leucotomised patients shows that approximately one-third of the cases make a complete recovery, and are able to resume normal life. A further third are improved, and are often able to go home, though not to return to work. A third are not improved, and of these a small number are made worse.

[1] Since the late 1950's, the operation has been less often resorted to, owing to the great advances in drug therapy.

The outstanding characteristic of most leucotomised patients, when they have recovered from the operation, is their care-free and insouciant attitude towards life, and their complete lack of self-consciousness. There is little evidence of purely intellectual impairment, but there are usually certain characteristic personality defects which stem from reduced symbolic functioning—defects such as irresponsibility, lack of foresight and initiative, and a lack of consideration for others. These weaknesses, however, are far from uncommon among "normal" people; and, as has already been stated, they do not prevent many leucotomised patients from returning to work—even, in some cases, to professional occupations such as accountancy and teaching.

Electrical Convulsant Therapy

Another new treatment that has given striking results is electrical convulsant therapy (commonly abbreviated to ECT). This method originated from the observation of von Meduna that there was an apparent antagonism between epilepsy and the type of insanity known as schizophrenia. When, as sometimes happened, a schizophrenic patient suffered an epileptic convulsion, his mental condition seemed temporarily to be improved. This led von Meduna to try the experiment of inducing convulsion artificially, by injections of cardiazol: a method which has now been replaced by electrical convulsant therapy, in which convulsions are induced by passing an electric current through the patient's brain by means of electrodes, with a potential difference of 150 volts, applied to the temples.

The treatment is highly empirical, since no one knows precisely what physiological effect the convulsions produce. The psychological effect, though it is less permanent, is similar to that produced by leucotomy: so it is probable that the convulsions temporarily obstruct the passage of nervous impulse from the pre-frontal areas to the thalamus, either by raising synaptic resistance or by putting certain neurons out of action. With repeated shocks the temporary interruption may become permanent, but it is noteworthy

that post-mortem examination discloses no changes in the brains of people who have undergone ECT.

The treatment has proved dramatically successful with certain types of insanity, particularly the melancholic psychoses, and it is now being increasingly used, in conjunction with psychotherapy, in the treatment of neurotic[1] conditions, such as anxiety and depressive states (see Chapter XVIII).

Electro-Encephalography

Another important development is electro-encephalography. At all times, even when we are asleep or unconscious, waves or pulses of electrical activity are occurring in the cortex: thus incoming stimuli do not initiate the brain's activity, but merely modify activity that is already going on.

The existence of these "brain waves" was first revealed in 1925 by Berger, who showed that if electrodes are attached to the scalp, the waves can be picked up, amplified and recorded. The resulting record (Fig. 14) is known as an electro-encephalogram (EEG). The first waves to be recorded in this way were the so-called alpha-waves—regular waves of small amplitude, occurring at an average rate of about ten per second. Alpha-waves occur in subjects who are completely relaxed—which in most cases involves lying in a quiet room with closed eyes. The waves are usually banished by any form of attention or effort—for example, if the subject opens his eyes, or, with his eyes still shut, listens attentively to sounds or conversation, or starts to think out a problem or do sums in his head.

When the subject is awake but relaxed, the cortex may be thought of as "ticking over"—relatively inactive at the moment, though ready for action when needed. In these circumstances, probably large numbers of nerve cells are active and inactive at the same time, thus giving a regular rhythm. When the subject attends to sensory (particularly visual) stimuli, or engages in concentrated symbolic activity,

[1] "Neurotic" (as distinct from "psychotic") does not mean "insane." The neurotic patient is failing to adjust to reality, but he has not lost touch with it completely. The psychotic, on the other hand, usually has some form of delusion and hallucination, and is not living mentally in the real world.

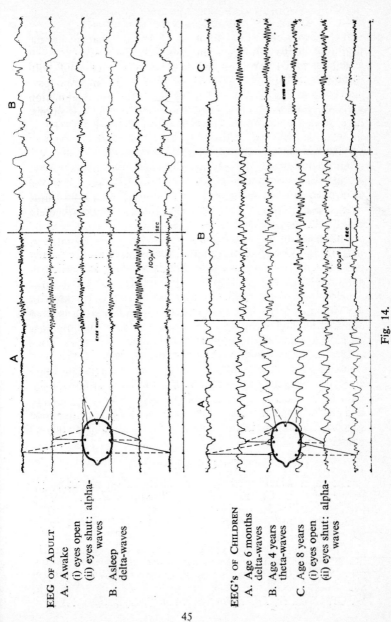

EEG of Adult

A. Awake
  (i) eyes open
  (ii) eyes shut: alpha-waves

B. Asleep
  delta-waves

EEG's of Children

A. Age 6 months
  delta-waves

B. Age 4 years
  theta-waves

C. Age 8 years
  (i) eyes open
  (ii) eyes shut: alpha-waves

Fig. 14.

45

the uniform rhythm stops, and the cells break up into small groups or patterns with different rhythms, which are too faint to be detected by electrodes on the surface of the skull.

When we are deeply asleep or unconscious, large, slow, more-or-less random waves known as delta-waves predominate, and similar waves are almost continuously present in infants. In children aged two to five, more regular waves of smaller amplitude known as theta-waves appear, and are often predominant. In older children and adults, theta-waves are usually an indication of emotional disturbance. They can be evoked in most subjects in the laboratory by a mild irritation like a flickering light or a squeaking slate-pencil, or (a highly effective method with children) by proffering a sweet and then taking it away again.

If, in an older child or an adult, theta-waves are frequently present with no obvious cause, this is a strong indication of emotional instability. It probably indicates some failure of development of the CNS. In a group of sixty-six aggressive psychopaths, forty-three (65 per cent.) were found to have an abnormally high proportion of theta-waves, as against only 10-15 per cent. of the general population.

Electro-encephalography is still relatively in its infancy, and its main value at present is in diagnosing and locating brain abnormalities, such as tumours. But the EEG is now beginning to be used in the diagnosis of psychoneurotic children and adults, some of whom show abnormal EEG records which suggest that their difficult behaviour may be due mainly to constitutional factors.

NOTES ON READING

The most widely-used standard textbook on physiological psychology is C. T. Morgan, *Physiological Psychology* (McGraw-Hill: 3rd revised ed., 1964). J. S. Wilkie, *The Science of Mind and Brain* (Hutchinson: 1953), can also be recommended.

Stimulating and non-technical accounts of recent work in brain physiology are given in *The Physical Basis of Mind*, a series of B.B.C. talks edited by P. Laslett (Blackwell: 1950), and (with special reference to electro-encephalography) in W. Gray Walter, *The Living Brain* (Pelican Books: 1961).

CHAPTER III

ASSOCIATION AND THE CONDITIONED REFLEX

The Principle of Association

Study of the association areas of the brain leads to a once famous principle, the *Principle of Association*. In everyday language, this principle asserts that, when two experiences have occurred together, the occurrence of one will tend to revive the other. More formally: the simultaneous or temporally contiguous occurrence of two mental or neural processes *A* and *B* will result in a tendency for an event or process *A′*, similar to or symbolic of *A*, to evoke an event or process *B′*, similar to or symbolic of *B*.

However the principle is formulated, the facts it denotes are familiar enough. If two things or people are constantly seen together, the sight of one will tend to arouse an idea or image of the other. Emotions, thoughts, memories, etc., may be revived in our minds by the recurrence of some or all of the circumstances in which the original experience arose. To give more specific examples, a particular scent may recall the person who used it; a tune on the wireless may revive a memory of the singing class at school; the taste of ripe figs may recall the sun-warmed garden in which we enjoyed them in childhood; or the sound of a ship's siren revive the exciting sense of starting on a holiday.

Often the ground of the association is not immediately obvious. For example, I start to mow the lawn and at once find myself thinking about *Wuthering Heights*. Why? Because I was thinking about it when I last mowed the lawn a week ago—having then just read a *New Statesman* article on Emily Brontë.

If we are in the habit of attending to our own mental processes, we shall find that inconsequent associations of the latter type are constantly arising. Phrases, images or memories appear in consciousness with no apparent connection with what we are doing or thinking. Sometimes we can

47

track down the association, as in the above example of lawn-mowing and Emily Brontë: but often the source will elude us, since we have forgotten the experience from which the association originally arose.

Lloyd Morgan[1] gives an amusing example of an association which was eventually traced to its source. While listening to a string quintet at a concert, he was puzzled by a persistent image of monkeys climbing on a trellis. Investigation revealed that, as a child of eight, he had several times been present when this particular quintet was rehearsed. On these occasions, he was usually given a picture-book to keep him quiet. The book contained pictures of monkeys climbing on a trellis.

Free-Association

A common form of mental activity is free-association, or reverie. When we are not engaged in "directed" thinking— *i.e.* when we are not thinking about some particular topic or with some particular end in view—we are usually following out trains of association, in which one idea succeeds another with a minimum of logical control. Often we can catch ourselves in the middle of one of these trains of association and trace it to its source—an interesting exercise in introspection. It is possible that processes analogous to free-association are continually going on just below the level of consciousness, but subconscious mental processes will be discussed at a later stage.

Frequency, Recency and Intensity

Many facts about association are still obscure. Why, for example, are certain associations (such as Lloyd Morgan's association of music with monkeys) strong and persistent, while others fade away? The explanation formerly given was that the strength of an association between two ideas is a function, in the mathematical sense, of the frequency, recency and intensity with which they have been associated in the past. (Associated "with intensity" means, broadly speaking,

[1] In *The Animal Mind* (1930), pp. 154-5.

associated to the accompaniment of an "intense" experience, usually emotional.)

For example, if we frequently see a certain person, and, whenever we do so, he is smoking a pipe, we shall tend always to think of him with a pipe in his mouth (frequency). If we have recently been stung by a wasp, we shall be more chary of wasps (*i.e.* more inclined to associate them with pain) than if we have not been stung for some time (recency). If we have spent an intensely anxious half-hour in a hospital waiting-room, the smell of ether and antiseptic may forge an association that will last for years (intensity).

In the 19th century this explanation was generally accepted as adequate, but it has since come under heavy fire from many quarters. And it is obvious that there are many cases of association (often the more interesting ones) to which it can only be applied by an act of faith. Lloyd Morgan's "monkey" association, for example, has neither recency nor frequency in its favour. Therefore, we say, it must have been due primarily to intensity. But there is really no evidence that the association had any particular intensity: we simply have to postulate that it had, to make it fit the theory.

Discussion of this question, however, raises issues with which there is not space to deal. The essential point at the moment is that, whatever the factors involved, we do constantly associate elements in consciousness, not because of any logical or rational connection between them, but simply because they have been connected in some way in our past experience.

The Physiological Basis of Association

In the days before Lashley (cf. pp. 37-8) it was a relatively simple matter to express the facts just stated in terms of cerebral physiology. If two groups of brain cells, it was said, have often been excited together or in close succession, paths of lowered resistance will be formed between them, with the result that excitement of one group tends to produce a sympathetic excitement of the other.

But we have now substituted *patterns* for *groups* of nerve-cells, and the old theory of "association paths," formed by lowered synaptic resistance, must be fundamentally revised, if not wholly abandoned. All of which greatly complicates the attempt to give a physiological account of association. But the fact of association is as obvious as anything in psychology; so for the moment we must be content to accept it in its commonsense formulation, and leave later generations to unravel the mysteries of brain physiology that underlie it.

THE CONDITIONED REFLEX

The formation of associations under controlled, experimental conditions, has been demonstrated with superb laboratory technique by the Russian physiologist, Ivan Pavlov (1840-1936). Pavlov was originally experimenting with digestive secretions in dogs, and he devised a method (which will be described later) for measuring the amount of salivary secretion produced in response to various foods, such as bread, milk or meat. But a difficulty arose, in that many of the dogs were apt to secrete saliva, not only in response to the natural stimulus of the taste or smell of food, but also in response to any stimulus which had been regularly associated with food, such as the sight of the food-pan or the sound of the experimenter's footsteps. This led Pavlov to embark on a new line of inquiry; and in a famous series of experiments he demonstrated that a reflex response can be aroused, not only by the natural ("unconditioned") stimulus (UnCS), but also, in many cases, by a stimulus with which the natural one has been constantly associated—the "conditioned" stimulus (CS).

The experimental procedure was as follows. Pavlov made, under anaesthetic, a small incision in the cheek of each of his experimental dogs, and drew one of the salivary ducts through to the outside. By attaching a thin rubber tube, it was then possible to collect and to measure precisely, the saliva produced. Throughout the experimental periods, the dog was in a sound-proof room, restrained by a light harness which prevented it from moving about. It stood facing a hatchway which could be opened from outside, and through which the food-pan could be slid automatically. Throughout the training period, the dog was unable to see the experimenter.

Shortly before, or just as, the food (UnCS) appeared, some other stimulus such as a bell or a flash of light (CS) was given: and after several repetitions of this procedure, the dog learned to regard the bell or light as a signal for food, and to salivate on the appearance of the signal even though no food was given. Salivation to the signal is thus a "conditioned" response (CR). Similar conditioning processes occur constantly with domestic animals, as when a dog learns to regard outdoor boots as a signal for a walk, or crackling paper as a sign of biscuits.

The Principle of Conditioning

The basic principle of conditioning was originally stated somewhat as follows: if the natural stimulus to a particular response is frequently preceded by another stimulus, the first stimulus (CS) will eventually come to arouse the response originally evoked by the second (UnCS).

It is now realised, however, that this is misleading. The response to the CS *resembles* the response to the UnCS, but it is not identical with it. Pavlov's dogs salivated when they received the food-signal, but they did not chew or swallow; and even the salivation was less copious in response to the signal than it was to the food itself.

A more accurate statement of the principle of conditioning would be: after several pairings of the CS and the UnCS, the CS comes to arouse an *expectancy* of the UnCS, and hence to produce involuntary reactions *anticipatory* of the UnCS. When the UnCS occurs, the expectancy is confirmed, and the conditioned response is strengthened (or in Pavlov's term "reinforced"). Critics who feel that this formulation is too anthropomorphic are referred to the quotation from D. O. Hebb on p. 138.

Conditioned Fear-Responses

Nearly all Pavlov's experiments were carried out on the salivary reflex, which may be classed (with considerable appropriateness) as an "appetitive" response. Later experimenters investigated "aversive" conditioned responses, where a signal, such as a buzzer, was followed by a painful or frightening stimulus such as an electric shock. It was soon evident that fear can be conditioned just as readily as salivation. By the use of instruments such as the sphygmomanometer (which measures blood-pressure) and the plethysmograph (which measures breathing rhythm), it was shown that, after several pairings of buzzer and shock, the dog responded to the buzzer by making the involuntary responses that are characteristic of fear, such as increased blood-pressure, changes in breathing rhythm, and heightened muscular tension.

Physiological Basis of Conditioning

The physiological basis of conditioning is still under active study. Pavlov regarded conditioning as being entirely dependent on the cerebral cortex, and he held that it was due to some kind of link-up between the neural effects of the natural and the conditioned stimulus. This view was confirmed by the fact that a decorticate[1] dog lost all the conditioned reflexes formed before the operation. Recently, however, experimenters have succeeded, with great difficulty, in establishing conditioned responses in decorticate dogs and cats, thus showing that, in these animals at all events, certain rudimentary forms of conditioning can take place at a subcortical level. There can be no doubt, however, that in the intact animal the cortex plays a dominant part in the conditioning process.

Facts about Conditioning

Other important facts revealed by Pavlov's experiments were:

"Neutrality" of CS. Almost anything—a bell, a light, a buzzer, a ticking metronome, a touch on the skin, etc.—can serve as a conditioned stimulus, provided it is relatively neutral—*i.e.* that it does not evoke a strong response on its own account. If a stimulus is painful or frightening, it can seldom become attached to a response other than the natural one. Dogs, for example, cannot be conditioned to salivate

---

[1] Decortication (a less drastic process than decerebration) was performed by gradually washing away the cortex by a strong stream of water. One of Pavlov's dogs survived this operation for $4\frac{1}{2}$ years.

to a loud and alarming noise, or to a sharp electric shock, although they will salivate to a mildly painful stimulus, such as a pinprick.

Stimulus Generalisation. If a response has been conditioned to a particular stimulus, it tends to *generalise* to other, similar, stimuli. Thus if a dog has learned to salivate to a circle, he also salivates to an ellipse; if he has learned to salivate to a note of a particular pitch, he also salivates to notes higher or lower in the scale; and the amount of salivation is greater in proportion as the stimulus resembles the one to which he was originally conditioned.

Discrimination. The dog, however, can readily be taught to discriminate. If he regularly receives food after seeing a circle, but not after seeing an ellipse, he soon learns to salivate to a circle and to ignore an ellipse. This fact provides a valuable technique for testing dogs' powers of discrimination. If we want to know whether a dog can distinguish between two shapes, two colours, or two sounds, we can find out whether he is capable of learning to respond to one and not to the other. For example, when a dog has learned to make the circle-ellipse distinction we can present him with a series of ellipses approximating more and more closely to circles, and see at what point his powers of discrimination break down. Experiments on these lines show that a dog's powers of visual discrimination are much inferior to ours. His powers of auditory discrimination, on the other hand, are much greater. Most of Pavlov's dogs could learn, without difficulty, to respond to one musical note, and not to another which differed from it by only one-eighth of a tone (*i.e.* one-quarter of the difference between adjacent notes on the piano). These experiments have also confirmed the view (which was already fairly well established) that dogs are completely colour-blind.

If a dog is constantly given discrimination problems that are beyond his capacity, he squeals, struggles, and may try to bite the apparatus, and loses the ability to make even simple discriminations. He becomes, in fact, a canine neurotic, and must be treated by rest and sedatives.

Extinction. When a conditioned response has been established, it can be extinguished, temporarily at least, by repeatedly giving the CS without reinforcement—*i.e.* without following it by the UnCS. The results of one such experiment are shown in the table below. The CS—a metronome—was given at three-minute intervals without being followed by food.

Trial	Drops Secreted
1	13
2	7
3	5
4	6
5	3
6	2·5
7	0
8	0

In such cases, however, the reflex has been merely inhibited, not destroyed. If the stimulus is given again after a few hours' rest, a few drops are secreted ("spontaneous recovery"), and if the response is then reinforced it returns almost immediately to normal. Many series of non-reinforced trials are necessary before a well-established conditioned response can be extinguished to the point at which there is no spontaneous recovery; and, even then, if reinforcement is given, the animal re-learns the response in far less time than he took to learn it originally.

Delayed Conditioned Response. Pavlov found that, if the conditioned stimulus was continued—*e.g.* the bell kept ringing or the metronome ticking—for three minutes before food was given, the dogs soon learned to salivate, not at the first sound of the bell, but after it had been ringing for exactly three minutes. Again, if the bell was rung, and stopped, and there was a three-minute interval before food was given, the dogs salivated when precisely this interval had elapsed. In some cases, time-intervals up to half an hour were estimated with complete accuracy.

Summation of Stimuli. If a dog has acquired a conditioned salivary response to a bell, and also to a light, and the two stimuli are then given together, the response (in terms of drops of saliva secreted) is markedly greater than to either stimulus given alone. It is not, however, equal to the *sum* of the responses to the two stimuli given alone. This provides a further illustration of the fact, emphasised on p. 20, that when a number of stimuli occur together, their combined effect is not necessarily equal to the sum of their separate effects.

Reinforcement and Reward

As has already been stated, Pavlov used the term "rein-forcement" to denote the following of the CS by the UnCS, and the consequent strengthening of the CR. Among present-day psychologists, however, there is a tendency to use "rein-forcement" as though it were synonymous with "reward." This use is misleading, and has led to great confusion in some of the more advanced discussions of learning theory.

Prima facie, it does not sound unreasonable to say that the dog is rewarded for salivating by receiving food. But a moment's reflection shows that the term "reward" is not really appropriate, for food-getting is not *dependent* on saliva-tion; the dog receives food whether he salivates or not, and regardless of the amount of saliva produced. But it is in connection with fear-conditioning that the error of equating reinforcement with reward becomes most obvious. If a dog repeatedly undergoes, say, a buzzer-shock sequence, he soon makes involuntary fear-responses at the sound of the buzzer. These responses are reinforced when the shock occurs: but they are certainly not rewarded.

Instrumental Conditioning

It may seem strange that such an apparently obvious fact should be overlooked, but the issues have been somewhat tangled through the introduction, by later workers, of the concept of *instrumental conditioning*. Animals trained in conditions in which they are free to move about can learn not only to make involuntary reactions indicative of food or shock expectancy, but also to make voluntary movements designed to get food or to avoid shock. In one well-known apparatus, the Skinner box, the laboratory rat learns to press a lever which causes a food-pellet to drop into a pan. In another type of apparatus, an animal put into a box with an electrified floor presses a lever which switches off the electric current. Cases of this kind, where the response actually *produces* the UnCS (or, in the case of fear-conditioning, terminates or avoids it) are known as *instrumental conditioning*, to distinguish them from *classical conditioning* of the type described by Pavlov. Following Woodworth, we may sum up the distinction in commonsense terms: by classical conditioning the animal learns what to expect, and by instrumental conditioning it learns what to do about it.[1]

Instrumental conditioning clearly depends on the reward of obtaining food or avoiding shock. But it is unnecessary, and indeed highly misleading, to invoke the concept of reward in connection with classical conditioning—which, as has been stated, is essentially a form of association, whereby one stimulus becomes a signal or sign for another. In the writer's view, the term "instrumental conditioning" has been a source of confusion: the type of behaviour it is used to denote is really a form of trial-and-error learning, and is best treated under that head.

Conditioning of Human Subjects

Many other workers have experimented along Pavlovian lines, with both animal and human subjects. Watson, in America, carried out a famous series of experiments on the conditioning of fear-responses in children. He first found by experiment that instinctive fear-reactions are called out in infants by three types of experience only—namely pain, the sensation of being dropped, and sudden loud noises. He then showed that anything frequently associated with any of these experiences will become a conditioned stimulus to the fear-response.

Watson's first subject was an eleven-month-old infant, Albert B. Before the experiment, Albert had played confidently with rabbits, mice, rats, and various other fauna. The conditioning procedure may be described in Watson's own words. On the first day of the experiment,

> "The white rat, which he had played with for weeks, was suddenly taken from the basket (the usual routine)

[1] *Experimental Psychology* (1955), p. 554.

and presented to Albert. He began to reach for the rat with his left hand. Just as his hand touched the animal [a steel bar was struck by a hammer] immediately behind his head. The infant jumped violently and fell forward, burying his face in the mattress. He did not cry, however."

A week later, after several repetitions of this procedure, the rat was presented alone.

"The instant the rat was shown, the baby began to cry. Almost immediately he turned sharply to the left, fell over, raised himself on all fours and began to crawl away so rapidly that he was with difficulty caught before he reached the edge of the mattress." [1]

Albert's conditioning to rats had spread to many other objects of a furry kind. He now showed more or less marked negative reactions to a rabbit, a dog, a fur coat, and a package of cotton wool.

Fortunately, acquired fear-reactions of this type can be fairly rapidly deconditioned. Watson[2] describes the case of a three-year-old boy, Peter, whose fear of rabbits was removed by putting a rabbit (safely enclosed in a wire cage) at one end of a long hall, at the other end of which Peter was enjoying a meal. As the meal proceeded the rabbit was brought gradually nearer, but the process stopped as soon as Peter showed any signs of disturbance. The treatment continued for some time, the rabbit coming progressively nearer each day, until finally Peter was so thoroughly deconditioned that he would lift food to his mouth with one hand, and fondle the rabbit with the other.

Human adults, being more sophisticated, are usually less suitable subjects for conditioning experiments. Certain responses, however, can be fairly readily conditioned, among them the eye-blink response. If a sound-signal is immediately followed by a puff of air to the eyeball, causing blinking, most subjects develop the conditioned response of blinking to the sound. Still more successful results have been obtained in conditioning the galvanic skin response (GSR), which is a

[1] *Psychologies of* 1925, pp. 51-4.   [2] *Behaviorism* (1925), pp. 137-8.

very sensitive index of emotional tension. The GSR is measured by an instrument called the psychogalvanometer. The underlying principle is that any increase in emotional tension, whether of a pleasant or an unpleasant kind, is accompanied by increased activity of the sweat glands. Damp skin is a better conductor of electricity than dry skin, hence an emotional stimulus is usually followed, after an interval of 1 to $1\frac{1}{2}$ seconds, by a drop in the resistance of the body to the passage of an electric current. In a typical GSR experiment the subject is put in circuit with the psychogalvanometer, and is presented with various stimuli, while a pen moving over a revolving drum records the fluctuations from moment to moment in the electrical resistance of his body.[1] If a subject is repeatedly given a signal (say, a light) followed by an electric shock that is strong enough to be painful, he almost invariably develops a conditioned GSR to the light.

Man's command of language, however, and his greater capacity to be influenced by symbolic processes, make it impossible to get the same clear-cut and consistent results from human as from animal subjects. For example, if, when the conditioned GSR to the light has been well established, the experimenter says, "OK, no more shocks—I'm just going to try out the light now," the response to the light often ceases entirely. Man is less "stimulus-bound" than the animals—a fact which is sometimes inconvenient to laboratory psychologists, but which helps to explain his predominance in the animal world.

NOTES ON READING

Full accounts of Pavlov's experiments are contained in I. P. Pavlov, *Conditioned Reflexes* (Oxford Univ. Press: 1937), and in I. P. Frolov, *Pavlov and His School* (Kegan Paul: 1937). A valuable selection from Pavlov's writings is given in *I. P. Pavlov: Selected Works* (Moscow, Foreign Languages Publishing House: 1955), obtainable in London from I. R. Maxwell and Co.

[1] The so-called "lie detector" usually consists of a psychogalvanometer, working in conjunction with a sphygmomanometer, a plethysmograph, and other pieces of apparatus that record involuntary bodily changes.

CHAPTER IV

BRAIN AND MIND

In the early days of psychology, frequent reference was made to so-called "mental faculties," such as the memory, the imagination, and the will. These faculties were assumed to be mental entities of some rather obscure kind, and it was supposed that we remembered with our memories, imagined with our imaginations, and so on. The reader who has followed the chapter on the Nervous System can see how this misrepresents the facts. Terms like "the will," "the memory," etc., denote functions, not entities: they belong to the same logical category as terms like "the digestion". If I say "my digestion is out of order" I do not suppose that there is an actual entity called "my digestion" to which the statement refers; "my digestion" is simply a convenient shorthand term for "my digestive processes." Similarly, "the memory," "the imagination," etc., are convenient shorthand terms for processes of remembering and imagining.

There can be little doubt that, *mutatis mutandis*, the same analysis must be given of words like "consciousness" and "the mind." These, too, denote functions and not entities. "The mind," in other words, is not something which lies behind our mental processes, or in which mental processes occur. It is simply a convenient term to denote these processes.

This does not imply that terms like "the mind" or "the memory" should no longer be used. Like "the digestion" they are convenient expressions and save much circumlocution, but it is important that we should not misunderstand their logical function.

To-day, nearly all psychologists (and, for that matter, nearly all biological scientists) accept, tacitly or explicitly, the view that mental processes depend on processes in the brain.[1] The view in question may be termed for convenience

[1] This view does not imply, of course, that *all* brain-processes have mental effects. A great deal—perhaps most—of our cerebral activity is unaccompanied by consciousness.

the brain-dependence hypothesis. It cannot be conclusively proved, but it satisfies the essential requirements of a "good" hypothesis, in that it is consistent with all the observed facts, it explains the facts, and it has frequently made it possible to predict facts as yet unobserved. But though most psychologists accept the brain-dependence hypothesis in some form, we are still profoundly ignorant of the kind of dependence involved.

Forms of Brain-Dependence Hypothesis

Of the various theories that have been put forward, the most extreme is *epiphenomenalism*. This view, which is associated with the name of the great Victorian scientist, T. H. Huxley, holds that mental processes are epiphenomena, or by-products, of brain-processes: they are all caused by brain-processes and do not, themselves, cause anything. Mental processes, on this view, are produced by brain-processes in a way analogous to that in which a tune is produced by a musical-box. The notes, in other words, are all caused by processes in the box; they do not cause each other, or react causally on the instrument.

This view is impossible to disprove, but it leads to the paradoxical position that pain and pleasure are mere epiphenomena, and do not affect our behaviour. This is true as regards reflex action; as we have seen (cf. pp. 27-8) when we jump at a pinprick we are not really reacting to the pain. But it is a considerable step to extend the principle to voluntary action, and to say (for example) that when we have toothache and ring up the dentist, our action is due purely to brain-processes, and that the pain, as such, plays no part in causing it.

A more moderate form of brain-dependence hypothesis was held by William James. James agreed with Huxley that mental action is "uniformly and absolutely a function of brain-action, varying as the latter varies, and being to the latter as effect to cause." [1] But he denied Huxley's corollary that mental processes are causally ineffective. On James's view, mental processes, once in existence, can "react so as to

[1] *Textbook of Psychology* (1892), p. 6.

further or to dampen the brain-processes to which they are due" [1]—thus exerting what, in modern terminology, would be called a "feed-back" effect.

Yet another possibility may be provided by the double-aspect theory, put forward by C. D. Broad. This theory involves abandoning the assumption, which is usually made without question, that a process can be either physical or mental, but cannot be both. Broad suggests that some brain-processes may be *both* physical and mental—or, more accurately, that they can have both physical and mental characteristics. Thus on the double-aspect theory we have, not two series—a series of brain-processes and a parallel and dependent series of mental processes—but a single series of brain-processes, most of which are purely physical in character (cf. footnote, p. 59), but some of which have mental characteristics as well. The physical characteristics can be observed (or could in theory be observed, given sufficiently delicate instruments) by an outside observer: the mental characteristics can be observed only by introspection.

On the double-aspect theory, a brain-process which has mental characteristics may exert causal effects which are different from those exerted by a brain-process which is purely physical in nature. Thus the theory avoids the great difficulty of epiphenomenalism—that of asserting that our mental processes do not affect our actions.

It is difficult to see how these various hypotheses could be tested experimentally, and the current tendency in psychology (and philosophy) is to regard discussion of them as a waste of time. But the problem of the mind-body relationship will probably continue to fascinate those of a speculative turn of mind.

NOTES ON READING

The classical statement of the epiphenomenalist hypothesis was given by T. H. Huxley in an address to the British Association in Belfast in 1874 "On the Hypothesis that Animals are Automata, and its History," published in *Method and*

[1] *Op. cit.*, p. 104.

Results (Vol. IV of Huxley's Collected Essays) (Macmillan: 1894).

William James's criticisms of epiphenomenalism, and his statement of an alternative hypothesis, are discussed and quoted in Margaret Knight, *William James* (Pelican Books: 1950). The double-aspect theory is expounded by C. D. Broad, *The Mind and its Place in Nature* (Kegan Paul: 1925), which is still the standard work on the mind-body relationship.

CHAPTER V

THE DUCTLESS GLANDS

There are certain small organs in the body which exert a profound effect on intelligence and temperament, as well as on physical health and growth. These are the so-called ductless or endocrine glands. It was not until the end of last century that the importance of these glands began to be realised, and the science of endocrinology is still comparatively in its infancy.

The glands of the body are of two kinds: the duct glands, such as the salivary and sweat glands, which discharge their products through ducts to the inner or outer surface of the body; and the ductless glands, which discharge their products directly into the blood stream. The ductless glands operate like miniature chemical factories. Each takes from the blood the raw materials that it requires, and from them it manufactures its own characteristic product, known as a hormone (from Greek *hormao*, excite), which is then discharged again into the blood stream.

The most important of the ductless glands are the thyroid, the adrenals, and the pituitary. Their functions are closely interrelated, and, though they will be discussed separately, it must be borne in mind that over- or under-activity of any one gland inevitably affects the functioning of the others.

The Thyroid Gland

The thyroid gland is situated at the base of the neck, just below the larynx. It secretes two hormones—thyroxine and triiodothyronine—which both contain a large proportion by weight of iodine, and have similar physiological effects.

If development of the thyroid is arrested in infancy, the child becomes a cretin—a misshapen and imbecile dwarf. If the gland becomes deficient in later life, it leads to a condition called myxoedema, in which the heart-beat is slowed down, and there is a general fall in bodily metabolism. The face and hands become swollen and puffy, the skin becomes dry and rough, the hair falls out and the sufferer becomes slow, lethargic, unable to concentrate, and extremely sensitive to cold. One of the greatest practical discoveries of endocrinology has been that this condition can be effectively treated by the regular administration of thyroid extract. Even the unfortunate cretin, if he is taken young enough, can in this way be improved beyond recognition, though he seldom becomes completely normal.

Over-secretion of the thyroid is usually due to the fact that the gland has become pathologically enlarged. This condition, known as exophthalmic goitre or Grave's disease, is characterised by swelling at the base of the neck, and prominent staring eyes.[1] The effects are mainly the opposite of those produced by under-secretion of the thyroid. Heart-beat and body metabolism are speeded up, and the patient becomes over-active, tense, unstable, and insensitive to cold. Certain psychological states, such as anxiety, stimulate the action of the thyroid, and many cases of exophthalmic goitre have followed periods of intense emotional strain. In severe cases, part of the thyroid may have to be removed by operation.

A less dangerous form of goitre results from a lack of iodine in the diet. The thyroid secretions, as we have mentioned, contain much iodine, and if the supply of iodine in the blood stream is inadequate, the gland enlarges itself in the attempt to produce the necessary hormones. This condition was at one time endemic in certain parts of the world, such as Switzerland and the Peak District of Derbyshire, where the water is deficient in iodine. The incidence of endemic goitre has now been greatly reduced by the regular addition of small quantities of iodine to the drinking water or the table salt.

Besides the extreme cases of thyroid excess or deficiency, there are probably many cases differing slightly from the normal. Slight over-activity of the thyroid in childhood may cause rapid growth, while under-activity may lead to

[1] It is now known that the last-named condition is not a direct effect of thyroid over-secretion, but the result of over-secretion of anterior pituitary hormones (cf. p. 67).

slow growth and mental apathy. There may, however, be many other causes for the last-named condition, and it is important not to encourage the view that most dull children would benefit from thyroid extract.

The Adrenal Glands

There are two adrenal or suprarenal glands, each of which surmounts one of the kidneys, like a cocked hat. Each adrenal consists of two parts; the outer layer or cortex, and the core or medulla.

The adrenal cortex secretes a number of hormones (aldosterone, cortisol, corticosterone, etc.) which play an important part in bodily metabolism. There is evidence that these secretions are increased in amount when the individual is subjected to various kinds of stress. Destruction of the adrenal cortex (*e.g.* by tuberculosis) leads to a fatal condition, known as Addison's disease. Over-activity of the gland leads to accentuation of masculine sex traits. If it occurs in a woman, she tends to lose her feminine contours, her voice deepens, and she may find it necessary to shave.

Cortisol, one of the chief products of the adrenal cortex, has a marked effect in suppressing inflammatory reactions, and this hormone, and its chemical relative cortisone, which is found in adrenal tissue, are used with success in the relief of rheumatoid arthritis.

There is evidence that the mental illness known as schizophrenia is associated with a deficiency of certain cortical hormones, and some investigators have claimed that administration of these hormones is beneficial to schizophrenic patients.

The principal hormone secreted by the adrenal medulla is adrenaline. As already stated, the adrenal gland is closely linked with the sympathetic nervous system (cf. pp. 30-1), which controls the physical reactions induced by emotion. Certain emotions, such as fear, anxiety, and rage, have, through the sympathetic system, a strongly stimulating action on the adrenal medulla. This causes the blood stream to be flooded with adrenaline, which accelerates and strengthens the heart-beat, increases blood-pressure, counteracts fatigue in the muscles, opens wide the air passages in the lungs, suspends the activity of the stomach and intestines, and produces various other effects, all of them conducive to efficiency in flight or fight.[1]

The inhibiting effect of adrenaline on the stomach muscles explains why it is undesirable to eat a large meal if we are angry or "upset." The effect can be vividly demonstrated by giving a cat a meal, made visible to X-rays by the admixture of bismuth, and observing the contractions of the stomach as digestion proceeds. If a barking dog is introduced into the room, the contractions instantly cease, and are not resumed for half an hour or more, even though the dog is at once taken away.

Several investigators have studied the effects of injecting adrenaline into the blood stream. Human subjects injected with adrenaline displayed most of the observable physical symptoms of fear or anger, such as rapid heart-beat, pallor, trembling, sweating, and dilation of the pupils. In their accounts of their emotional experiences, however, they differed considerably. Most reported that they felt somewhat "tense" or "on edge," but some were aware of nothing more than physiological disturbances. Genuine fear or anger was seldom experienced in the absence of any situation that would provoke it, but persons under the influence of adrenaline were more easily frightened than they were in their normal state.

As a stimulus to brief spells of intense effort, adrenaline is wholly beneficial. But chronic fear or anxiety, with the consequent prolonged excess of adrenaline in the blood, may lead to pathological physical conditions such as disordered heart action, high blood-pressure, hyperacidity, and peptic ulcer.

Recent research has also suggested that schizophrenia, in some cases at all events, may be caused by abnormal functioning of the adrenal gland, leading to the production of

[1] Recent research has shown that the adrenal medulla in fact secretes two hormones, adrenaline and noradrenaline, which are very similar in their chemical properties. There is some evidence that adrenaline conduces primarily to the "flight", and noradrenaline to the "fight" reaction.

substances having an action somewhat similar to that of the drug mescaline. But this has not yet been confirmed.

The Pituitary Gland

The pituitary or hypophysis has been called the "master gland," not only because of the importance of its secretions, but because it exerts a measure of control over many other glands, particularly the thyroid, the adrenal cortex, and the sex glands. It is situated in a deep depression in the skull at the base of the brain. Its secretions are to a large extent controlled by the hypothalamus, with which it is connected by a stalk. It is made up of two lobes, the anterior and posterior.

The anterior lobe is now known to secrete six different hormones: thyrotropin and corticotropin, which stimulate the activity of the thyroid and the adrenal cortex respectively; two gonadotropins, which affect the functioning of the sex glands; prolactin, which stimulates lactation; and the growth hormone which influences bodily growth.

Deficiency of the growth hormone in childhood may produce "midgets"—dwarfs who, unlike cretins, are of normal intelligence and often quite attractive in appearance. While they are still young, their growth can be increased by pituitary extract. Over-secretion of the growth hormone during the growing period produces giants seven to nine feet tall. Over-secretion when growth has ceased causes enlargement of the joints and extremities, and a marked thickening and coarsening of the features. This condition is known as acromegaly.

Tumour or infection of the anterior pituitary may result in Simmonds' disease—a condition somewhat resembling myxoedema. The body metabolism is lowered, and there is loss of sexual function, and—in some cases—emaciation and premature senility.

Slight over-activity of the anterior pituitary is not a disadvantage. Persons of this type tend, as would be expected, to be above average height with strongly-marked features, and they are usually forceful, energetic, and clear-headed. Many of the world's famous men have been of this type.

The posterior lobe of the pituitary is less important, both physiologically and psychologically, than the anterior. Its main function is the regulation of the secretion of urine. It also produces an extract which stimulates the contraction of involuntary muscles, particularly those of the blood vessels and uterus, and injection of posterior pituitary are sometimes given to stimulate uterine contractions during childbirth.

Other Glands

The remaining glands—the sex glands, the pancreas, the parathyroids, the pineal gland, and the thymus—can be treated more briefly.

The sex glands, or gonads, function as both duct and ductless glands. As duct glands, they produce the reproductive cells, and, as ductless glands, they secrete hormones that promote the development of the genital organs and of secondary sex characteristics. The internal secretions of the gonads are directly connected with the experience of sexual desire.

The sex hormones are not completely sex-specific. Both male and female hormones are present in both sexes, the predominant hormone depending on the sex of the individual. An abnormally high proportion of the hormones of the opposite sex is one cause of virilism in women and effeminacy in men. Hens injected with male sex hormones showed a marked increase in dominant and aggressive behaviour, and at a later stage they stopped laying eggs and began to crow.

The pancreas is another example of a gland which, although it has a duct, also functions as a ductless gland. As a ductless gland it secretes the important hormone insulin, a deficiency of which results in diabetes melitus. An excess of insulin will lower the amount of sugar in the blood to such an extent that a disturbance of the CNS results, and some investigators believe that hyperinsulinism is quite often the cause of mental disturbance.

The parathyroids are four tiny glands that lie close to the thyroid. Their secretions affect calcium metabolism, and also act on the CNS so as to prevent over-excitability. Disease or removal causes a tense and tremulous condition with

painful muscular spasms, while over-secretion produces a
general condition of torpor.

The pineal gland, attached to the hind part of the brain, is
possibly a relic of a third (cyclopean) eye, which is still found
in certain lizards. Little is known of its functions, and it is
apparently of minor importance.

The functions of the thymus gland (situated behind the
breast-bone) are also obscure. It has recently been discovered, however, that when the gland is functioning abnormally it secretes a product which acts like the arrow poison,
curare, and causes a block at the point where nerve-impulse
activates muscle. A rare disease, myasthenia gravis, in which
this blockage occurs, has been relieved in some cases by
removal of the thymus gland.

NOTES ON READING

Most psychological textbooks, and all textbooks of general
physiology and biochemistry, deal with the ductless glands.
A clear account in non-technical language, well suited to the
beginner, will be found in the chapter on The Endocrine
Organs in V. H. Mottram, *The Physical Basis of Personality*
(Pelican Books, 2nd revised ed., 1952), and there is a fuller
treatment in A. Stuart Mason, *Health and Hormones* (Pelican
Books, 1960). The article on the Endocrine System in
Chambers's Encyclopaedia can also be recommended.

CHAPTER VI

THE SENSE OF SIGHT

Besides the accepted five senses of sight, hearing, taste, smell, and touch, there are at least five more, namely heat, cold, pain, the kinaesthetic or muscle sense, and the sense of balance. An adequate account of the structure and function of the various sense-organs would require a book to itself, but the beginner in psychology needs no more than an outline of the relevant facts.

STRUCTURE OF THE EYE

The human eyeball, of which only a small part is normally visible, is actually an approximate sphere. A cross-section is shown in Fig. 15.

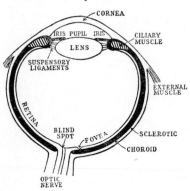

Fig. 15.

The rotation of the eyeball in its socket is controlled by three pairs of external muscles. The eyeball is surrounded by three coats. The tough outer coating, the *sclerotic*, forms the white of the eye. At the front of the eye, this coat has a transparent portion, the *cornea*. The sclerotic is lined by a light-excluding membrane, the *choroid*, which consists mainly of tiny blood-vessels. Beneath the choroid is the sensitive film of the eye, called the *retina*. The *iris*—the coloured part of the eye, which lies behind the cornea—is really an extension of the choroid. Behind the iris is the *lens*. Light is admitted to the lens through the *pupil*, which looks like a small black dot in the centre of the iris, but is in fact an aperture like that of a camera. By the reflex action of the muscles of the iris, this aperture contracts when the light increases, and expands when the light is reduced.

The shape of both cornea and lens is such as to refract or bend inwards the light rays that enter the eye. The "natural" shape of the lens is spherical, but it is flattened and held in position by suspensory ligaments.

The lens is highly elastic, and the shape can be altered according to the nearness of the object being focused. The greater the curvature of the lens, the sharper the refraction. Distant objects require no adjustment, but objects less than 20-30 feet away give a blurred image when the lens is flattened,

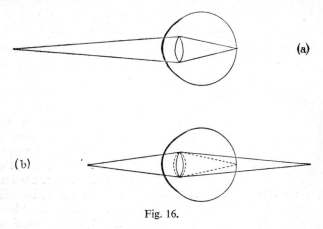

Fig. 16.

and the curvature has therefore to be increased. This is shown diagrammatically above.

Fig. 16(a) shows a "pencil" of rays diverging from a point, falling on the lens of the eye, and being brought to focus on the retina. The nearer the point is brought to the eye, the more divergent is the "pencil" of rays coming from it, and the greater must be the curvature of the lens for the point to be focused correctly. Fig. 16(b) shows a pencil of rays from a point close to the eye, brought to a focus well behind the retina by the unadjusted lens (continuous lines), and focused correctly on the retina when the curvature of the lens is increased (dotted lines).

This adjustment of curvature is known as *accommodation*, and is carried out by the *ciliary muscle*, which is shown in Fig. 15. Contraction of the muscle has the effect of loosening the suspensory ligaments, and allowing the lens, in virtue of its natural elasticity, to bulge outwards and assume a more spherical shape.

The diagrams on p. 71 are over-simplified, since in practice we do not see points, but objects of definite size. Each point on such an object gives rise to a corresponding point on the image, which is always inverted. The reason for this will be clear from Fig. 17, where the paths of rays from the extremities of the object are shown. The fact that we see objects the right way up, although the retinal image is inverted, was once regarded as a major problem, and we shall return to it later.

The retina—the sensitive surface on which the image of

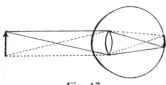

the object is thrown—is a complex structure of neurons. Light-waves affect the sensitive nerve-endings and cause nerve-currents to be transmitted along the optic nerve to the visual areas of the brain. The nerve-cells

Fig. 17.

of the retina are of two main kinds—cones and rods. The cones are used in normal daylight vision, and the rods in twilight vision. The process of "dark adaptation"—such as occurs, for example, when we enter a cinema in the daytime—is a process of replacing cone by rod vision. When the eye is adapted to full light, it is said to be in a photopic condition; when it is "dark-adapted" (or, more strictly, adapted to twilight), it is said to be in a scotopic condition. For the eye to pass from the photopic to the scotopic condition takes, normally, some twenty minutes (the greater part of the adaptation having been completed at the end of ten); the reverse process is almost instantaneous.

The rods have no colour-vision: to the scotopic eye, the world appears in differing shades of grey. We can, it is true, see luminous colours (such as traffic lights) in the dark, but this is because the light is strong enough to rouse a few cones into activity.

Rods and cones are not evenly distributed over the retina. The cones are concentrated in the centre, and are infrequent towards the edges of the retina, while the reverse is true of the rods. The central part of the retina, known as the *fovea*, contains a great concentration of cones and very few rods, and this is the point of clearest vision in the light-adapted eye. But when the eye is dark-adapted, the fovea is almost blind. If we are trying to distinguish an object (such as an aeroplane in the sky) in semi-darkness, we shall see it more clearly if we look slightly to the right or left of it, than if we look at it directly.

COLOUR-VISION

Colour-vision is due to the fact that the cones, unlike the rods, give a different response to light of different wave-lengths. The wave-length of light is measured in millionths of a millimetre (written $m\mu$). Light-waves between approximately 760 and 390 $m\mu$ give rise to colour-sensations in the normal human eye. Within this range lie all the colours of the spectrum, which are, in descending order of wave-length, red, orange, yellow, green, blue, indigo, and violet. Waves longer than 760 $m\mu$ are called *infra-red*; they give heat, but no light, sensations. Waves shorter than 390 $m\mu$ are called *ultra-violet*; they produce certain well-known effects, such as tanning of the skin, and they can damage the human eye if they are present to excess; but they give rise to no colour-sensations.

Purple and carmine, which are mixtures of red and violet, fall outside the spectrum, in the sense that they cannot be produced by any single light-wave, but only by a mixture.[1] If we add these colours to those of the spectrum, we have a complete, closed series, which can be represented by a circle, as in Fig. 18.

[1] Strictly speaking, the same is also true of "pure" red. The red of the spectrum is not quite what we commonly regard as the primary red, but is slightly yellowish.

Ordinary white light is a mixture of all the wave-lengths in the spectrum. The different colours of different objects are really due to selective absorption. A white surface reflects all the light-waves that fall upon it; a black surface reflects none; a coloured surface reflects predominantly a particular band of the light-waves in the spectrum, and absorbs the rest. (The term "predominantly" must be emphasised, as some coloured surfaces reflect *all* spectral light-waves to some extent, appearing paler or less saturated in proportion as they do so.)

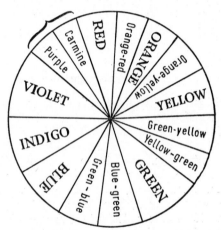

Fig. 18.   COLOUR CIRCLE.

In compound colour-names, by convention, the dominant colour is put last, *e.g.* " blue-green " means green with a trace of blue, and " green-blue " means blue with a trace of green.

Brightness

Colours differ, not only in hue and in saturation, but also in brightness or luminosity. Brightness depends in part on the energy or intensity of the stimulus: two light-waves of the same wave-length but of different amplitude (as shown in Fig. 19) will give rise to two colours of the same hue, but different brightness.

But brightness is not wholly dependent on energy: it is also affected by wave-length. The human eye is most sensitive to wave-lengths towards the middle of the spectrum, and a stimulus of given intensity, if its wave-length is medium, will give a far brighter sensation than a stimulus of the same intensity in the longer or shorter wave-lengths. Yellow, in the middle of the spectrum, is the colour with the greatest "intrinsic" brightness, and there is a continuous decrease in brightness on either side of it, the darkest colour being violet.

The Purkinje Phenomenon

When the eye becomes dark-adapted, the point of maximum sensitivity shifts slightly towards the short end of the spectrum: consequently there is a change in the relative brightness-values of the different colours. In scotopic vision, of course, all colours are replaced by greys, but a green surface (*i.e.* a surface that is green in daylight) will appear a lighter grey than a yellow surface, and a blue surface will give a

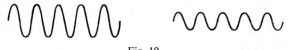

Fig. 19.

lighter grey than a red. This change in relative brightness is called the *Purkinje phenomenon*, from the Austrian investigator who first drew attention to it.

Colour Mixing

Colour mixing is usually performed in the laboratory by means of a colour-wheel of the type shown in Fig. 20. This apparatus enables a disc containing two or more differently coloured sectors to be rotated at a high speed, so that the different sectors stimulate the eye in rapid succession. There is always a slight time-lag before the effects of retinal stimulation die down, consequently the rapid alternation of stimuli has the same effect as if the various wave-lengths were affecting the eye simultaneously. When colours are mixed in this way, the effect is often different from that obtained by mixing paints. For example, if all the colours of the spectrum are mixed on the colour-wheel, the result is white or a very pale grey; but if the colours of the spectrum are mixed in a paintbox, the result is a muddy brown. The explanation is, that, when we use a colour-wheel, we are adding light-waves, and, when we mix pigments, we are subtracting them. If a disc containing segments of every spectral colour is rotated on the wheel, the light-waves of all seven colours strike the eye in rapid succession. But, if the seven actual pigments are mixed, the light-waves of the seven colours are all, or nearly all, absorbed. As already explained, each pigment reflects a certain range of the wave-lengths in the spectrum, and absorbs the rest. Consequently when pigments are mixed, one absorbs what another reflects, and a number of pigments in combination absorb between them nearly all the waves in the spectrum. Thus a mixture of many different pigments always tends towards black, whereas a mixture of many differently-coloured sectors on a colour-wheel tends towards white.

Fig. 20.
COLOUR-WHEEL.
Differently-coloured cardboard discs are slit along one radius, so that they can be fitted together to give sectors of any desired size.

When colours lying close together in the spectrum are mixed on the wheel, the result, as would be expected, is a colour intermediate between them. For example, if we mix a yellowish-red of wave-length about 700 mμ with a golden-yellow of wave-length about 600 mμ, we get an orange colour indistinguishable from that produced by the single wave-length of 650 mμ. If, however, we mix colours that lie opposite one another in the colour circle, both colours disappear and we get white or neutral grey.

Complementary Colours

Pairs of colours that combine to yield a colourless sensation are known as *complementaries*. Every colour in the spectrum, whether pure or a mixture, has its complementary, either in the spectrum or outside it in the carmine-purple range. As can be seen from the colour-circle, red and blue-green are complementaries, as are also yellow and indigo, blue and orange-yellow,[1] and green and carmine-purple.

Red and green are often spoken of as complementary, but this is not strictly accurate. As we have said, the complementary of pure red is blue-green, and the complementary of green is carmine-purple. If pure red and pure green discs are rotated on the colour-wheel, the result, rather surprisingly, is yellow—usually a somewhat dingy greyish-yellow, owing to the low saturation of most colour-discs used in laboratories.

Contrast Phenomena

There is an interesting, and not yet wholly understood, tendency for the sensation of any colour to induce the sensation of its complementary, though the complementary stimulus is not actually present. This fact is evident in the phenomena of successive and simultaneous contrast.

(i) *Successive Contrast.* If we fix our eyes on a coloured patch for about twenty seconds, then turn them to a white or

[1] The fact that certain blues and yellows combine to form white has puzzled generations of students who know that if we mix blue and yellow paints the resulting colour is green. The explanation is this. Most yellow pigments reflect primarily the yellow light-waves, but also a certain proportion of the light-waves on either side of yellow, as far round the colour circle as red and green. (The reader is advised to refer to the colour circle on p. 74). Similarly, most blue pigments reflect primarily the blue light-waves, but also a certain proportion of the light-waves on either side of blue, as far round the colour circle as green and violet.

When blue and yellow pigments are mixed (subtractive mixture), one absorbs what the other reflects, and only the green light-waves are reflected by both. Thus the resulting colour is green. But if discs coloured with the identical blue and yellow pigments are rotated on the colour-wheel (additive mixture), both sets of light-waves, covering between them the entire range of the spectrum, strike the eye in rapid succession, and the resulting colour is white.

But why is the resulting colour not green, since green light-waves are reflected by both discs and are therefore present twice over, so to speak, in the resulting mixture? The answer will become clear by reference to the colour circle. The yellow disc reflects some red light-waves, and the blue disc reflects some violet light-waves. These red and violet waves are not absorbed, as they would be in a subtractive mixture, but are both present. In combination, they give carmine-purple: and carmine-purple is the complementary of green, and cancels it out.

neutral grey surface, we "see" a patch of the same shape and size as the original, but of the complementary colour. This secondary patch is usually known as the *negative after-image*, though the term *after-sensation* would be more accurate.

This phenomenon is probably due to retinal fatigue. If part of the retina has been stimulated for some time by a patch of (say) red, it becomes less sensitive to red light-waves.[1] If the eyes are then turned to a white surface—*i.e.* a surface which reflects all the light-waves in the spectrum—the "red-fatigued" part of the retina gives only a minimal response to the red light-waves, but responds normally to the orange, yellow, green, blue, indigo, and violet light-waves, which together give a sensation of blue-green.

(ii) *Simultaneous Contrast.* If a small piece of neutral grey paper is placed on a coloured background it usually appears faintly tinged with the complementary colour of the background. This latter effect is not so striking as successive contrast, particularly when a red or green background is used; but the "induced" colour becomes more obvious if the patch and the background are covered with a thin sheet of tissue paper (see Frontispiece).

The simultaneous contrast effect is usually seen immediately, if it is seen at all; no prolonged staring is necessary. It cannot, therefore, be explained in the same way as successive contrast, as the result of retinal fatigue. The cause of the phenomenon is still unknown. It has received comparatively little attention in recent years, perhaps owing to the behaviourist tendency to fight shy of investigations that too obviously involve introspection. But it is a matter of considerable theoretical interest.

Contrast phenomena are also of practical interest, since they are at the root of the fact, of which most people are aware, that a colour juxtaposed with others may look quite different from the same colour in isolation. This applies

[1] Colours usually appear less saturated when we have stared at them for some time. The student can verify this by covering the left half of the yellow rectangle in the Frontispiece with a sheet of paper, and staring fixedly at the right half for 30-60 seconds. If he then, *without moving his eyes*, removes the paper, the two halves of the rectangle will look surprisingly different in colour.

particularly to complementaries, which always tend to heighten each other: a red, for example, looks more intense beside its complementary blue-green than it looks by itself.

Colour-Blindness

Some people, owing to defective development of the cones, are wholly or partially colour-blind. The totally colour-blind person sees the world only in black, white, and grey. This condition is rare, but red-green blindness affects about one man in 25, and about one woman in 1,000. A few people are colour-blind in one eye only; and they have proved a godsend to colour-theorists, since, by comparing the sensations of their colour-blind eye with those of their normal eye, they have been able to give facts about the sensations of the colour-blind which otherwise could never have been discovered. The information provided by these monocularly colour-blind persons has made it reasonably certain that, to most red-green blind people, all colours at the red-orange-yellow-green end of the spectrum (from approximately 760 to 500 mμ) appear as different shades of yellow.

Colour-blind people are blind only to the tone or hue of a colour, not to other qualities, such as brightness. A clear strong red, for example, is easily distinguished from a dull green, even though neither looks to the colour-blind person as it looks to us. By attending closely to such differences, red-green blind people are often able to pick out and match many colours with reasonable accuracy, and many of them go through life without ever suspecting that their colour-sense is abnormal.

Retinal Zones

Even the normal eye is colour-blind in certain areas. The retina can be roughly divided into three "zones," as indicated in Fig. 21. The central area (C), in and around the fovea, is the area of clearest vision in the light-adapted eye, and the only part that can see all colours. The intermediate area (B) is sensitive to blue and yellow, but not to red and green. The outer area (A) is completely colour-blind. This "zoning" is certainly connected with the distribution of cones and rods over the retina, but other factors may play a part as well.

The existence of the zones can be demonstrated by a well-known laboratory experiment. By means of an apparatus called a colour perimeter, a small coloured stud is moved slowly from the edge to the centre of the subject's field of vision. When the subject first catches sight of the stud "out of the corner of his eye," he usually sees it simply as something moving, which looks white or an indeterminate grey. When it has moved a little further inwards, a blue or yellow stud is usually named correctly, but a red or green stud is tentatively described as yellow. Only when it has moved almost into the centre of his visual field is a red or green stud seen in its "true" colour.

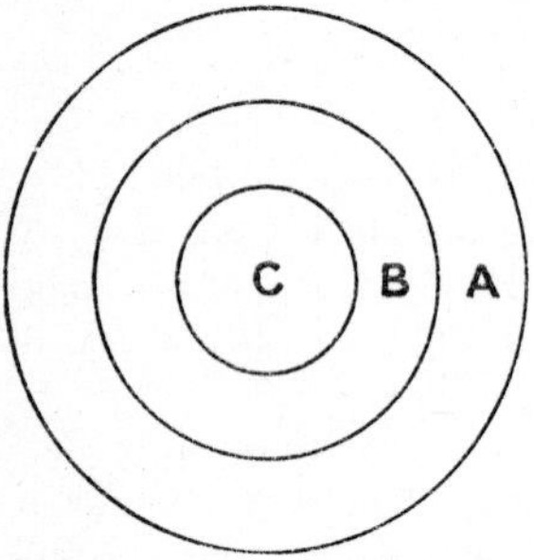

Fig. 21. RETINAL ZONES.

Colour-Vision in Animals

Pavlov's experiments appear to have established beyond doubt that dogs are colour-blind, and it was held at one time that the same was true of all mammals except man and the higher apes. Around 1935, however, experiments with rats suggested that they probably have some degree of colour vision, though it is less developed than that of human beings.

The retinae of many animals consist mainly of rods, and these animals, quite apart from their undeveloped colour-vision, are greatly inferior to human beings in their powers of visual discrimination in daylight. In twilight, however, they have the advantage. It is not strictly true that they can "see in the dark," for no creature can see in complete darkness, but their vision in semi-darkness is far clearer than ours.

Birds, unlike animals, have keen vision and a well-developed colour-sense, though they are less sensitive than humans to the blue-violet end of the spectrum. The fact that birds have colour-vision might be suspected from their vivid plumage, which is in striking contrast with the greys and browns which are all that most animals affect. Bees (and probably many other insects) are insensitive to the red end of the spectrum; but their sensitivity to the violet end is so much keener than ours that they can see ultra-violet. Proof of this fact is that they can be trained, by the sort of conditioning technique described in Chapter III, to discriminate almost unerringly between two pieces of white paper (indistinguishable to the human eye) one of which reflects ultra-violet waves while the other does not.

The Ladd-Franklin Theory

The fact that all mammals except the highest are colour-blind supports the theory, first put forward by the American psychologist Ladd-Franklin (1847-1930), that colour-vision is an evolutionary phe-nomenon. (This view is not, as might be supposed, incompat-ible with the fact that "lower" creatures like birds and insects have colour-vision, for in-

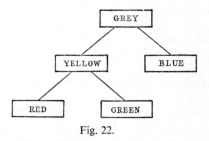

Fig. 22.

sects, birds, and mammals are on different branches of the tree of evolution.) According to Ladd-Franklin, the wave-lengths in the spectrum originally produced only sensations of white and grey. Later, blue became visible at the "short" end of the spectrum, and yellow towards the "long" end; and later still, yellow split into red and green, as indicated in Fig. 22. When red and green are mixed, they revert to the more primitive colour out of which they are evolved, just as blue and yellow revert to grey.

Ladd-Franklin suggested, also, that the three zones in the human retina correspond to the three main stages of evolu-tion. The outermost zone is still in the primitive stage, the intermediate zone in the second stage, and only the innermost zone in the final stage of development. The colour-blind eye, on this view, is a throw-back to a more primitive evolutionary level. Since there is no reason to suppose that the evolutionary process has stopped, it would follow, if the Ladd-Franklin theory be true, that if man survives for a few more aeons, he may derive colour-sensations from infra-red and ultra-violet.

The Ladd-Franklin theory is highly convincing at some points. It accounts better than any other theory for the fact that colour-blindness usually takes the form of blindness to red and green, and that red-green blind persons see red and green as yellow. A weak point of the theory is that it certainly post-dates the evolution of the colour sense. Ladd-Franklin held that man himself was originally colour-blind, but this is quite improbable in view of the fact that apes have colour-vision. If colour-vision evolved, it did so at the pre-human level.

The Ladd-Franklin theory is also weakened by the fact that, up to the present, no species of mammals has been discovered to be red-green blind, as distinct from totally colour-blind. But, although the theory is open to criticism in these and other respects, it may well be true in essentials.

THE BRAIN IN VISION

It is important to realise that we see with the brain as well as with the eyes. The formation of an image on the retina is only the first stage of vision. The final stage occurs when a nerve-current is transmitted by the optic nerve to the brain. We have very little detailed knowledge of what takes place in the brain at this stage, but, whatever it is, it is an indispensable part of the total process. If the visual areas of the brain are destroyed, sight is completely lost.

There is also a further sense in which sight depends on the brain. Not only is the brain's activity essential if we are to see at all; the nature of our visual experience depends partly on the brain. The brain, in other words, is more than a mere recording instrument. It makes an active contribution to what we see, so that our final experience is not a mere copy of the retinal image, but is, so to speak, a joint product of the eye and the brain, deriving some of its qualities from one source and some from the other.

One example of this has already been given: namely, that the retinal image is inverted, yet we see things the right way up. This was once considered a great mystery, but it is no more than a specially striking instance of the principle just stated. A further example of the same principle is the fact that the retinal image is two-dimensional, yet we see objects as solid, and as at different distances from us. This fact requires some further explanation.

Depth-Perception

(i) *The Binocular Cue*. Tridimensional perception depends on the use made by the brain of various so-called "depth-cues" and "distance-cues." The most important of these is the *binocular cue*. When we look at an object that is not too far away, the right eye sees a little further round to the right of the object, and the left eye a little further round to the left. From the

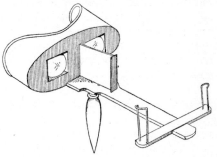

Fig. 23. STEREOSCOPE.

fusion of these two retinal images the brain produces the effect of solidity, though how it does so is as yet wholly obscure.

This principle is employed in the stereoscope, illustrated in Fig. 23. Two photographs of the same scene or object are taken from points about $2\frac{1}{2}$ inches apart (*i.e.* about the same distance apart as the two eyes).[1] These are mounted side by side on a card and placed in the stereoscope. The bridge down the centre of the instrument ensures that the right eye sees only the right-hand picture, and the left eye only the left-hand picture; and the result is a striking effect of solidity.

The binocular cue is undoubtedly the principal depth-cue.

[1] For long-range views, the depth-effect is enhanced if this distance is increased.

Monocular depth-perception is very inaccurate, as can be shown by various simple experiments. For example, we may take a pencil in each hand and, starting with the hands some distance apart, try, with one eye closed, to bring the points of the two pencils as close together as possible without allowing them actually to touch. When we open both eyes, we usually find that there is room for improvement.

(ii) *The Focusing Cue.* Although monocular depth-perception is inaccurate, it is not completely lacking. Persons who have lost one eye are able to drive cars, play ball games, and do many other things that they obviously could not do if they had no power at all to judge distance. For near vision, one-eyed people probably make considerable use of the so-called *focusing cue.* As has already been explained, we bring a near object into focus by contracting the ciliary muscle. The nearer the object, the greater the contraction, so that sensations of tension in the ciliary muscle will provide some indication of the distance of the object from the eyes. This cue is probably not much used by those with normal vision, but is developed by practice in the one-eyed.

(iii) *The Perspective Cue.* The focusing cue is ineffective at distances of more than about 20 feet, since beyond this distance no focusing is required; and the binocular cue becomes ineffective at about 100 feet, as at this distance the two retinal images are not sufficiently different for the cue to operate. In distant vision, depth-perception depends mainly on perspective cues. We implicitly make use (as we do in looking at pictures) of such obvious facts as that distant objects appear smaller than objects close at hand, that they are seen in less detail, and that they are often partly concealed by nearer objects.

Retinal Rivalry

The phenomenon known as retinal rivalry provides further evidence of the part played by the brain in vision. If we look through the stereoscope at a card containing two squares of different colours—say, blue and yellow—one eye sees only the blue square, and the other sees only the yellow. What will the brain make of these two different stimuli?

Results vary from different subjects; usually, however, the blue and yellow squares appear alternately, at fairly regular intervals, during most of the experimental period, but from time to time the two colours fuse to form grey. These periodical shiftings are not due to any change in stimulus, or in the retina. Throughout the experiment, there is a blue image on the retina of one eye, and a yellow image on the retina of the other. It is the brain which selects now one and now the other image for attention, or which combines them to produce a sensation of grey. This last fact is particularly significant, for it shows that colour-mixing does not necessarily involve any physical mixture of light-waves, but that in certain circumstances it can be performed by the brain alone. The theoretical importance of this fact is not yet, perhaps, fully appreciated.

Ambiguous Figures

Still further evidence of the part played by the brain in vision is provided by ambiguous figures of the type shown

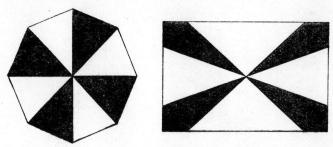

Fig. 24.

above. The designs in Fig. 24, for example, can each be seen in two ways, according to which part we regard as the "figure" and which as the "ground": and, up to a point, we can change voluntarily from one way of seeing the designs to the other.

Now, here, as in retinal rivalry, the stimulus does not change when our experience changes, and it is highly improbable that there is any change in the retina: the change, whatever it is, must occur in the brain. Other ambiguous figures, which involve a suggestion of perspective, are shown in Fig. 25.

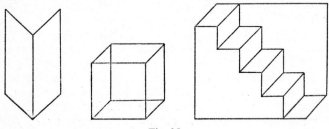

Fig. 25.

Optical Illusions

Still further examples are provided by the familiar optical illusions. Here the qualities we experience may be entirely different from the "real" qualities of the object seen. In Fig. 26, for example, the vertical lines are straight, but they look bent.

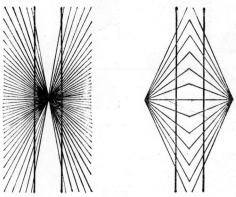

Fig. 26.

In Fig. 27 (the famous Müller-Lyer illusion) the two horizontal lines are of equal length, but the top line looks longer.

In Fig. 28 (Sander's parallelogram illusion) the lines *OP* and *PQ* are equal, but *OP* looks longer.

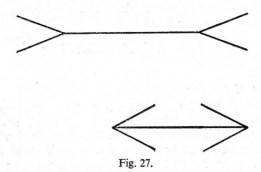

Fig. 27.

Another phenomenon that should perhaps be classed with the illusions is the well-known cinematographic effect. A series of still views, presented in rapid succession, gives us the experience of seeing movement.

Finally, the brain plays an essential part

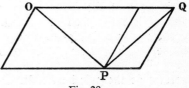

Fig. 28.

in what is technically known as the organisation of the sense-field. This topic, however, will be more appropriately treated under perception. Enough has already been said to make it clear that we do not see with the eyes alone.

NOTES ON READING

Vision and the other special senses are fully treated in almost every standard textbook of psychology. Among the best accounts are those in C. T. Morgan, *Introduction to Psychology* and *Physiological Psychology*. G. Conrad and G. Mueller, *Sensory Psychology* (Foundations of Modern Psychology Series. New Jersey and London, Prentice-Hall: 1965) can also be recommended.

CHAPTER VII

THE OTHER SENSES

HEARING

Structure of the Ear

The structure of the ear is shown in Fig. 29(a).

Sound-waves pass along the outer canal and strike the drum, causing it to vibrate. These vibrations are transmitted by a chain of linked bones (known, by their shape, as the hammer, the anvil, and the stirrup) across the middle ear, to the oval membrane at the entrance to the inner ear. The inner ear is filled with fluid, and, from the oval window onwards, the waves are transmitted through liquid. The main part of the inner ear is the cochlea or spiral coil, shaped like the shell of a snail. Along the coils of the cochlea runs a tightly-stretched membrane, the basilar membrane, which consists of thousands of fibres which are thrown into vibration like piano-strings. The coils of the cochlea narrow as the spiral ascends; the basilar membrane, however, widens from base to apex, the longer and looser fibres being at the tip of the spiral, and the shorter fibres, under greater tension, at the base. It is probable that different parts of the membrane are tuned to different wavelengths, so that sounds of different pitch cause different parts of the membrane to vibrate. Strong evidence for this view is the fact that damage to particular parts of the membrane causes deafness to notes of particular pitch. The fibres of the basilar membrane are linked by small nerves, known as hair-cells, with the ends of the nerve-fibres that lead to the brain. The final stage in hearing, as in sight, is the transmission of a nerve-current to the brain, in this case to the auditory area of the temporal lobe.

Deafness may be due to injury to the ear-drum, to stiffness or malformation of the bones of the middle ear, to disease or injury of the oval window, the cochlea or the auditory nerves, or to many other causes. Where the cause of deafness lies in the outer or middle ear, the defect may be short-circuited by bone conduction. An appliance is used which

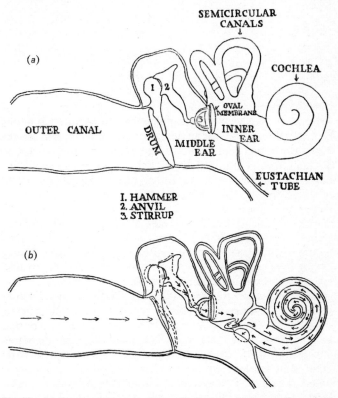

Fig. 29. (a) STRUCTURE OF THE EAR. (b) SECTION, SHOWING COURSE OF A SOUND-WAVE. (Adapted from *The Children's Encyclopaedia*.)
Note arrows showing direction of vibration through fluid of inner ear. Having stimulated the basilar membrane on their way up the cochlea, the sound-waves pass down again, and terminate at the point shown.

amplifies the sound-waves and transmits them to a vibrating diaphragm, which is held in contact with the head behind the ear. The waves are thus transmitted through the bones of the skull direct to the inner ear.

Two features in Fig. 29 have not yet been mentioned—the Eustachian tube and the semicircular canals. The Eustachian tube connects the middle ear with the throat. Air is supplied to the middle ear through this tube, and, if it becomes blocked (*e.g.* by catarrh), pain and deafness may result from the fact that the air-pressure on the two sides of the drum is unequal. The semicircular canals have nothing to do with hearing, but are concerned with the sense of balance, which will be treated separately.

Sound-Waves

Hearing, like vision, is stimulated by waves or vibrations, but sound-waves differ in many respects from light-waves. Light can travel in a vacuum, but sound requires a material medium for its transmission. This medium is usually air, but sound-waves can also travel through fluid and many other media, such as bone or metal. Sound-waves are much larger and slower-moving than light-waves. Light travels at 186,000 miles a second, or some 670 million miles an hour; sound travels through the normal atmosphere at what seems by comparison the modest speed of some 700 miles an hour.

Sound-waves may be regular or irregular. Irregular sound-waves produce noises, regular sound-waves produce musical notes or tones. There is, however, no clear-cut separation of tones and noises; what we hear are sounds, some of which are predominantly tonal and some predominantly a-tonal in character. The pitch of a musical note depends on the frequency of the sound wave; the greater the number of vibrations per second, the higher the pitch of the note. The lowest note audible to the human ear has a vibration rate of about 20 per second; the highest, about 20,000 per second. The range of the ordinary grand piano is from about 25 to 4000.

Sensitivity to notes of high pitch is at a maximum in early life, and begins to decrease at about the age of 25: it is said that no one over 40 can hear the squeak of a bat. Many animals have an upper limit far higher than that of humans, and can hear notes with vibration-rates up to 50,000 per second. Poachers have been known to make use of this fact by controlling their dogs with special whistles, which emit a high note inaudible to the gamekeeper.

Pitch-Discrimination

Pitch-discrimination—*i.e.* the power to distinguish between notes with different vibration-rates—varies widely from one individual to another; but the most musical human being cannot compete in pitch-discrimination with the average dog (cf. p. 53). Pitch-discrimination is most accurate within the range of about 500 to 5000 vibrations per second. Just as the eye is most sensitive to the wave-lengths in the middle of the spectrum, so the ear is most sensitive to sound-waves in the middle range. Within this range, most people can distinguish differences of about ·3 per cent. in frequency rate; that is to say, they can distinguish between two notes whose respective vibration rates are 1000 and 1003, or 2000 and 2006, or 3000 and 3009. With frequencies higher than 5000, the percentage difference must be slightly greater before it can be appreciated, and for the lowest audible frequencies it must be as great as five per cent.

Combination and Analysis of Sounds

When two notes are sounded together, we do not hear a single note of intermediate vibration-rate, as would be the case if sound-waves behaved like light-waves: we hear a chord. Whether the result is pleasing or discordant depends largely on the mathematical ratio between the vibration-rates of the two notes, though other factors, such as familiarity and "setting," are also involved.

In ordinary life, we constantly hear a medley of different sounds at the same time. When this happens, the various sound-waves do not enter the ear separately, but are combined into a single complex wave-motion, which is communicated to the drum of the ear. This being the case, it is remarkable how easily we can pick out individual sounds, such as a particular instrument in an orchestra, or a friend's voice against a background of miscellaneous noises. It is generally held that this power of analysis depends on the differential tuning of the basilar membrane. If different parts of the membrane respond to different wave-lengths, the wave of a mixed sound will throw many different parts of the membrane into vibration, and each part will correspond to one of the original components of the complex sound-wave. Some psychologists reject this explanation, however, and hold that the analysis must take place entirely in the brain.

Loudness and Timbre

Sounds differ in other qualities besides pitch. They differ in loudness, and in timbre. Loudness depends on the amplitude of the vibration: the relation between pitch and loudness in sounds is similar to the relation between hue and brightness in colour. Two sound-waves of the same vibration-rate, but different amplitude, produce two notes of the same pitch, but different loudness.

Timbre is the characteristic quality of different instruments —the quality which makes a note played on a violin, for example, sound quite different from the same note played on a piano. Timbre is a matter of overtones. Every regular sound-wave is accompanied by other vibrations whose rate is an exact multiple of that of the original wave—*i.e.* a wave vibrating at 100 per second produces secondary vibrations at 200, 300, 400, etc. These subsidiary waves are called overtones; and it is the number and strength of these overtones that give each instrument its peculiar timbre. A tuning fork gives a perfectly pure tone, but no musical instrument does so. The nearest approach to a pure tone is that of the flute, and it is for this reason that the flute sounds a little thin and colourless when it is played as a solo instrument.

The Localisation of Sound

Our power to locate the source of a sound depends largely on our use of cues from binaural hearing. In judging the direction from which a sound has come, we unconsciously make use of the fact that a sound from the right sounds slightly louder to the right ear, and strikes the right ear a fraction of a second sooner than it does the left. If, however, the sound comes from directly behind or in front, or from directly above or below, sound-waves will reach the two ears at the same time and with the same loudness, and the binaural cue cannot operate. In real-life situations, the eyes come to the aid of the ears in such cases; or, if the source of sound is not visible, we may turn our heads and so convert a front-back into a right-left direction. But if these aids are debarred, localisation is very uncertain when the sound comes from any position in the median plane (*i.e.* the plane equidistant from the two ears).

This can be demonstrated in the laboratory with an apparatus called a sound-cage; but, if nine people can be induced to co-operate, it can be demonstrated, as far as the front and back positions are concerned, without any apparatus at all. One person, blindfolded and keeping his head motionless, sits in the centre of a circle and the remaining eight group themselves around him in the

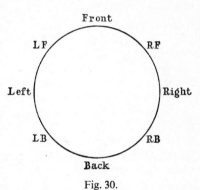

Fig. 30.

positions shown in the diagram (Fig. 30). The members of the circle then, singly and in irregular order, make some slight sound, such as can be made by tapping two pennies together; and each time the sound is made, the subject points to the direction from which he thinks it came. Almost every subject will be found to locate sounds from the right and left positions with accuracy and confidence, but to confuse sounds from the front and back. When mistakes are made with the intermediate positions, they occur in the front-back rather than in the right-left direction: *RB*, for example, may be confused with *RF*, but scarcely ever with *LB*.

THE SENSE OF BALANCE

The sense of balance depends partly on the muscle sense, which will be discussed later, but primarily on the *semi-circular canals* of the inner ear, which open into the *vestibule*. Both the vestibule and the canals are filled with fluid.

The canals, which are shown in the diagram of the ear on p. 89, are set in three planes: one is horizontal and the other two are vertical, and at right angles to each other. Thus every possible movement of the head has a corresponding effect on the fluid in the canals. Each canal contains a bunch of hair-cells, whose hairs lie in the fluid, so that when the fluid is affected by head movement, the hairs are swayed and bent like reeds in a stream. In contact with the bodies of the hair-cells are the ends of sensory nerve-fibres, which connect with the cerebellum. Movement of the hair-cells causes nerve-current to be transmitted to these fibres, and by them in turn to the cerebellum, which, as stated in Chapter II, is the part of the brain responsible for maintaining bodily posture and equilibrium.

The semicircular canals are affected only when the head is moved: our awareness of static position depends on the vestibule, which also contains hair-cells. The tips of the hairs in these cells are matted together, and in the mats are embedded particles of stone called *otoliths*. The otoliths exert a continual gravitational pull or pressure on the hairs, and the nature of this pull or pressure varies with the position of the head. Thus, even when the head is stationary, there is constant stimulation of vestibular nerve-cells, which connect, like the nerve-cells in the canals, with sensory nerve-fibres that run to the cerebellum. Rapid rotation, and certain other types of movement, affect the semicircular canals and the vestibule, and temporarily disturb the balance sense, producing giddiness and nausea.

The fact that the organs of balance form part of the ear becomes less surprising when we realise that the two have a common origin. Fishes, for example, have neither cochlea nor semicircular canals, but a single organ which is affected both by water-waves and by sound-waves in water. At a higher evolutionary level, this organ is divided into two parts, one of which is concerned with hearing and the other with balance.

TASTE AND SMELL

Taste and smell are stimulated, not by waves or vibrations, but by actual contact—of sapid substances with the taste-buds in the sense of taste, and of minute particles with the sense-organs inside the nostrils in the sense of smell. Thus these two senses, unlike sight and hearing, cannot operate at a distance.

Taste

The receptors for the sense of taste are taste-buds. These are situated mainly in the tongue, though there are a small number in the soft palate and around the tonsils. If we were to examine the surface of the tongue with a mag-

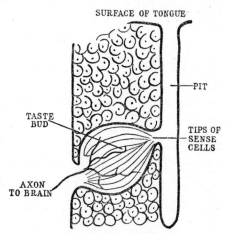

Fig. 31. TASTE BUD.
[After Woodworth, *Psychology* (Methuen).]

nifying glass we should see that it is full of little pits, and the tips of the sense-cells which compose the taste-buds run into the sides of these pits, as indicated in Fig. 31.

Strictly speaking, we can taste only liquids. Solid food, before it can give rise to taste sensations, must be sufficiently dissolved in saliva to run down into the pits and make contact with the taste-buds.

There are only four fundamental tastes—sweet, sour, salt, and bitter. Flavour, or savour, is a compound of taste and other sensations, primarily smell. The characteristic flavour of coffee, for example, depends almost entirely on smell. The

only taste-sensation yielded by unsweetened coffee is bitter, and if the nose is plugged, and the eyes are shut, coffee cannot be distinguished from a weak solution of quinine.   The flavour of an onion depends similarly on smell, and with the nose stopped we cannot distinguish the taste of an onion from that of an apple.   As well as receptors for taste, the tongue contains receptors for touch, heat, and cold, and these, too, often contribute to savour.   The revulsion induced by castor oil, for example, is due partly to touch sensations, and many kinds of food and drink become quite unpalatable if they are served at the wrong temperature.

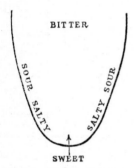

Fig. 32.   The Location of Taste Cells on the Human Tongue.

The taste-buds of the tongue do not all yield all four of the fundamental tastes.   Some yield only two or three, and others only one.   These specialised taste-buds are not evenly distributed over the tongue, consequently certain parts of the tongue are specially sensitive to particular tastes.   The distribution of these areas is shown roughly in Fig. 32.   A drop of sweetened lemon-juice tastes sweet to the front part of the tongue, and sour to the sides.   The central part of the tongue is relatively insensitive.

Smell

Smell is a sense about which we know comparatively little, apart from the fact already stated, that it makes an important contribution to flavour.   The receptors for smell are olfactory cells situated at the top of the inside of each nostril.   Gaseous particles in the inhaled air arouse a chemical action in these cells, and cause nerve-current to be transmitted by the olfactory nerve to the brain.

In man, the sense of smell is relatively unimportant; so it is not surprising that the olfactory areas of the human brain are much simpler in structure than the other sensory areas. It is noticeable that, whereas language abounds in specific names for visual qualities, like shapes and colours, there are very few epithets for smell. If we want to describe a smell, we usually have to do so by reference to its source: we say that it is a smell of cigar-smoke, or lavender, or petrol, or fish. But when we are dealing with visual qualities we use terms like "round" and "red"; we do not describe things as moon-shaped or blood-coloured.

A Dutch psychologist, Henning, has attempted to divide smells into six fundamental classes, namely (i) fragrant (*e.g.* flower smells), (ii) spicy (*e.g.* cloves or cinnamon), (iii) fruity, (iv) resinous (*e.g.* pine), (v) burned (*e.g.* tar), and (vi) putrid. But smells do not lend themselves to classification as readily as tastes, and the proposed division is not wholly satisfactory.

A minor, but interesting, point about the olfactory sense is that it is very rapidly fatigued. We cannot continue smelling any particular smell for long. If we come into a room that is heated by a foul-smelling oil-stove, we become quite unconscious of the smell after about ten minutes; and the same, unfortunately, holds for more attractive smells, like the scent of hay or roses.

THE CUTANEOUS SENSES

The cutaneous or skin senses are those of touch, heat, cold, and pain. The last three are not, as is commonly thought, mere variants of the touch sense; they are separate senses, each with different types of receptor.

The receptors for the cutaneous senses consist mainly of various types of small bulbs or corpuscles at the end of the sensory nerve axons. These are illustrated in Fig. 33.

There are three different types of touch receptor. In the regions of the body that are covered with fine hairs, the hair follicles are provided with specialised nerve-endings, which are stimulated whenever the hair is moved; these act as receptors for light pressure. In the hairless regions of the body, the receptors for light pressure are the *Meissner corpuscles*. In all parts of the body, *Pacinian corpuscles* are

the receptors for deep pressure. Other corpuscles, known as
Ruffini and *Krause* corpuscles, are probably the end-organs
for warmth and cold, though this is not fully established.

In addition, there are free nerve-endings, which act as
receptors for pain. Pain is unique among the senses in having
no specialised end-organ, and also in the fact that it can be

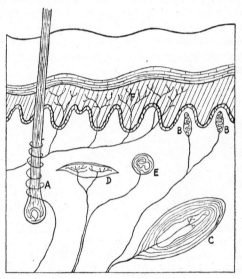

Fig. 33. CUTANEOUS RECEPTORS.

A, hair follicle with nerve ending. B, Meissner corpuscle, receptor for
light pressure. C, Pacinian corpuscle, receptor for deep pressure. D,
Ruffini corpuscle, and E, Krause corpuscle, probably receptors for
warmth and cold respectively. F, free nerve endings, receptors for pain.
[Adapted from Sandiford, *Educational Psychology* (Longmans).]

aroused by over-stimulation of all other types of receptor,
even those for sight and hearing.

If we take a fine-pointed pencil, with the point at about the
temperature of the skin, and with it lightly touch different
spots on the back of the hand, the position of the various
end-organs can be roughly determined. Occasionally, the
contact of the pencil can hardly be felt; but usually we feel

touch sensations, and at certain points (when the pencil happens to touch the relevant end-organ) we have clearly-marked sensations of heat, cold, or pain. These heat-, cold-, pain-, and touch-spots (as they are called) are more numerous in some parts of the skin than others. In general, the front parts of the body have more touch-spots than the back. The lips and finger-tips are particularly rich in touch-spots and the fingers and cheeks in heat-spots. The tongue and the inside of the mouth have comparatively few heat-spots, so we are able to drink very hot liquids without discomfort. If we test the temperature of a cup of tea with our finger, we may get an instructive shock.

THE KINAESTHETIC SENSE

The kinaesthetic or muscle sense is the sense that informs us of the position and movement of our limbs. The muscles and tendons are provided with receptors and nerves that are stimulated by muscular movement and tension. If it were not for the sensations transmitted by these nerves, we should have no means of knowing, for example, the position of our limbs in bed, except by looking to see. Until comparatively recently, the muscle-sense was not clearly distinguished from the touch-sense, but there is now no doubt that it has its own specific sense-organs, yields its own specific sensations, and is a sense in its own right. The "feel" of driving a tennis ball, or throwing a stone, for example, clearly involves something more than skin sensations. In the disease called locomotor ataxia, the muscle-sense is entirely lost.

NOTES ON READING

See *Notes on Reading* for the previous Chapter.

CHAPTER VIII

SENSATION AND PERCEPTION

In the section on the association areas of the brain, an attempt was made to describe, in physiological terms, the experience of recognising a friend's voice. Certain nerve-cells in the auditory area are directly stimulated, and fibres running from these cells to the association areas stimulate other cells, and induce symbolic processes which give rise to images, memories, etc., of such things as the appearance of our friend's face, the sound of his name, and so on (pp. 36-7).

This account skates over many difficulties, and will have to be made more precise at a later stage. But, as it stands, it provides a starting point for discussion of the difference between sensation and perception. The total experience—broadly speaking, a combination of auditory sensations with symbols of various kinds—is perception. The part that consists simply of hearing the sounds made by our friend's voice, is sensation.

In more general terms, sensation is the experience we have when nerve-cells in one or other of the sensory areas of the brain are stimulated, whereas perception is sensation plus a great deal more—plus the experience produced by stimulation of nerve-cells in the association areas. Perception, in other words, is sensation reinforced by memories, images, etc., derived from past experience and called up by association. We have already seen (p. 39) how damage to the association areas can cause grave disturbances of perception, though sensation is unaffected.

To take an example from the sense of sight. When we perceive a house, the retinal image that gives rise to the perception may be no more than a greyish, more-or-less-oblong shape. But "perceiving a house" means much more than having a sensation of a greyish oblong shape. A house means to us something with a back and an inside, something that contains rooms, doors, passages, and the rest: and all this knowledge is involved in, and forms part of, our experience—it is part of what we mean when we say we "see a house." When we perceive an object, in other words, we attribute to it, implicitly or explicitly, qualities that we have come to expect it to possess, but that we are not, at the moment, sensing.

The distinction would be clearer if sensation and perception occurred as two separate and distinguishable stages—if we began by having a mere sensation, and then passed on to recognition of objects. But this scarcely ever happens, at all events where the sense of sight is concerned. Normally, sensation and perception are but two aspects of a single process. We can *think* of them separately, as we can think of the shape of an object apart from its size, but we cannot *experience* them separately. Perhaps the nearest we can get to actually experiencing the difference, is by looking at such drawings as the one shown in Fig. 34. At first glance, it is just a meaningless chaos of lines: but usually after a moment the lines seem to fall into shape and sensation gives place to perception of—what?

"Implicit" Ideas and Images

The above outline is considerably over-simplified. Sense-perception raises some of the most difficult theoretical problems in psychology, and a really adequate treatment would take us beyond the scope of the present book. But on two points, at least, the account just given must be amplified.

Often, the qualities that we attribute to an object in perception are not merely *additional to*, but *incompatible with*, the qualities that we are actually sensing. For example, a penny seen from an angle looks elliptical, but we perceive it as round. A piece of coal strongly illuminated may reflect more light to our eyes than a piece of white paper in shadow, yet we unhesitatingly perceive the coal as black and the paper as white. This phenomenon is known as *perceptual constancy*.

Again we have so far spoken of perception as involving "images," "memories," "the attribution of qualities," and so forth. It is hard to avoid using language of this kind, but it must now be made clear that the ideas, images, etc., in question, are often implicit rather than explicit. When we see a house from the front, we do not necessarily think of the back, or form an image of the back. Nevertheless, the fact that we

(Winter Thomas Advertising Co., Ltd.)

Fig. 34.

know that houses have backs is somehow involved in our perceptual experience.

The point is not easy to grasp, but it can perhaps best be made clear by considering cases of so-called "disappointed perceptual expectation." When we see a friend coming, we do not consciously attribute to him the possession of a certain kind of voice. But if he were to speak to us in a voice that was not his own, we should be considerably surprised. Again, if we perceive a jug of water, we do not, as a rule, form consciously any image of its weight. Nevertheless, there is undoubtedly a sense in which we perceive it as heavy: for if we go to pick it up, and what we perceived as a full jug turns out to be empty, disappointed perceptual expectation occurs in a rather comic form. Evidently, there was *something* with which the experience is discordant: not necessarily an image, but at least some kind of preliminary mental and physical "set."

In terms of cerebral physiology, one might tentatively express the facts thus. When we perceive something (say, a house), a complex pattern of cortical nerve-cells is stimulated. Now, as we have already seen (p. 20), when a number of nerve-cells are stimulated together, their combined effect does not necessarily equal the sum of their separate effects. Among the nerve-cells that are involved in perceiving a house are small groups or patterns, which, if stimulated separately, would give rise to images of the back, the rooms, the walls, etc. But when they are stimulated as part of a larger system, the conscious counterpart of their stimulation is less definite: it consists, for the most part, of no more than implicit or latent images.

In more general terms—when a complex pattern of cortical nerve-cells is stimulated, the resulting experience is *sui generis*. It is not simply the sum of the experiences that would arise if the various component nerve-cells were stimulated separately. The whole point will be clearer to the reader when he has read the section on the *Gestalt* theory (pp. 106 ff.).

Subjective Factors in Perception

Perception may be greatly influenced by the preliminary direction of our attention, by expectation, or by desire.

This fact accounts for many cases of misperception, as when a haystack in twilight is perceived as a house, or distant thunder as the rumbling of a train. If we were to attempt a physiological explanation, we might say that through familiarity, expectation, or interest, certain brain-patterns are in a state of sub-excitement before the perception occurs. They can thus be "touched off" very easily, even by an inappropriate stimulus, as a runner set on the mark may leap forward if a spectator snaps his fingers. If we are out mushrooming, every scrap of paper looks like a mushroom, and if we are waiting anxiously for the sound of a returning car, any light sound outside is liable to be mistaken for the crunch of wheels on the gravel.

In recent years, considerable attention has been paid to the subjective element in perception, and many experiments have been carried out. Some of these involve presenting the subject with a stimulus that is too vague, or too short in duration, to be clearly recognised, and asking him what he "sees." In these conditions, the fullest possible scope is given to subjective factors. A schematic drawing representing little more than a cube on four legs, for example, may be seen by one person as a television set, by another as a filing cabinet, and by another as a medicine chest. Hungry subjects confronted with a blurred out-of-focus pattern on a screen tend to see in it a variety of food-objects. Words thrown on to a screen for a fraction of a second tend to be interpreted in accordance with the subject's interests. A religious person, for example, might read the word "scared" as "sacred," while a horror-film addict might read it as "scarred."

Some of the current techniques for assessing personality depend on observing, and interpreting, the subject's reaction to an "unstructured" stimulus. This is further discussed on p. 209.

The Organisation of the Sense-Field

Clearly, when we perceive objects our experience depends largely on the brain. But it must not be supposed that the brain plays no part before this stage. As has already been emphasised (pp. 82-7), the brain plays an essential role in seeing long before we reach the stage of perception, as defined above.

Not all seeing involves the recognition of familiar objects. Our whole visual field, for example, might be filled with a formal design that does not represent any actual object. But in such a case, what we saw would not be a mere jumble of unrelated sensations. We should see the design *as* a design—in other words, we should regard certain shapes and patches of colour as belonging together, and we should see some parts of the design as figure and others as background. In more formal language, the sense-field would be organised, not chaotic.

This organisation depends on the brain, though whether it involves the association areas is uncertain. The main factors leading us to group elements of the sense-field together appear

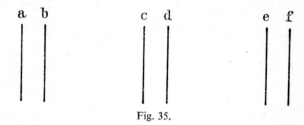

Fig. 35.

to be five in number, namely (i) proximity, (ii) similarity, (iii) continuity, (iv) completeness, and (v) symmetry.

Proximity. In Fig. 35, for example, we unhesitatingly see the pairs of lines, and the space between them, as "figure" and the rest as "ground." It is almost impossible to make ourselves group lines *b* and *c*, and *d* and *e* together. Similarly, certain stars which lie close together, like the Pleiades, are seen as "belonging" together and as forming a group.

Similarity. In Fig. 36, we see the left-hand group of dots as consisting of vertical, and the right-hand group as consisting of horizontal rows. In each case, that is to say, we group the similar elements together.

Continuity. This factor, also, can be illustrated from the stars. Stars that lie in a straight line (like Orion's Belt), or on a continuous curve, will tend to be seen as forming a group.

Completeness and Symmetry. A complete, closed figure, particularly when it is symmetrical, always tends to be seen as a unit, and to stand out from the background. A baby is far more likely to notice the round moon than an irregularly shaped cloud, even though the cloud is just as bright.

The Gestalt Theory

Much controversy has raged over the question whether the tendency to organise the sense-field in the ways described above is innate, or whether it must be learned by experience. The classical psychologists took for granted that it must be learned by experience. The sense-field of an infant, they

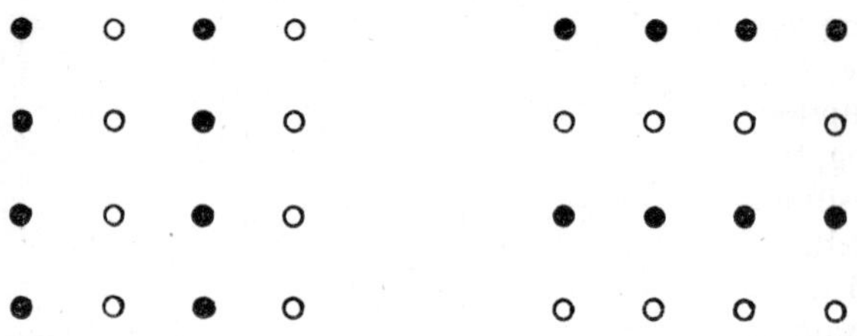

Fig. 36.

held, is a chaos of atomic sensations, and the baby learns gradually by experience to group certain elements together and to see them as forming a segregated, subordinate whole within the total sense-field.

This view was criticised by Stout[1] as long ago as 1896, but in the nineteen-twenties it sustained a concerted onslaught from a group of German psychologists known as the *Gestalt*[2] school. One of the fundamental tenets of this school is that awareness of pattern or structure in the sense-field is innate. We have, of course, to learn by experience to

[1] In *Analytic Psychology.*
[2] The word *Gestalt* is somewhat difficult to render in English. It means essentially "whole-made-of-related-parts," and is sometimes translated as "form," "pattern," or "configuration"; but usually the German word is retained.

recognise and identify objects, but a totally unfamiliar object will still appear to a baby as a *Gestalt*: in other words, it will be seen, not as a jumble of disconnected sense-elements, but as a segregated form or figure.

This view is difficult to establish with certainty, as we cannot get introspections from babies. Some evidence is obtainable, however, from the study of people born blind, who have later gained sight by operation. This evidence does not unambiguously support the *Gestalt* view, as such patients find it impossible at first to distinguish by sight between even the simplest shapes, such as a square and a triangle, with which they have long been familiar by touch. On the other hand, there seems no doubt that the primitive figure-ground organisation—*i.e.* the ability to see a square or a triangle as a separate "something" standing out from the background— is there as soon as the patient becomes able to see at all.[1]

The view the *Gestalt* school is attacking is based on the assumption, which is implicit in much older psychological writing, that the seeing of relations, or of elements-in-relation, is in some way subsequent, and secondary, to the seeing of the elements themselves. But this assumption has only to be stated to be questioned. When we look at Fig. 35 on p. 105, for example, we do not first see a number of lines, and then see that they are grouped in pairs. What we see immediately are *pairs* of lines—and the seeing of them *as* pairs is just as immediate as the seeing of them as lines.

Further evidence for this view has been obtained from experiments with animals, which show that they, too, respond immediately to relations. Hens, for example, were trained to go for food always to the darker coloured of two grey trays (to a medium, rather than to a light, grey tray). A dark grey tray was then substituted for the light grey, so that the medium grey, which was formerly the darker, was now the lighter of the two. Which tray would the hens go to now? Most of them went unhesitatingly to the new, dark grey, tray—showing that they had learned to respond to the darker of two things in relationship, rather than to a particular shade of greyness.

[1] For a fuller discussion of this question, see Young, J. Z., *Doubt and Certainty in Science* (1951).

The essence of the *Gestalt* theory is its insistence that form is as important as content. The classical psychologists had been curiously blind to this fact, largely because of their pre-occupation with analysis. They had aimed, in their own words, at making psychology a kind of "mental chemistry," and they assumed that all that was needed to learn the truth about any complex entity, mental or physical, was to reduce it to its elements. The *Gestalt* school oppose this atomistic approach. They point out, with perfect justice, that the nature of any complex whole or *Gestalt* depends as much on the relations between the elements that compose it, as on the elements themselves. We learn little more about a tune, for example, by separating it into isolated notes, or about a design by reducing it to separate shapes and bits of colour: and the main result of making such an analysis is to destroy the internal structure on which the nature of the *Gestalt* depends. A complex whole is not a mere aggregate of parts. Every *Gestalt* has, *qua Gestalt*, qualities that are not possessed by its elements, and about which we can learn little by studying its elements separately.

Conversely, an element in isolation may differ from the same element when it forms part of a *Gestalt*. For it is affected by its background and setting and by its place in the total structure, just as a colour, for example, is affected by the colours that surround it.

The more detailed applications of *Gestalt* theory involve much that is obscure and controversial, but its main tenets are now widely accepted, and they have been extended far beyond the field of sense-perception: for example, to learning (which will be discussed later), to the higher thought-processes, and to social psychology. Indeed, the whole current of thought, in both psychology and physiology (not to mention the physical sciences) seems to be setting in this direction. Lashley's views on cerebral physiology, for example, have a strongly *Gestalt* flavour, though they were reached quite independently; and all modern writers on the nervous system show the *Gestalt* tendency to treat a complex stimulus or response as an integrated whole, rather than as an aggregate of discrete elements.

NOTES ON READING

A comprehensive account of theory and experiment in the field of perception is given in M. D. Vernon, *The Principles of Perception* (Pelican Books: 1962). Work on the subjective element in perception is described in R. R. Blake and G. V. Ramsey, *Perception: an Approach to Personality* (New York, Ronald Press Co.: 1951).

The classical works on the *Gestalt* theory of sense perception are W. Köhler, *Gestalt Psychology* (New York, Liveright: 1929), and K. Koffka, *Principles of Gestalt Psychology* (Kegan Paul: 1935). A collection of writings by leading members of the *Gestalt* school is contained in Willis D. Ellis, *A Source Book of Gestalt Psychology* (Routledge and Kegan Paul: 1938). There is a valuable chapter on Gestalt psychology and its later developments in R. S. Woodworth and M. R. Sheehan, *Contemporary Schools of Psychology* (Methuen: 9th revised ed., 1965).

CHAPTER IX

ATTENTION

At every moment of our waking lives, we are being bombarded by sense-stimuli, and are experiencing perceptions, thoughts, images, and emotions of many kinds; but only a few of these are in the focus of consciousness. The student at a lecture will usually, one hopes, have his attention focused on the lecturer's utterances. But at the same time he is vaguely aware of many other facts—the picture that his next-door neighbour is drawing in his notebook, sounds of traffic in the street below, the hardness of the lecture-room seats, and the attractive wave in the hair of the student in front. If any one of these facts becomes sufficiently interesting or insistent, attention may be focused upon it instead of upon the lecturer, and the latter's voice fade temporarily into the margin of consciousness.

Thus attention may be described as the selective activity of consciousness; like a beam from a searchlight, it focuses now this item and now that among the miscellaneous contents of the mind. Not only sensations and perceptions, but emotional and cognitive experiences of all kinds, may at one moment be sharply focused in the centre of attention, and then, as the spotlight shifts, fade into the confused and dimly-illuminated background.

The factors that lead us to attend to one thing rather than another are of two main kinds: objective factors, depending on the nature of the object attended to; and subjective factors, depending on the interests, tastes and mood of the individual. Advertisements—which depend for their success very largely on their power to catch and hold attention—provide a valuable field in which the operation of these various factors can be studied.

Objective Factors in Attention

The principal objective factors are: (i) intensity, (ii) size, (iii) change or movement, (iv) repetition, (v) systematic form, and (vi) novelty—though the last-named might equally be classed as subjective. The direction of attention at any given moment depends on the interaction of these various factors, some of which may pull in one direction and some in another.

(i) *Intensity* and (ii) *Size*. It is obvious that, other things being equal, an intense stimulus—a loud sound, or a bright colour—will attract more attention than one which is less intense; and the same holds good, within limits, for size.

(iii) *Change or Movement*. Anything that moves or changes has attention-value on that account. If we are out in the country, and a rabbit starts up on one side of us, we shall at once turn to look at it. Again, electric signs that move or change colour, or a moving display in a shop window, all obviously attract attention; and the open coal fire, we may suggest, owes much of its popularity to the constant movement of its flames.

The above examples relate to the sense of sight, but, *mutatis mutandis,* the same principle applies to the other senses. For example, we soon cease to attend to a continuous sound; but, if the sound stops, becomes louder or softer, or changes in pitch, attention is at once reawakened. This fact is important to the public speaker. A voice that varies in pitch, stress and rhythm will hold attention far more easily than one that is, literally, monotonous.

(iv) *Repetition*. A stimulus gains in attention-value by being repeated—until with frequent repetition it becomes too familiar. A persistent tapping, for example, may arouse attention when a single tap would not; but, if the tapping is long continued, it will fade into the background of attention like the ticking of a clock or the continuous rumble of traffic. An effective advertising device is the use of a stock phrase (such as "My goodness, my Guinness"), which recurs as a constant *motif* in a variety of situations, and thus combines the attractions of repetition and novelty.

(v) *Systematic Form*. As has already been emphasised, we have a tendency, which is probably innate, to pick out, and to attend to, closed figures and symmetrical patterns. Thus a systematic, clear-cut arrangement will always have the

advantage over one that is shapeless and vague. An advertisement that consists of a formless huddle of small print will
have little chance of arousing attention in competition with
one that is well spaced and set out—particularly if the latter
is surrounded by a border which frames it and makes it stand
out from the rest of the page.

(vi) *Novelty.* Attention is always aroused by an unfamiliar
object, or by a familiar object in an unusual setting. We
should be unlikely to overlook a kangaroo in the garden, or
a uniformed policeman in a swimming-pool.

Subjective Factors in Attention

Attention, however, does not depend wholly on objective
factors. Anything that appeals to our instinctive propensi-
ties, or to our acquired tastes and interests, will have
attention-value on that account. Advertisers make full use
of this fact. There are few successful advertisements that do
not make a strong appeal to one or more of the instincts. It
may be self-assertion ("X appeals to men of discrimination"),
curiosity ("Watch this space"), fear ("Four out of five have
pyorrhoea"), the maternal instinct (cherubic infants figure in
a large number of the advertisements in women's journals),
or, very frequently, the sex instinct. Pictures of glamorous
girls in romantic situations are used to advertise an extraordinary variety of products, from chocolates to radio sets;
and the pictures serve to attract attention (and of course to
secure a favourable response) even when they have little
direct bearing on the goods they are helping to sell. Any
widespread temporary interest, such as a coronation or a
presidential election, is also exploited to the utmost by
advertisers.

If something makes a strong appeal to our instincts or to
our acquired interests, it will arouse attention even though its
objective attention-value may be slight. The enthusiast for
old furniture will at once spot the valuable antique in the
corner of the junk shop; the naturalist will observe the rare
bird or butterfly that no one else has noticed; a mother's
attention will be aroused by a cry, however faint, from her

baby; and we are all of us instantly aroused to alertness by the sight or sound of our own name.

And not only our interests, but our general mood or attitude, may affect the direction of our attention. If we are depressed and disgruntled, we tend to notice things—mud on the carpet, unpleasing expressions on the faces of others, sinister omens such as crossed knives and single magpies—which normally would never get beyond the margin of consciousness.

In short, we often attend to things, in themselves inconspicuous, if they happen to interest us or to sort with our dominant mood. And the converse is also true: we are often surprisingly blind even to the most conspicuous objects, if they make no appeal at all to our interests. A large, vividly-coloured poster advertising oil-engines or cattle-cake may completely fail to register, if we happen to be quite uninterested in these commodities. These facts have an important bearing on the psychology of testimony, which is discussed in Chapter XIII.

"Divided" Attention

Strictly speaking, we cannot attend to two things at once, for at any given moment attention can have only one focus. Thus the term "divided attention" is really a misnomer. Although we sometimes appear to be distributing our attention among different objects or activities, in such cases one of three things, none of which entails division of attention, is really happening.

The first possibility is that one of the two activities requires no attention. Those skilful knitters who can knit and read at the same time, have learned by long practice to knit quite automatically. When the knitting requires attention—for example, if a stitch is dropped, or the pattern goes wrong—reading has temporarily to cease.

The second possibility is that attention is rapidly oscillating between two objects. In a gathering of people, we may engage in a tête-à-tête conversation with the person beside us, and at the same time catch the drift of a general conversation that is going on around. At no time, however, are we listening to two conversations simultaneously: what happens in such cases is that from time to time we mentally switch off our neighbour and tune in to the general conversation, then pick up our neighbour again in time to catch the drift of what he has been saying. The efficiency of such "disparate" attention, as it is termed, can be roughly measured in the laboratory. A subject adds columns of numbers while a story is read aloud, and afterwards reproduces what he can remember of the story. Individual results differ somewhat, but, on the average, the attempt to combine the two tasks results in about a 40 per cent. loss of efficiency in each.

The third possibility, when attention appears to have been divided, is that we are attending, not to a number of different objects, but to a single complex object. The conception of "an" object, after all, is ambiguous. A spoke, a wheel, and a car are all objects, of ascending degrees of complexity. If three cars are parked side by side they are, of course, not structurally connected like the parts of a single car, but they, too, may be seen as *a* group, and held collectively in the focus of attention.

The Span of Apprehension

One of the oldest experiments in psychology attempts to determine how large a group we can take in completely at a glance, in the sense of not merely perceiving the group *qua* group, but of discriminating the separate units. The apparatus generally used is a *tachistoscope* (from Greek *tachistos*, quick, and *skope*, see) which exposes, for a fraction of a second, cards containing a number of dots or other simple figures. As each card is exposed, the subject attempts to say how many units it contains. The maximum number that he can discriminate clearly is commonly known as his *span of attention*, though *span of apprehension* is a better term.

Results show that, if the units composing the group are arranged haphazard, the normal span of apprehension is about four or five: beyond this number, errors become frequent, and correct responses are largely a matter of chance. If the cards contain letters instead of dots, about four or five are again as many as can be distinguished in a single exposure.

If, however, the units are organised—*e.g.* if the dots form a pattern, or the letters a word or phrase—a far larger number may be reported correctly. Few people, for example, would have any difficulty with the sixteen dots shown below:—

But in such cases the span has not really been increased; all that has happened is that the units have become more complex. The subject has not distinguished sixteen separate units, but four complex units, and the total of sixteen is reached by calculation. The same considerations apply to words and letters. Four words, especially if they form a familiar phrase, can be read as easily as four letters, since the subject recognises each word (or the whole phrase) as a *Gestalt,* without attending to the separate letters. As every proof-reader knows, the tendency to see words as wholes often makes it very difficult to detect misprints, provided they do not affcet the genenal outline of the word. Many readers, for example, may not have noticed the two misprints in the previous sentence.

The span of attention for auditory material can also be measured. If a number of taps are made, too rapidly to be counted, subjects can usually discriminate correctly up to five or six: though here again the number may be greatly increased if the taps form a rhythmical pattern.

The Distraction of Attention

Many experiments have been carried out on the distraction of attention, particularly by noise. Results, on the whole, suggest that the effects of distraction are less than is often supposed. Subjects have carried out various types of mental work to the accompaniment of intermittent crashes, bells, sirens, gramophone music, humorous anecdotes, hammering, or many other types of distraction. Many subjects reported that they found the noise extremely irritating and disturbing, but performance, on the whole, was surprisingly little affected, and in some cases it was actually improved.

Certain types of noise, as would be expected, were more disturbing than others. Intermittent noises, particularly when they were sudden and startling, produced more effect than continuous noise; and meaningful sounds, such as conversation and music, were more distracting than meaningless noises, such as the hum of traffic.

It would be dangerous, however, to conclude hastily from these results that the effects of noise are negligible. Many of the experiments involved working only for short periods at comparatively simple tasks, such as adding together pairs of numbers, or cancelling all the e's in a sheet of letters. No adult is fully extended by tasks of this kind, and the subjects probably had ample reserves of energy, on which they could draw to counteract the effects of the noise. This would explain the fact that in some cases output was actually higher under distraction.

This view is confirmed by investigations into the effect of noise on energy expenditure. Effort may be measured in terms of muscular tension or breathing rate, or, more accurately, in terms of oxygen consumption, as shown by chemical analysis of the subject's exhaled air. Such experiments all tend to show that energy expenditure is higher in noisy conditions, even when the noise is of the continuous and meaningless kind (like the clatter of typewriters), which most subjects find least disturbing.[1] This increased physiological cost does not greatly matter for short periods or simple tasks, since the subject is probably still working well within his limits, and has plenty of energy in hand. But when we are engaged on concentrated intellectual work, the increased

[1] Cf., for example, Laird, D. A., "Experiments on the Physiological Cost of Noise," *J. Nat. Inst. Indust. Psychol.*, 1928-9, **4**, 251.

energy-expenditure required to resist distraction may lead to greatly increased fatigue.

It must always be remembered, however, that there are wide individual differences in what constitutes distraction. *A*, for example, might find it quite impossible to work during a broadcast of *Figaro*, since the music would exert a constant pull on his attention: whereas to *B*, who is less musical, it might be no more than a vaguely pleasant noise on the margin of consciousness. But it can safely be said that it is better, if possible, to remove a distraction than to try to train oneself to ignore it. We can, if necessary, force ourselves to do effective intellectual work in the most disturbing conditions, but the cost in fatigue is usually quite disproportionate to the result.

The Attentive Set

Concentrated attention usually involves a characteristic physical "set." The sense-organs are adjusted for clearer perception; there is increased muscular tension, particularly around the neck and shoulders; small bodily movements cease; breathing becomes shallower and more rapid; and the individual, if he is seated, tends to lean forward. When attention is strongly aroused, this "set" is adopted unconsciously: we may watch it being gradually assumed, for example, by someone who is seated in an armchair, watching a television programme which increasingly grips his interest. When we are finding concentration difficult, it is sometimes helpful to keep the body deliberately in the attentive posture.

NOTES ON READING

More space is devoted to attention in the older than in the more recent textbooks. There is a stimulating chapter in James, *Principles of Psychology*, and a detailed discussion from the philosophical point of view in G. F. Stout, *Manual of Psychology*. The chapter on attention in M. Collins and J. Drever, *Experimental Psychology* (Methuen: 1926) can also be recommended.

CHAPTER X

IMAGERY

Besides sensation and perception, in which our mind is in contact with things in our immediate, present environment, we also have mental images of absent objects and past events, as well as of things that have never actually existed. These mental images are dependent on symbolic processes in the association areas.

Images may be classified in two different ways. First, there is the distinction between memory-images and constructed images; and, secondly, there is the distinction between the different images associated with the different senses.

Memory-Images and Constructed Images

If we visualise a friend's face, or have an auditory image of the sound of his voice, we are experiencing a memory-image. If we have a mental picture of a city with gates of pearl and streets of gold, or of an animal with the head of an eagle, the body of a rabbit, and the tail of a cow, we have formed a constructed image. Such images occur in connection with other senses than sight: notably with hearing, as when a composer mentally hears a sequence of sounds that he has never actually experienced.

It is sometimes said that, whereas memory-images all reproduce or resemble something that we have experienced in the past, constructed images do not, and are novel. But although a constructed image *as a whole* is novel, its various elements all have their counterparts in our past experience. We have never seen gates of pearl or streets of gold, but we *have* seen gates and pearl and streets and gold, and the constructed image is a new creation only in the sense that it combines these elements in a new *Gestalt*.

Images Associated with the Different Senses

There are as many different kinds of mental images as there are different kinds of sensations. We can see pictures in the mind's eye, hear sounds in the mind's ear, and call up images associated with all the other special senses—as for example of the taste of chocolate, the scent of violets, the "feel" of emery paper, the heat of a radiator, the cold of a window-pane in winter, the pain of a burn, or the muscular effort involved in pulling a garden-roller. Many attempts have been made to estimate the relative clearness of the different types of imagery, but such comparisons are difficult, since images, like the other data of introspection, do not lend themselves to exact measurement. However, most people find it possible to grade images roughly into five classes (very clear, clear, moderately clear, not at all clear, no image); and, when large numbers of images of different types are graded in this way by large numbers of subjects, results show that, though there are wide individual differences, there is a well-marked general tendency for visual imagery to be the clearest, with auditory second, and images of pain and smell at the bottom of the list. This result is quite consistent with the predominance of vision in man, and the relatively low development of the olfactory sense (cf. pp. 96-7).

Visual images are not only clearer, but also more frequent and more intrusive, than other types. They tend to arise spontaneously in connection with most other kinds of imagery, whereas the reverse does not hold good. We can hardly imagine the taste of chocolate or the muscular effort of pulling a roller, without also having a mental picture of chocolate, or of the roller, but, if we have a visual image of a tree, we do not inevitably have an image of the feel of its bark, the rustle of its leaves, or the scent of its blossom.

The extent of individual differences in imagery must, however, be emphasised. Although, for most people, visual imagery is the most important, there are many individuals for whom it is less important than auditory, kinaesthetic, or other types of imagery. There are people who remember their friends by the sound of their voice rather than by their appearance, and they experience in geometry or map-reading an inability to visualise clearly conic sections, spherical triangles, or contours. There are others, skilled in the movements involved in cricket or dancing, or in welding or lathe-turning, who, because they think of these movements in terms of kinaesthetic images (images of their inner muscular "feel"), not in terms of the pictures that they present to a spectator, are sometimes unable to teach or to describe them to pupils whose images of movement are predominantly visual.

Verbal Images

In much of our thinking, especially when it is abstract, we employ images of words more than images of things or events, and these verbal images require special mention. They must not be confused (as they have too often been confused) with the incipient movements of the vocal cords, tongue, lips, and other organs of speech, which often accompany our mental processes. These movements may occur when we are reading or thinking—indeed, the subvocalisation to which they give rise is one of the main avoidable causes of a slow speed of silent reading—but they are no more mental images than is any other bodily movement. What is meant by a verbal image is, quite simply, an image of a word; and this may be a visual image of its written or printed appearance, or an auditory image of its sound, as well as a kinaesthetic or motor image of the movements involved in its expression in speech, writing, or gesture.

Images and Sensations

An image (which has been described as a sort of centrally-aroused sensation) is normally less steady, less vivid, and less distinct than the corresponding sensation. Nevertheless, it is possible in certain circumstances to mistake an image for a sensation, and *vice versa.*

A hallucination, which is only an image of marked vividness and intensity, is regarded as a sensation by the hallucinated individual. Moreover, we may all fail to distinguish between a sensation and an image of a very soft sound; and, as Gardner Murphy records,[1] under appropriate experimental conditions in a dark-room, we cannot tell when we are actually seeing, and when we are merely imagining, a faint picture on a screen. No doubt the isolation of the auditory or the visual sensation in these experiments contributed to

[1] *Introduction to Psychology* (1951), p. 251,

its seeming to be an auditory or visual image. Nevertheless, these experiments demonstrate that sensations and images are not always discernably different.

Individual Differences in Imagery

As has already been said, while in most people visual imagery is the best developed, and auditory imagery comes second, some people depend more on imagery of one of the other kinds, and again, as thinking becomes more abstract, images of words or other symbols become more important than images of objects or events. These differences at one time led to an attempt to divide people into "types" in respect of their predominant imagery, and to label them "visiles," "audiles," etc. But more recent work has shown that people with more or less vivid images of different kinds are more numerous than those in whom one kind of imagery is sufficiently pervasive to justify their being assigned to a definite type.

On the other hand, there are certain oddities of imagery, which do exist in some people, but not in the majority. First, some individuals have *number-forms*—visual images in which the different numbers are arranged in a definite, unvarying form or map—and, whenever they think of a number, this map comes before their mind's eye, and they mentally look at the number in its appropriate place. Galton,[1] who first systematically studied these number-forms (as he studied other aspects of imagery) found that they tended to fall into a few main types, to run in families, and to be unconnected with any special method of learning numbers in childhood. He also noted that people with number-forms are as astonished to find that number-forms are uncommon as the majority, without number-forms, are to learn that some people have them. Later investigators have failed to provide any evidence that the possession of number-forms is associated with exceptional competence in mental arithmetic.

A second oddity is *synaesthesia*, or the tendency to associate images belonging to one sense with sensations, images

[1] *Inquiries into Human Faculty* (1883).   Reprinted in Everyman's Library, 1907.

or ideas that belong to another. The most frequent form of synaesthesia is chromaesthesia, or "coloured thinking," in which images of different colours are associated with different sounds, different people, the different months of the year or days of the week, or the different letters of the alphabet. Scriabin, the composer, associated different colours with different musical keys, and there have been several chromaesthetic musicians who have thought that the enjoyment of a pianoforte solo would be greatly increased if each of the keys in the piano operated a switch for a differently coloured light, so that the sequence of sounds would be accompanied by a sequence of colours. Synaesthesia is presumably only an extreme form of the common tendency to think and talk of "warm reds," "cool blues," "heavy blacks," "free lines," etc., and to judge dark-coloured cubes to be heavier than light-coloured cubes of the same size and weight. In all these instances, images of one sense are associated with sensations or images belonging to another.

Thirdly, some people have images that are unusually detailed, realistic and vivid, and are definitely localised in external space—images that differ from hallucinations only in that they are not mistaken for actual percepts. These *eidetic* images, as they are called (from Greek *eidos*, thing seen), may be rigid, obsessive and disturbing; or they may be plastic, controllable and consonant with the individual's purposes. In its most characteristic form, an eidetic image occurs immediately after the corresponding percept. But eidetic images are not all immediate reproductions of percepts. Often they persist or recur, over a considerable time; and some of them belong to the "constructed," not to the "memory" category.

The detailed and vivid character of eidetic images may be illustrated by a "letter square" experiment of the type described by Gardner Murphy.[1] A square of letters, such as

$$X \quad R \quad B$$
$$L \quad J \quad Z$$
$$C \quad F \quad Q$$

[1] *Op. cit.*, p. 256.

is exposed to a group of subjects, and they are asked to look at it steadily until they feel that they can call up a clear visual image. Most people are confident that they can do this after about a minute, and in fact they have no difficulty in repeating the letters X, R, B, L, J, Z, etc., in the order in which they learned them. But, if they are asked to begin at the top right-hand corner and read the columns *downwards*, most subjects are nonplussed. An eidetic subject, however, would be able from his image to read off the letters vertically, diagonally, backwards or in any order desired.

Eidetic images are quite common among children (they occur in approximately 60 per cent. of children between the ages of ten and fifteen), but they usually wane in adolescence. Allport[1] has experimented with eidetic children, and found that if they look at a complicated picture for 35 seconds, they usually have no difficulty in projecting a clear and detailed image of it on to a grey screen. The picture used in Allport's experiment was a German street scene, which included, not very conspicuously, an inn-sign bearing the word *Gartenwirth-schaft*. Ten of the thirty children tested (who knew no German) were able to spell out this word, either forwards or backwards, from their image, with no more than two errors.

Eidetic imagery is not unknown among adults, although it is rare. Thouless[2] quotes the case of a blindfold chess player who employed eidetic imagery of the board and pieces. When he was playing two games at once, he could banish one image and summon the other as required. Some public speakers read off their speeches from an eidetic image of the manuscript. Galton mentions one statesman who employed this method, and who attributed certain hesitations in his speech to corrections in the script from which he was "reading." Many poets and artists, too, have had rich eidetic visions, which have helped to determine their vocation, and have influenced their actual poems and pictures.

[1] "Eidetic Imagery," *Brit. J. Psychol.*, 1924, **15**, 99.
[2] *General and Social Psychology*, 1958, p. 136.

The Functions of Images

At least as important as the nature of images are their functions, to which, in recent years, Allport, Bartlett and Pear, among others, have given special attention.

First, images are essential ingredients in all distinct thinking (perhaps in *all* thinking) about objects or events that are not present and actual, but past, future or merely possible. It was once keenly debated whether there are "imageless thoughts," thoughts unaccompanied by any form of imagery; and, although the debate is now less keen than it was, the question cannot be regarded as settled. James and Stout both held that in many mental processes there are "imageless transitions"—indeterminate, vague states containing no definite images. But both these psychologists agreed that clear thinking, as distinct from these vague transitional states, always involves some sort of imagery, if only verbal imagery; and more recent experimental work[1] has, on the whole, strengthened this view.

Secondly, images are an aid to memory. We can remember more easily what we can visualise, or image in auditory, kinaesthetic or other ways. Many systems for improving the memory, though they often pay too little attention to other kinds of images, make great play with the value of visual images in memory-training; and many experiments have proved the value of visual aids in learning. Valentine,[2] for example, has devised an interesting lecture experiment, in which two short historical passages of equal length and difficulty are read aloud to the class. During the reading, one passage is illustrated by a map on the blackboard, while the other is not. (Both passages are provided with maps, and it makes no difference which is used.) After each passage has been read, the class is invited to answer thirteen questions about its content—the map, of course, being then concealed. Invariably, a far higher proportion of right answers are given to the piece with the map.

---

[1] Cf. Friedländer, H. F., "The Recalling of Thoughts," *Brit. J. Psychol.*, 1947, **37**, 87.

[2] *Introduction to Experimental Psychology* (4th edit., 1947), pp. 42-6.

Thirdly, verbal images, as has already been stated, assist abstract thought, as for example, in mathematics and the other sciences, where we should be hamstrung if we could not mentally image words, numbers and other symbols. "If I think of life," said Stout,[1] "I think of a general kind of process manifested in an indefinite diversity of special ways. The word 'life' enables me to fix attention on the common form of process in contradistinction to its manifold modes of presentation. A mental picture imitative of the object is less adapted to fulfil this function than the word 'life.'" Some psychologists, however, and notably Pear,[2] urge that concrete non-verbal images are much more useful in abstract thought than has sometimes been supposed. They emphasise the value of actual and imaged models in many branches of science, and they point out that we often employ non-verbal images for abstract ideas (e.g. an image of scales for justice), and that visual statistics make many abstractions clear to those who might otherwise never understand them.

Fourthly, images are an aid in invention, problem-solving, and all other mental manipulation of actual or possible objects. An architect envisaging a new building, a mechanic imagining what is wrong in the invisible interior of a faulty machine, a chess player foreseeing what the position will be after a series of possible moves and counter-moves, and a boy imagining what his muscular sensations will be if he jumps down from a twelve-foot wall: all these are using images to guide their thought and behaviour.

Fifthly, images enter into our appreciation of literature, painting, sculpture and all the other arts. When we are look-ing at a picture or a statue, we are having, not only visual sensations and percepts, but also a variety of images deriving from the other senses, as when we mentally experience, however dimly, the sound, taste, smell, touch, temperature or movement of what is portrayed. Again, when we are reading poetry or prose of artistic merit, our experience includes images of the sounds of the words, and images of the objects and events to which the words refer. Some poets

[1] *Manual of Psychology* (5th, rev. edit., 1944), pp. 149-50.
[2] *The Place of Imagery in Mental Processes* (1937).

(*e.g.* Shelley and Tennyson) make great use of visual images, others (*e.g.* Swinburne, but not Browning) are specially attentive to auditory images, others (*e.g.* Longfellow) paint word-pictures, while others again (*e.g.* Pope in *The Essay on Man*) are more concerned to convey thoughts than to evoke definite images of particular things. But all poetry and prose employs images to a greater or lesser extent, and speech or writing that is designed to affect our feelings or behaviour makes use of the fact that concrete, vivid images have much more power than abstract, general terms to excite emotion and instigate action.

NOTES ON READING

Peter McKellar, *Imagination and Thinking* (Cohen and West: 1956), is an important recent contribution to the study of imagery. T. H. Pear, who has repeatedly emphasised the importance of non-verbal imagery, gives an interesting account of imagery in *Remembering and Forgetting* (Methuen: 1922). On eidetic imagery, E. R. Jaensch, *Eidetic Imagery* (Kegan Paul: 1930), is the original authority, but subsequent experiments, like those of Allport to which we have referred, have greatly clarified the facts.

CHAPTER XI

INTELLIGENCE AND INTELLIGENCE TESTING

"Intelligence," like "instinct," is a word that is freely used but seldom defined. If we were to say that intelligence is the factor that is common to all mental abilities, the reader would not feel greatly enlightened. But, in fact, this definition enshrines one of the most important psychological discoveries of the century.

Spearman's Theory of Intelligence

In 1904, Spearman (1863-1945) brought mathematical evidence to show that all measurable mental abilities are related.[1] His earliest inquiries dealt with a somewhat limited range of activities, but later investigations, covering musical capacity, aptitude for mathematics, grasp of mechanical principles, logical memory and many other abilities, have amply confirmed the view that they all tend to go together. The relationship need not be close, but, in statistical language, the correlation, however small, is always positive[2]—in other words, the fact that a person possesses any particular mental ability makes it more likely, not less likely, that he possesses any other. This discovery conflicts with the popular view that nature works on a compensatory principle, so that ability in one direction is balanced by weakness in another.

Spearman went on to maintain (as the result of a statistical argument too complex to summarise here) that the degree and type of the correlation that exists can be explained only on

[1] In *Amer. J. Psychol.*, 1904, **15**, 284.

[2] The degree of relationship is expressed by the correlation coefficient, which lies between $+1$ and -1. Perfect *positive* correlation, as between the readings of two thermometers under identical conditions, gives a coefficient of $+1$. Perfect inverse or *negative* correlation, as between the amount of sand in the two bulbs of an hour glass, gives a coefficient of -1. Complete absence of relationship (as between, say, hair colour and intelligence) gives a coefficient of 0. Imperfect positive correlation gives a coefficient between $+1$ and 0, and imperfect negative correlation a coefficient between 0 and -1.

the hypothesis that all mental abilities have some factor in common. He called this common factor g; and he held that each of our mental abilities depends partly on g, and partly on a second factor specific to itself. Some abilities, such as ability in mathematics, depend mainly on g: others, such as ability in drawing, depend mainly on specific factors. Later research has brought out the fact that, in addition to the general factor g and the specific factors, there are also group factors, each of which enters into some, but not all, intellectual activities. Thus any particular mental activity depends partly on g, partly on the group factors which it shares with related mental tasks, and partly on factors specific to itself. Among the most firmly established group factors are: (i) verbal ability, which involves facility in the comprehension and use of words, (ii) numerical ability, which enters largely into arithmetic, but not so much into other forms of mathematics, such as geometry, (iii) mechanical ability, (iv) the ability to grasp spatial relationships and (v) musical ability. Many forms of intellectual activity depend more on group factors than on g.

The Nature of g

According to Spearman, g consists essentially of the capacity for relational thinking. Slightly modifying his original definition, we may describe it as *the capacity to discern relevant qualities and relations, and to educe relevant correlates.*

This definition requires some elucidation. If we are asked "What is the relation of black to white?" and reply "Opposite," we have discerned a relation. If we are asked "What is the opposite of black?" and reply "White," we have educed a correlate. In the first case we have been given two terms or, more technically, "fundaments," and asked to state the relation between them. In the second case, we have been given one fundament and a relation, and asked to supply the second fundament. If we symbolise any statement of a relationship (such as "black is the opposite of white") by XrY, then in the first case we have been given X and Y and asked to supply r, and in the second case we have been given X and r, and asked to supply Y.

The evidence for this definition of *g* is, once again, mathematical. Statistical analysis shows that tasks are saturated with *g* in proportion as they involve analytic and constructive relational thinking—that is, the sort of thinking involved in the solution of problems.

Spearman regarded *g* as broadly equivalent to what is generally meant by intelligence, and study of common usage supports this view. The sorts of activity that would be universally admitted to involve intelligence include, for example, solving a chess problem, working out the proof of a theorem in geometry, or thinking out improvements to the design of a machine. All these activities clearly involve grasping the relevant relations between the fundaments of a situation, and bringing new fundaments into consciousness by a process of eduction.

The proviso that the relations discerned, and the correlates educed, must be relevant, is an important one. A charwoman known to the writer was advised to cover the wireless set during a thunderstorm. She decided to take no risks and covered the non-electric gramophone also. She had engaged in relational thinking, but the relation discerned was irrelevant.

Intelligence Tests

Modern intelligence tests consist mainly of problems that involve the discerning of relations, the eduction of correlates, or both. One of the best examples is the analogies test, first used by Burt: *dog* is to *puppy* as *cat* is to mouse, tail, kitten, milk—the testee being required to underline the correct word. Here the testee has first to discern the relation between dog and puppy, then to educe a correlate—*i.e.* to find what bears the same relation to cat as puppy does to dog. More difficult examples of the same type are "motive is to method as why is is to manner, try, wherefore, how"; and "sparrow is to animal as leaf is to flower, bird, vegetable, tree."

A low score in tests of this kind is often due partly to the tendency to be misled by irrelevant relations. In the last-quoted analogy, many people seize on the common but irrelevant association between "leaf" and "flower" or "leaf" and "tree," to the neglect of the less obvious relation between "leaf" and "vegetable" which, in this context, is the only relevant one.

The fundaments related need not necessarily be words. They may be numbers—*e.g.* a series of numbers is given such as 1, 3, 2, 5, 3, 7, 4, 9, and the subject is asked to continue the series for two numbers more. This requires him to find the relating principle of the series, and to supply two more items related in the same way. Analogies and other types of test may also be presented in the form of diagrams. For example,

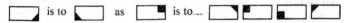

It is impossible to devise problems that do not demand some group factor (such as verbal ability or numerical ability) as well as *g*; and most intelligence tests in general use consist of a variety of problems, presented in different forms and involving different types of material, so that the influence of the various group factors may cancel out. For some practical purposes, however, this is not entirely satisfactory, since in many fields of intellectual activity success depends as much on group factors as on *g*.[1] A recent development, made possible by improved statistical techniques, is to devise tests that will measure the influence of each of the group factors, as well as of *g*, instead of seeking to reduce the influence of these group factors to a minimum.

Standardisation of Intelligence Tests

An intelligence test is of no value until it has been standardised. The fact that a boy has scored, say, 127 in an intelligence test tells us nothing in itself, since we do not know if this is a normal, an exceptionally high, or an exceptionally low score for a boy of his age. We require a norm or standard with which an individual's performance can be compared.

Clearly, there is no method of determining *a priori* what a "normal" person "ought" to score in a particular test. The "normal" score is simply the average score (or a score in the

[1] Some critics go further, and suggest that the concept of *g* can be dispensed with: intelligence, in their view, is simply the name given to one or another combination of group factors. For a statement of this view, see H. J. Eysenck, *Uses and Abuses of Psychology* (1953).

middle range). Accordingly, every test must be given to a large and representative sample of those for whom it is intended, and the average, range and distribution of scores must be discovered; and, if the test is intended for children of various ages, we must discover the scores of each separate age group. Then, and only then, shall we possess the knowledge which will enable us to evaluate any particular score.

Mental Age and the IQ

Pioneer work in standardisation was done by Binet, who, in 1905, in collaboration with Simon, set out to devise a series of tests to determine which Parisian children were incapable of profiting from the ordinary type of school education. Binet was not greatly concerned to define what he was trying to measure, and many of his original tests were unsatisfactory by modern standards, since they measured acquired knowledge rather than intelligence.[1] They had also the practical disadvantage that, being given orally in question-and-answer form, they could not be applied to groups of children simultaneously. For the purpose for which they were designed, however, the tests were highly successful, and in a revised form, they are still widely used for individual testing. The latest revision (the Terman-Merrill New Stanford Revision) was published in America in 1937.

In the present context, the most important fact about Binet's tests is that they embodied a scale. It is to Binet that we owe the conception of "mental age." Briefly, the mental age (MA) of a child is the age at which the average child obtains the score that he makes. For example, if a child of 10 achieves the score of the average child of 12, his MA is 12. The intelligence quotient (IQ) is the MA expressed as a percentage of the real or chronological age $\left(\dfrac{MA}{CA} \times 100 \right)$—in this case,

[1] Tests of information often provide valuable indirect measures of intelligence. Growth of vocabulary, for example, is correlated with growth of intelligence among children, and a vocabulary test is a prominent feature of the various versions of the Binet Scale. But the modern tendency is to eliminate tests of this type in favour of those that directly involve the discernment of relation and the eduction of correlates.

120. In the average child the MA and CA are, of course, the same, so that the IQ will be 100: but any IQ between 90 and 110 falls within the average range, in the sense that it is not in the top or bottom quarter.

The distribution of IQ's among children is roughly[1] as follows. (The 25 per cent. "above 110" includes the 10 per cent. "above 120" and the 2 per cent. "above 130"—and similarly with the "below 90" group.

IQ	%
above 130	2
,, 120	10
,, 110	25
90-110	50
below 90	25
,, 80	10
,, 70	2

Intelligence does not increase after the age of 16 or 17. In other words, the intelligence test score of the average adult is no higher than that of the average youth or girl of 17, although the adult doubtless has the advantage in acquired knowledge, experience and self-confidence. It is impossible, therefore, to apply the conception of mental age to an adult; some other method must be found of relating his score to a norm.

Percentile Ranking

The method commonly employed is that of percentile or decile ranking. If a person's score gives him a percentile rank of 70, this means that, of the representative sample of the population on whom the test was standardised, 69 per cent. made lower scores than he made, and 30 per cent. made higher scores. Percentiles are commonly grouped into deciles. Those with percentile rankings ranging from 91 to 100 compose the tenth decile, and so on. Thus, when we know a person's percentile or decile ranking, we can see at once how his score compares with that of other adults.

[1] The word "roughly" must be emphasised. The proportions, especially at the extreme high and low ends of the scale, vary appreciably with the type of test employed, since some tests give a greater dispersion of scores than others.

Percentile ranks can be translated into IQ's, if we assume, as we reasonably may, that intelligence is distributed among adults in the same way as among children. Referring to the table on p. 132, we see that only 2 per cent. of children have IQ's above 130. So if an adult's score puts him in the top 2 per cent.—*i.e.* if his percentile rank is 99 or 100—we may say that his IQ is more than 130. If he is in the top 10 per cent.—the tenth decile—he has an IQ of over 120, and so on. But, since with the adults the IQ is no more than an indirect method of expressing the percentile rank, it is now more usual to state the percentile rank directly.

Intelligence and Heredity

There is abundant evidence that intelligence depends largely on heredity. The following table shows the correspondence (expressed in terms of the correlation coefficient)[1] that has been found to exist between the intelligence of people of different degrees of relationship.

Identical twins ...	...	·90
Other siblings[2] ...	...	·50
Cousins ...	...	·27
Unrelated	...	·00

This does not imply, however, that intelligence is entirely hereditary, and that the environment plays no part. Heredity sets an upper limit to intelligence, but it is environmental factors that determine whether that limit shall be reached. The effect of these factors is relatively small in civilisations like our own, where few people are undernourished and everyone goes to school; but in countries where malnutrition and illiteracy are widespread, the effect of environmental factors may well be considerable.

Also, D. O. Hebb[3] has suggested that the effects of the environment may vary with age. In early childhood, when the brain is growing rapidly and synaptic connections are being established, intellectual stimulation may have much

[1] See footnote, p. 127.
[2] *I.e.*, children of the same parents.
[3] *The Organization of Behaviour* (1949).

more effect in developing intelligence than it has in later childhood and adolescence.

This is clearly a most important hypothesis. It is difficult to test experimentally with human subjects, but it has received considerable support from experiments with animals. For example, Hebb himself, in an early experiment, found that rats brought up as pets, and given the run of the house, were markedly superior in problem-solving ability to their litter-mates brought up in cages: and he concluded that "the richer experience of the pet group during development made them better able to profit by new experiences at maturity."[1] Later experimenters found similar, irreversible, effects of early experience on the problem-solving ability of dogs.[2]

Facts Revealed by Intelligence Testing

Other facts of interest revealed by intelligence testing may be briefly recounted.

(i) There is little evidence of significant differences in intelligence between people of different European nations. Negroes, on the average, score lower than white men in intelligence tests, but this may be due to the fact that most intelligence tests were designed by white men in a "white" environment, and are not wholly suited to men with a different cultural background. In any case, there is considerable over-lapping: many negroes score above the average for whites, and many white men score below the average for negroes.

(ii) There is no difference between the average intelligence of men and women.

(iii) The popular belief that intelligence is associated with frail physique is quite unfounded. Actually, there is a slight positive correlation between intelligence and physical development. It is true that the children at the top of the class are often smaller and lighter than those at the bottom, but no

---

[1] *Op. cit.*, pp. 298-9.
[2] Thompson, W. R., and Heron, W., "The Effect of Restricted Early Experience on the Problem-solving Capacity of Dogs." *Canad. J. Psychol.*, 1954, **8**, 17-31, quoted by Barnett, S. A., in "Exploratory Behaviour," *Brit. J. Psychol.* 1958, **49**, p. 300

inference can be drawn from this fact until we compare their respective ages. The brightest children in a class may be considerably younger than the dullards.

(iv) There is a definite relationship between delinquency and mental dullness. By no means all delinquents are unintelligent, but 8 per cent. of delinquents (as against 2 per cent. of non-delinquents) are mentally defective, in that their I.Q's are below the recognised border-line of 70; and the average intelligence of child delinquents is appreciably lower than that of the general child population.[1] During the Second World War, a similar relation between delinquency and dullness was found in the Army.

Uses of Intelligence Tests

Intelligence tests are employed for many practical purposes. They are of great value to the vocational psychologist, as an aid to determining the types of occupation for which an individual is best fitted. Occupational success, of course, depends on many factors besides intelligence: it depends also on special aptitudes, attainments, physical qualities, interests and character traits. But there are many occupations in which high intelligence is a prerequisite, though not a guarantee, of success. A boy of no more than average intelligence who attempts to train for one of the higher professions is wasting his time. Conversely, where a person of high intelligence is employed on routine work, his talents are lost to the community, and he himself may suffer great unhappiness and frustration. In doubtful cases, an intelligence test may save years of misdirected effort.

Educational psychologists are making increasing use of intelligence tests. For example, such tests are used (in conjunction with the ordinary examination) in selecting pupils for different types of secondary education. They are of great value, too, in the investigation of educational backwardness and the diagnosis of mental deficiency. They can help to determine whether poor achievement is due primarily to low intelligence, or to other causes such as bad teaching or emotional conflict. Tests of intelligence are also employed

[1] Cf. Burt, *The Young Delinquent* (1925), pp. 296 ff.

in the guidance of "problem" and difficult children. Here, as in occupational guidance, intelligence is, of course, only one of many factors that must be investigated. But in many cases the child's troubles are due primarily to the fact that he is of mediocre or low ability, and that his parents, unwilling to recognise this, are trying to drive him towards a level of achievement that he cannot reach.

NOTES ON READING

Fuller discussions of the nature of intelligence will be found in R. H. Thouless, *General and Social Psychology*; R. Knight, *Intelligence and Intelligence Tests* (4th revised ed., 1948); and P. E. Vernon, *Intelligence and Attainment Tests* (Univ. of London Press: 1960). Comprehensive accounts of the design, standardisation, use and interpretation of intelligence tests are given in Anne Anastasi, *Psychological Testing*, and Lee J. Cronbach, *Essentials of Psychological Testing* (Harper and Row: 1964), and there is a useful short treatment in L. Tyler, *Tests and Measurements* (Foundations of Modern Psychology Series. New Jersey and London, Prentice-Hall: 1963). Detailed instructions on the application and scoring of Binet tests are given in L. M. Terman and M. A. Merrill, *The Stanford-Binet Intelligence Scale: Manual for the Third Revision* (Harrap: 1961).

CHAPTER XII

ANIMAL LEARNING

Some of the liveliest psychological controversies of recent years have raged around the theory of learning. We know that learning occurs, and we know a great deal about the factors that facilitate it. But when we tackle the basic questions, "What is learning? And what physiological changes take place in the brain and nervous system when we learn?", we find ourselves beset by problems.

Habit Learning and True Learning

We must begin by distinguishing two senses of learning—habit or motor learning (the sense in which we learn how to swim, or to ride a bicycle) and true or ideational learning (the sense in which we learn how an engine works, or understand the proof of a theorem in geometry). The distinction is not as clear-cut as it appears at first, since many familiar forms of learning fall into an intermediate category; but this point will be discussed later.

Investigations into the nature of learning usually begin with the relatively simple learning processes of animals, and here there are two main schools of thought. The first school lays all the emphasis on habit learning, and maintains that animal learning—at all events below the level of the higher apes—results simply from a blind process of trial and error. This view is associated with the names of E. L. Thorndike (1874-1949) and C. L. Hull (1884-1952). The *Gestalt* school, on the other hand, lays all the emphasis on true learning, and maintains that an element of "insight"[1] or "seeing how" is apparent in animal learning even at a comparatively low level. W. Köhler (1887) and E. C. Tolman (1886-1961) are the chief exponents of this view.

[1] The precise relation of "insight" (in the *Gestalt* sense) to intelligence is discussed on pp. 149-51.

The Background of Animal Psychology

It may help to clarify the issues to glance at the background of animal psychology. Until the latter part of the 19th century, there was a widespread tendency to explain the behaviour of animals along anthropomorphic lines. Animals were regarded, to quote Julian Huxley, as "little human beings with just the same thoughts and emotions as ourselves, which they are, for some reason, unable to express." The quotations from Romanes on pp. 8-9 provide examples of this anthropomorphic approach.

Later, however, a reaction set in. It was argued that inferences about the cognitive states of animals are at best precarious, and that the behaviour of most animals can be explained quite adequately without assuming that they have intellectual processes similar to our own. In 1891 Lloyd Morgan, a pioneer in this field, laid down his famous Canon of Parsimony, which asserts: "In no case may we interpret an action as the outcome of the exercise of a higher psychical faculty, if it can be interpreted as the outcome of the exercise of one which stands lower in the psychological scale." [1]

The reaction went so far that it has led some theorists to feel that the only really scientific approach to animal psychology is to proceed on the assumption that animals are automata without consciousness: thus they will never allow themselves to say (for example) that an animal "wants," "fears" or "expects" something. But this view is now losing ground in its turn, and we appear to be working our way towards a more balanced outlook, which combines the elements of truth in both the anthropomorphic and the automaton theories. The current attitude has been well summed up by D. O. Hebb: "The true objection to anthropomorphism is not to discovering a similarity of mechanism in human and animal behaviour, but to inventing similarities that do not exist." [2]

Thorndike's Experiments on Animal Learning

One of the pioneer experimenters on animal learning was E. L. Thorndike. In 1897-98, when he was only 23, he

[1] *An Introduction to Comparative Psychology*, p. 59.
[2] "Emotion in Man and Animal," *Psychol. Rev.*, 1946, **53**, pp. 88-105.

carried out a number of experiments, and put forward various
conclusions, which, though they are no longer widely accepted,
have provided the starting-point for nearly all subsequent
discussions on the subject.

Thorndike's experimental animals were usually cats, and
he worked with trick-cages or puzzle-boxes. These were
boxes with sides made of bars or wire, and doors which could
be opened from within by lifting a latch, pulling a loop, or
some similar action. His method was to put a hungry cat in

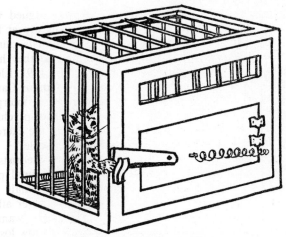

Fig. 37. CAT IN PUZZLE-BOX.
(From B.B.C. Talks Pamphlet, *The Study of the Mind*, by Cyril Burt.)

the box with food outside, and to observe how soon, and by
what means, the cat learned to get out.

In every case, the cat begins by clawing and scratching
about the box in a more or less random manner. To quote
Thorndike's own description, which has now become classical:

"The cat shows evident signs of discomfort and of an
impulse to escape from confinement. It tries to squeeze
through any opening; it claws and bites at the bars or
wire; it thrusts its paws out through any opening and
claws at everything it reaches; it continues its efforts

when it strikes anything loose or shaky; it may claw at things within the box." [1]

In the course of these activities, the cat sooner or later claws at the latch or loop so as to open the door. At the next trial the same sort of thing happens, but the number of random movements is less; and in subsequent trials the decrease continues, though irregularly, until finally, when the cat is put into the box, it goes straight to the latch and claws it, and

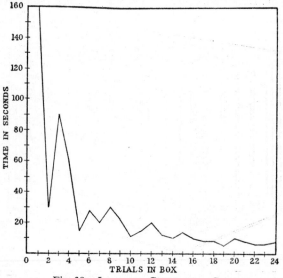

Fig. 38. LEARNING CURVE OF A CAT.

this particular learning-process is complete. The hungrier the animal, the more rapidly it learns; and, as later experiments have shown, an immediate "reward," in the shape of food, has a far greater effect in speeding up learning than a reward that is not given until some time after the problem has been solved.

If the time taken in successive trials is measured, and the results plotted in the form of a graph, we get a "learning curve" of the type shown in Fig. 38.

[1] *Animal Intelligence* (1911), p. 35.

This is typical of the curves produced by most laboratory animals in most types of experimental learning—for example, by rats learning to run mazes, or chicks learning to escape from confinement by scrambling through a piece of stovepipe set at an angle. The number of trials necessary for success will vary with the difficulty of the problem and with the strength of the incentive, but nearly all the curves show the characteristic tendency to fall gradually (though irregularly), rather than suddenly.

Thorndike's chief contention was that animal learning takes place purely by trial and error, and does not involve any element of insight. The cat has learned to get out, rather as we learn to balance on a bicycle—he does not "see" how to do it, but has merely formed a series of motor habits. Trial-and-error learning, on Thorndike's view, takes place in accordance with three Laws: (i) The Law of Frequency: movements most frequently performed tend to be repeated; (ii) The Law of Recency: movements most recently performed tend to be repeated; (iii) The Law of Effect: right movements tend to be "stamped in" by the satisfaction of success, and wrong movements to be "stamped out" by the dissatisfaction of failure. The Law of Effect, more elaborately formulated and renamed the Principle of Reinforcement, has played a central part in the work of another proponent of habit learning, C. L. Hull.

The "Laws of Learning" and the Principle of Association

Thorndike's Laws of Learning have a familiar sound. They recall that corollary of the Principle of Association (cf. pp. 48-9), which states that the strength of an association between two ideas is a function of the frequency, recency and intensity with which they have been associated in the past. The Principle of Association deals with connections between ideas, and Thorndike's Laws with connections between stimuli and motor responses. But, except for this difference, the "Laws" are little more than a special application of the older doctrine. As such, they are open to most of the objections that have been urged against it, as well as to certain others peculiar to themselves.

The great difficulty about Thorndike's Laws, as about Hull's Principle of Reinforcement, is that, since ostensibly they relate to motor responses and not to symbolic processes, they imply that learning has been in purely motor terms—in other words, that what the animal has learned is a particular sequence of movements. And this is emphatically not the case. The cat in the puzzle-box, for example, does not always make precisely the same movements to get out. A cat that has learned to pull a loop may sometimes pull it

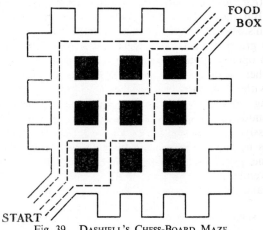

Fig. 39.   DASHIELL'S CHESS-BOARD MAZE.

The alleys were only slightly wider than the rat's body, so that there was no possibility of cutting corners.

with its right paw, sometimes with its left paw, and sometimes with its teeth.

Many subsequent experiments have confirmed this finding. One of the most striking was carried out by J. F. Dashiell, who trained rats in a chess-board maze (Fig. 39), in which there are twenty different routes, all of equal length, from the starting-point to the food-box. (Three of these routes are shown by dotted lines.) On the Hull-Thorndike principle, it would be predicted that a rat would learn one particular path through the maze, and consistently follow it. But, in fact, the rats varied their routes from one run to the next.

Brain-injured rats showed less tendency to variation, but even they were far from exhibiting the complete stereotypy of behaviour that the Hull-Thorndike theory demands.

These facts conclusively refute the purely "motor" theory of animal learning. But Thorndike's Laws of Learning may still be valid in a modified form, and it is still possible to defend the view that all animal learning is essentially blind. Many psychologists would explain the facts somewhat as follows. The cat has gradually come to associate a particular action (*e.g.* pulling a loop) with a particular result (*i.e.* getting out). But the association is quite non-rational—like Lloyd Morgan's association of music with monkeys (p. 48). The cat has no grasp of cause and effect. If it had, it would "see" how to open the door when once it had done it by accident, and when next put into the box would go straight to the loop without further trial and error. But, in fact, as the learning curves show, trial-and-error behaviour does not stop suddenly in this way. All that happens is that it progressively decreases. Thus all the evidence suggests that there is no sudden moment of insight—no "aha" experience, as some psychologists have called it—but only a gradual improvement as the correct association is slowly built up in accordance with the Laws of Frequency, Recency and Effect.

Köhler versus Thorndike

This view, or something like it, was for years fairly widely accepted. About 1920, however, a powerful antagonist entered the field in the person of the *Gestalt* psychologist, Wolfgang Köhler. Köhler argued[1] that Thorndike got the results he did get, simply because he put his cats in situations that were quite unnatural (from an animal's point of view) and set them problems that were beyond their capacity. An animal cannot be expected to "see," after a single experience, that pulling a loop will cause a door to open. But, with simpler problems, there is often clear evidence of insight. Sometimes trial and error ceases after one success, and sometimes the animal solves the problem immediately, without any trial and error at all.

[1] In *The Mentality of Apes* (1925), and elsewhere.

For example, if, as a simple experiment, we put a dog behind a short length of wire fencing with food on the other side, he will at once "see" the solution and run round the end of the fence. This is admittedly a very simple problem, but it is a genuine one: a hen in the same position often makes frantic efforts to force its way through the wire. Köhler argues that when we are experimenting with animals, whose intelligence is at best only rudimentary, we *must* use simple problems; and he also points out that Thorndike loaded the dice against his experimental animals by setting them problems in which they could not "inspect the total situation"— *i.e.* in which the elements necessary for solution were not all simultaneously before them. Even a human being, if he were placed in a maze or a puzzle-box, could adopt no other method than trial and error. As McDougall said: "Let us imagine twenty college professors shut in as many cages in a condition of 'utter hunger,' while a table is temptingly spread before the line of cages. And let us suppose that each one can secure his release only by scratching a hole in the ground with his finger-nails and rummaging with his nose at the bottom of this hole. The conditions would be comparable to those imposed on his cats by Professor Thorndike. Is it not possible that a Martian observer, knowing little of human nature, might infer from the behaviour of the professors that they were creatures of small intelligence, much given to random movements and meaningless vociferations?"[1]

Köhler's Experiments with Apes

Köhler himself carried out a large number of experiments with apes, setting them problems which were of fundamentally the same kind as the one of the dog and the food. They all involved confronting the animal with a "goal" (usually food), to which the direct path was barred, but an indirect path left open, and visible to the animal. Solution of the problem lay in taking the indirect path.

In such situations, apes showed unmistakable evidence of insight. They would use bamboo sticks, for example, to draw in bananas lying out of reach beyond the bars of their

[1] *An Outline of Psychology* (1923), p. 195.

cage. One ape successfully joined together two sticks for this purpose. Other apes piled up boxes and climbed on them to reach bananas hanging from the ceiling. These experiments are not in themselves a refutation of Thorndike, since Thorndike himself, unlike many of his disciples, did not deny insight to apes. But results similar in nature, though less striking, have been obtained with rats and other animals, when they were given problems appropriate to their powers.[1]

Krechevsky,[2] for example, trained rats in a "discrimination box," in which they had to choose between two pathways, one of which was a blind alley while the other led to food. By means of movable doors, the "food" path was changed irregularly from right to left, but its position was always indicated by a low hurdle at the entrance, which the rats had to cross. Woodworth[3] describes experiments on similar lines, where rats were confronted with two doors, only one of which led to food. The "food" door was changed irregularly from right to left, but was always marked by a light burning above it. The learning curves of the rats in these experiments differed significantly from those of Thorndike's cats. Since only two choices were open, about 50 per cent. of correct responses could be expected by chance alone, and this was in fact the proportion usually obtained in the earlier runs. But when the rise did come, it came, in many cases, comparatively suddenly. There was not a slowly increasing proportion of right choices, but a rapid advance from 50 per cent. to nearly 100 per cent. successes. This result strongly suggests insight—as though, after a period of bewilderment, the rats had suddenly "got the idea" of responding to the hurdle or the light, and ignoring the right-left position.

Levels of Insight

Thorndike tended to speak of insight as something that must be possessed either completely or not at all. But, in

---

[1] Cf., for example, Adams, D. K., "Experimental Studies of Adaptive Behaviour in Cats," *Comp. Psychol. Monographs*, 1929, **6**, No. 27; and "A Restatement of the Problem of Learning," *Brit. J. Psychol.*, 1931, **22**, 150.

[2] "'Hypotheses' versus 'Chance' in the Pre-Solution Period in Sensory Discrimination-Learning," *Univ. Calif. Pub. Psychol.*, **6**, No. 3, 1932.

[3] *Psychology: a Study of Mental Life* (1940), p. 300.

fact, there are degrees of insight. There may, for example, be many levels of insight into the working of a wireless set— from that of the trained radio-engineer to that of the child who knows which knob he has to turn to switch on. When the domestic wireless set fails to function, we may try to put it right by trial-and-error activities not very unlike those of the cat in the puzzle-box.

> "*Homo sapiens* showed evident signs of displeasure, and of a desire for music. He twiddled the knobs in a more or less random manner, pulled out the H.T. plugs and replaced them, fingered connections, pulled and shook anything loose, and occasionally thumped the cabinet. In the course of these activities, he happened to move a loose valve (the cause of the trouble) and thus restored a broken contact. He was clearly startled by the burst of sound that ensued, and had no grasp of the relation between his action and the result. The stamping-in effect was, however, obvious. In subsequent breakdowns, random movements were progressively reduced, and activity tended to centre on the valves."

This is not a wholly frivolous parallel. It is intended to bring out two points: (i) The cat that has learned to pull a loop to escape from a puzzle-box, cannot have complete insight, since it cannot be expected to understand the mechanism of the box; but it has the same sort of rudimentary insight as the man who knows that when his wireless goes wrong he can sometimes start it again by fiddling about in the neighbourhood of the valves. (ii) Although in both cases the solution was reached by trial and error, it is begging the question to describe the activities involved as "random." What we are witnessing in both cases is *experimental behaviour*. Much of it, no doubt, seems to an expert ludicrously inappropriate, but this does not alter the fact that the activities of both cat and man (apart from those that are mere expressions of annoyance) are conative movements, directed by their grasp (admittedly very rudimentary) of possible means to ends.

The Nature of Insight

So far, we have not attempted to give a precise definition of "insight" as the *Gestalt* psychologists use the term. Essentially, it seems to consist of a reorganisation of the perceptual field—elements, previously separate, being seen as an actual or potential *Gestalt*. This reorganisation may come about in different ways. A simple *Gestalt* may be enriched and made more complex by the incorporation of new elements ("integration"); or what at first appeared chaotic may come to reveal a definite internal structure ("structurisation"). (This last experience is one that many of us have with unfamiliar music or modernist paintings.) With the experimental animals, reorganisation occurred when, for example, the loop was seen as a thing-to-be-pulled, or when what was once a mere box or stick was suddenly seen as a link with the desired banana.

Insight, as thus defined, is present in nearly all animal learning, even in that simple form involved in the conditioned reflex. The perceptual field of Pavlov's dogs is reorganised when a bell has ceased to be a mere noise and become a signal for food. Similarly, with the "natural" conditioned responses that arise outside the laboratory, as when a puppy learns to regard outdoor shoes with joy, and carbolic soap with uneasiness.

In the above examples, insight has dawned gradually, but in its most characteristic (and advanced) forms it occurs in a sudden flash—as when the ape suddenly realised that he could reach the banana if he stood on a box. In some cases (as in the example of the dog and the wire fence on p. 144), this "flash" is not evident, as the solution is seen as soon as the problem is presented. But when there is a sudden transition from "not seeing" to "seeing," the experience may be compared with those sudden shifts of perception that occur, for example, with Fig. 34 on p. 102: or with "puzzle-pictures," like that in Fig. 40, when the hidden figure springs out from the background.

Köhler found, as would be expected, that it is much easier for animals to organise elements into a *Gestalt* when the elements lie close together in space. An ape, for example, was more likely to use a stick to pull in a banana, if the stick and banana were simultaneously in view. If the stick lay behind the ape, so that he could not see it without turning away from the banana, the problem was more difficult, since some of the elements necessary for solution had to be represented symbolically. A still more difficult problem required the ape to transfer an element mentally from one *Gestalt* to another. Some apes that had solved the stick-and-banana problem were put in a cage where no bamboo stick was available, but where there was a tree with long thin branches that

Fig. 40.   PUZZLE: FIND TWO FACES.

could be easily snapped off. In this situation, only the most intelligent apes broke a branch off the tree.

Physiological Basis of Insight

The *Gestalt* school have put forward a tentative explanation of insight in terms of brain physiology. They suggest that the relational properties of the *Gestalten* we perceive have their counterparts in similar relational properties— similar "patterns of excitation"—in the nerve-cells of the brain. This is a most daring speculation, but at present it is little more, and it is impossible here to discuss it in detail. We may note, however, that this theory (known to the *Gestalt* school as the "isomorphism"[1] of cerebral processes and perception) receives a certain amount of experimental support from the work of Lashley (cf. pp. 37-8).

Insight and Intelligence

Insight, in the *Gestalt* sense, has obviously much in common with intelligence, as already defined. But the term "insight" has a wider connotation, since it is applied to types of learning (such as those involved in conditioning) that most writers would hesitate to call intelligent.

The following hypothesis would link the two concepts together. Animals and (to a lesser degree) humans are determined by the innate constitution of their nervous systems to pick out, and to attend to, certain patterns in the sense-field, and to respond to them in particular ways. So long as animals do no more than this, they are behaving mechanically or instinctively, not intelligently—like the fishes, described by James, which are no sooner cast back from the hook into the water than they automatically seize the hook again.[2] The first glimmerings of intelligence appear when the innate stimulus-response mechanisms become extended and modified as the result of individual experience. This occurs in all the simpler forms of learning, as when a chick, which is innately disposed to peck at everything it sees, learns to regard bits of orange-peel as things-to-avoid. At a higher level, creatures may react spontaneously and successfully to new situations—*i.e.* to stimulus-patterns that have not been experienced before, and that do not evoke an innate response. Köhler's apes had clearly reached this stage, and animals lower in the scale of development also reach it occasionally, when the problem is sufficiently simple—as with the problem of the food and the wire fence, mentioned on p. 144.

Behaviour at either of these levels may be described as "adaptive." At the second level, insight is clearly present;

---

[1] Isomorphism is a term employed in chemistry in relation to substances that are similar in their crystalline form.

[2] James remarks that these fish "would soon expiate the degradation of their intelligence with the extinction of their type, did not their extraordinary fecundity atone for their imprudence."

and, even at the first level, since there has been a reorganisation of the perceptual field, there is insight of a rudimentary kind. But insight of this type is related only distantly to intelligence, in the human sense. Undoubtedly, a creature behaving adaptively is reacting to a complex percept that has been formed by individual experience. Yet the creature is not reasoning. The relations between the elements have been grasped only unconsciously or implicitly: they have not been clearly cognised.[1] A fish that has several times taken the angler's bait and rejected it, may eventually learn by experience to avoid flies of a certain type. But it has not grasped the fact that flies of this type tend to be unpalatable, and to contain sharp points. All that has happened, probably, is that such flies have ceased to look attractive. It is a different matter when a human being refuses, say, pickled onions, because they disagreed with him last week. In this case, recognition of the relation between pickled onions and discomfort is not merely implicit, but conscious.

The same distinction may be drawn in more advanced and more obviously insightful forms of animal learning, such as that of the rats described on p. 145. Rats are strongly disposed by nature to attend to locations, but they are not strongly disposed to attend to lights. In learning to respond to a light and ignore location, therefore, the successful rats had made a drastic revision of their normal modes of perception. But this was probably all that had happened. We need not assume that the rats had consciously grasped the fact that the relation between food and light was constant and the relation between food and location was not: though the suddenness of the rats' learning makes explanations of the latter kind less obviously preposterous than they would be in the case of the fish.

To sum up: adaptive behaviour is the most primitive form of intelligence. It implies the capacity to form and to react to percepts as a result of individual experience, but it does not imply reasoning: it does not imply, in other words,

[1] This implicit awareness of relations is a familiar experience, even among humans. For example, if a friend alters the position of the furniture in his room, we may realise that the room looks different, but be unable to say just what the difference is.

that the elements of the percept have been, or could be, explicitly discriminated and the relations between them grasped. Fully intelligent behaviour involves the capacity to grasp, and to attend to, relations as such, and to educe correlates (pp. 128-9). On this view, there is no clear dividing line between adaptive and intelligent behaviour. As we ascend the animal scale from the amoeba to the ape, one type of behaviour passes over gradually into the other.

Animal Memory

Memory and learning are two aspects of the same process, and many of the distinctions made with regard to learning—*e.g.* between habit learning and true learning—apply also to memory. We have tried to show that animals are not confined to habit memory, but it is doubtful whether they have ideational memory or recollection in quite the same sense as human beings.

Obviously, animals have no *verbal* memory, but ideational memory is not necessarily verbal. When we remember where we put our fountain-pen, or whether a particular house is on the right or left of the road, we are probably remembering mainly in terms of visual, non-verbal imagery. Do animals remember in this sense? Common sense would unhesitatingly say that they do, and certain experiments (known as "delayed reaction" experiments) confirm the common-sense verdict. Food, for example, may be placed in one of various receptacles while the animal is looking on, and the animal released after an interval. Rats, cats, dogs and apes will in these circumstances go straight to the hidden food, provided the interval before release is not too long. The maximum interval varies with different animals, but with apes it may be as much as seventeen hours.

The natural inference seems to be that the animal remembers seeing the experimenter conceal the food. But it is not strictly necessary to assume that the animal has conscious recall. What he is experiencing may be no more than associative revival. This distinction, which is an important one, can best be made clear by example.

Recall and Revival

We have all had the experience of meeting someone in the street and recognising his face as familiar, but being quite unable to remember who he is. This is associative revival. If we finally succeed in "placing" him—in remembering, let us say, that he is the postman in mufti, or the new cashier in the bank—we have passed from associative revival to recall. It is probable that memory in animals consists almost entirely of associative revival. When a dog recognises an acquaintance, human or canine, it is unlikely that he has any conscious memory of their former meetings. The acquaintance looks, and smells, pleasant and familiar, and that is probably all. Similarly, when a cat returns to a mousehole, this does not necessarily mean that she remembers catching a mouse there yesterday. But, perceptually, the mousehole area has altered for her. It has associations of excitement and interest that it did not have before. In more general terms, the animal may retain a "set" towards a goal without any clear conscious memory of what the goal is. This situation is not unknown among human beings. Most of us, for example, have at some time opened a drawer or cupboard and suddenly realised that we have forgotten what we were looking for. Similarly, the animal in the delayed-reaction experiment may retain a strong feeling that the food-box is a thing-to-explore, without any conscious memory of what it contains. It seems likely, on general grounds, that conscious recall appears at about the same evolutionary level as "true" intelligence, though some writers, in obedience to the Canon of Parsimony, would deny that animals (even apes) have any conscious recall at all.

Differences between Animal and Human Learning

Man's greater intelligence, his power of abstract thought, and his greater capacity for forming and using symbols, are the basis of the differences between human and animal learning. These differences may be summarised briefly: (i) man uses more insight in the solution of problems; (ii) to a much greater extent than the animals, man can make use of past experience, and apply to present problems techniques that he has learned elsewhere; (iii) man can solve problems by the use of symbolic processes, whereas animals must usually solve them in terms of overt behaviour; (iv) by his power of abstraction, man can eliminate a whole class of solutions at once: when a suggested solution has proved unsatisfactory in some particular respect, all other solutions that resemble it in this respect can be ruled out; (v) man, by the use of language, can learn from explicit instruction.

NOTES ON READING

The *Encyclopaedia Britannica* article on Comparative Psychology by T. C. Schnierla gives a useful account of experimental studies of animal learning. Köhler's experiments are described in detail in his book *The Mentality of Apes* (Kegan Paul: 1925; reprinted in Pelican Books: 1957). Recent developments and controversies in the field of animal and human learning are discussed in S. A. Mednick, *Learning* (Foundations of Modern Psychology Series. New Jersey and London, Prentice-Hall: 1964), P. L. Broadhurst, *The Science of Animal Behaviour* (Pelican Books: 1963), and at a more advanced level in E. R. Hilgard, *Theories of Learning* (Methuen: 2nd revised ed., 1958), and W. H. Thorpe, *Learning and Instinct in Animals* (Methuen: 2nd revised ed., 1963).

CHAPTER XIII

HUMAN LEARNING AND MEMORY

The distinction between habit or motor learning, and true or ideational learning (which involves symbolic processes), has already been drawn, but it is an over-simplification to regard the two types as sharply contrasted. They are rather the extremes of a continuous scale. Towards the middle of the scale lie many familiar forms of human learning, such as learning to typewrite or to drive a car, which involve both an element of insight and an element of habit-formation.

The part played by trial and error in learning increases as we move towards the "motor" end of the scale. But among human beings (and possibly among many animals also) there is no such thing as pure trial-and-error learning. Trial-and-error behaviour is controlled and directed by insight. The beginner at tennis, for example, does not make purely random movements with his racket. The sort of movements he makes are controlled from the first by his knowledge of what he wants to do to the ball, and of how balls behave when rackets strike them. Within these limits, the laws of frequency, recency, and effect may operate, in conjunction with insight, to "stamp in" successful strokes, and to "stamp out" those that land the ball in the net.

Motor Learning in Human Beings

Many experiments have been made with human learning of a predominantly "motor" kind. Typewriting provides a particularly good field for experiment, since improvement, in both speed and accuracy, can be precisely measured. A typical learning curve for a beginner in typewriting is shown in Fig. 41.

This shows clearly two of the characteristic features of human learning curves. These are (i) rapid rise (or fall)[1] in

[1] Whether a learning curve falls or rises depends on the way in which improvement is measured. It may be measured in terms of the time taken to complete a standard number of units (or a prescribed task, as with the cat in the puzzle-box) or in terms of the number of units completed in a standard period of time (as with Fig. 41).

the early stages, followed by a slower rise as the limit of achievement is approached, (ii) periodical "plateaux"—*i.e.* short periods in which no measurable improvement takes place. These plateaux occur in most forms of human motor learning. They are a familiar phenomenon, for example, among athletes, by whom they are usually attributed to "staleness," fatigue or loss of interest. But the explanation probably goes deeper. Acquiring a highly developed skill,

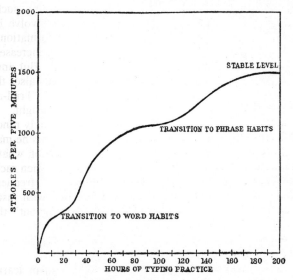

Fig. 41. LEARNING CURVE FOR TYPEWRITING.
[Adapted from R. B. Cattell, *Your Mind and Mine* (Harrap).]

in athletics, typewriting, or any other predominantly motor activity, usually involves forming a series of habits or movement-patterns that are increasingly complex and finely adjusted. Plateaux tend to occur when the subject has mastered a simple pattern and is feeling his way towards a new level of complexity or co-ordination: or, as Cattell puts it, when a simple habit has been mastered and a higher habit is incubating.

In typewriting, for example, the novice has at first to attend to each letter as he strikes it. He then passes to a stage where the word or syllable, rather than the individual letter, becomes the unit; and finally, if he becomes expert, he will type whole phrases with a single rhythmical pattern of finger-movement. In the curve in Fig. 41, the first plateau marks the transition from letter-habits to word-habits, and the second the transition from words to phrases. Similar plateaux occur, for broadly similar reasons, among children learning to write. It is important that this fact should be realised, and that children should not be unduly pressed during these incubation periods; for, though there is no visible improvement, new and more complex neural co-ordinations may be developing internally.

Rote Memory

A somewhat different form of habit-learning is involved in *rote learning*—*i.e.* the memorising of verbal material that is (*a*) meaningless (at all events to the learner), and/or (*b*) disconnected. Some writers class learning of this kind as ideational, mainly on the ground that it involves words: but we can use words without having the corresponding ideas, and some forms of rote learning involve considerably less ideation than are involved, for example, in learning how to start a car on a steep hill, or how to impart top spin to a tennis ball.

If we learn by heart a passage in a foreign language that we do not understand, we are doing little more than forming motor habits of the speech-organs. This is an extreme form of rote learning. Slightly further along the scale towards ideation is learning a disconnected string of words in our own language: here the separate items have meaning, but there is no coherence in the series as a whole. Further still in the direction of ideation would be memorising a passage such as the following, from the specification of a radio-gramophone:

> "The cathode transformer is coupled to four power triodes operated in Class A parallel push-pull with additional negative feed-back."

Here the sentence-structure gives a measure of coherence, and most of the individual words convey some meaning, but the passage as a whole means almost nothing to the uninitiated reader.

Learning at any of these levels is what is popularly known as "parrot-learning." There has been a minimum of ideation; little more has been acquired than a series of verbal habits. Some students have a regrettable tendency to fall back on verbal memorising when they encounter passages in textbooks or lecture-notes that they do not understand. This is most undesirable, even from the relatively sordid point of view of passing examinations. If the student has not grasped the meaning of what he has memorised, his hold on it will at best be precarious; and, as every examiner knows, if the student happens to have written down and uncritically learnt by heart an erroneous, nonsensical note of a lecture, and then reproduces this nonsense in the examination-room, he at once shows himself up as a parrot-learner.

Experiments on Rote Learning

The classical experiments on rote learning were carried out at the end of the last century by the German psychologist Ebbinghaus—one of those patient Teutonic investigators who, in James's phrase, "could never be bored." Most of Ebbinghaus's experiments were conducted with himself as subject: the material memorised consisted of nonsense syllables, such as *lom, buf, seb, gar,* etc., which were carefully constructed to avoid, as far as possible, all resemblance to actual words. Much of Ebbinghaus's work was of mainly academic interest, since the memorising of nonsense syllables bears little relation to any "real-life" activity. The most interesting facts that emerged were: (i) As might be expected, ease of memorising varies almost directly with the meaningfulness of the material. A stanza of poetry could be learned with only one-tenth the number of repetitions that were required for learning an equivalent number of nonsense syllables. (ii) Forgetting is very rapid at first, immediately after learning, and then becomes slower.

A third point, more emphasised by later investigators than by Ebbinghaus, is that subjects faced with strings of nonsense syllables or similar meaningless material, nearly always try to ease the task of learning by imposing some sort of meaning or order on the chaos. If any syllable resembles (however remotely) an actual word, the resemblance is seized upon and this syllable becomes a landmark in the list. Again, when the list is repeated, the time intervals may be varied, and certain syllables accented, so that the separate items are linked in a rhythmical pattern. There is a continual effort, in short, to enlist the help of ideation, and to impose meaning, or at least structure, on the jumble of separate units.

Ideational Memory

It is with ideational memory that the student is mainly concerned. Such memory often involves words, but, as has already been emphasised, does not necessarily do so. Remembering how a tune goes, or what so-and-so looks like, or where the post office is, may involve no verbalisation at all.

It is common to speak of a person as having "a good memory" or "a bad memory," implying that memory is a single function. This is true up to a point: statistical analysis of the results of memory experiments shows that there is a general factor of memory, just as there is a general factor of intelligence. But there are also important group and specific factors. It is probable that the group factors relate to the particular sense through which the material is presented —that is to say, that there are group factors of visual memory, auditory memory, kinaesthetic memory, etc. It is also probable that there are specific factors such as memory for faces, memory for places, memory for numbers, or memory for tunes. The evidence, however, is not yet complete, and it must always be borne in mind that in real-life, as distinct from laboratory, situations, it is emotive rather than cognitive factors that mainly determine remembering. In other words, we remember things primarily because they interest us. Whether the material is presented visually or aurally, or whether it relates to numbers or places or names, are factors of minor importance. A doctor, for example, may find it easy to remember the names of his patients, but difficult to remember the names of people met at social gatherings; and the schoolboy who cannot remember the date of the Battle of Naseby may have no difficulty in remembering his own batting average, or the date of the half-term holiday.

Assimilation, Retention and Recall

Memory, whether rote or ideational, involves at least three elements, namely (i) assimilation, (ii) retention, and (iii) recall and/or recognition. If we are now to remember the main facts about the size and population of Australia, we must at some previous time have assimilated these facts; we must have retained them during the interval; and we must now be able to reproduce them, or at least to recognise them as familiar.

Assimilation, as measured by the amount retained immediately after learning, is highly correlated with intelligence, where meaningful material is involved. *Retention* can be estimated by expressing the amount retained after an interval as a percentage of the amount assimilated. Such retention, it is obvious, will be greatly affected by the number of times the material is mentally reviewed during the interval; but, if such conditions are kept uniform as far as possible, results suggest that retention depends mainly on organic factors, and that it is but slightly correlated with intelligence. It is greatly affected by variable physiological conditions such as fatigue and ill-health, as well as by emotional factors. *Recall and recognition* must be distinguished. Often, though we cannot recall a fact or a name, we can recognise it unhesitatingly when it is put before us. Some memory experiments use recognition rather than recall as a criterion of retention. The nonsense syllables (or whatever the material is) that have been learned, are intermingled with new and unfamiliar syllables, and the subject is asked to pick out those that he recognises. A similar technique is employed in some "new-type" examinations, where, instead of being required to write answers in essay form, the candidate is presented with a series of statements such as "The first Parliament of Great Britain was formed in 1654, 1707, 1745, 1776," and is required to underline the correct year.

Recall differs from recognition in two respects. It is a more arduous and less passive process (scores in memory experiments are invariably higher when recognition, not recall, is demanded): and, except in the simplest forms of memory, recall is essentially a selective activity. In real-life situations, we seldom want to reproduce material in the exact form in which we learned it. Usually, we search our minds for memories that are relevant to some present problem or interest. Is there anything we learned about dynamics at school, for example, that bears on the problem of how to siphon the last few inches of water out of the garden tank? In such cases, the recall of accurate but irrelevant information may be a hindrance.

Relevance of recall is obviously closely related to intelligence. An accurate but unselective memory is the mark of the second-rate student. Every examiner knows the type of candidate who makes little attempt to relate his answers to the question asked, but simply reproduces *verbatim*, so far as he can, any remotely connected passage from his notebook. Unselective recall is also the hall-mark of the bore. James speaks with feeling of "those dry and fanciless beings who spare us no detail, however petty, of the facts they are recounting, and upon the thread of whose narrative the irrelevant items cluster as pertinaciously as the essential ones."

Causes of Forgetting

The converse of learning is forgetting, and the causes of forgetting are numerous. But they fall into two main categories, namely (i) fading, and (ii) blocking.

The physiology of memory is still almost entirely obscure (pp. 20-1 and 38). The most we can say with confidence is that memory is in some way connected with the after-effects of neural activity in the brain. These after-effects are commonly known as *brain-traces* or *memory-traces*, but their nature is a matter of speculation, so we must beware of speaking of them as though they were observable phenomena.

The main cause of forgetting is probably the gradual fading of brain-traces that are not reactivated: Woodworth has described it as a return to normal, analogous to the healing of a wound. A trace that is too weak to produce recall may still suffice for recognition; but, if it is not reactivated, it will gradually fade to the point at which it can no longer, under normal conditions, give rise to any conscious experience at all.

Some psychologists assert that no brain-trace ever fades out completely. This is the sort of statement that it is impossible to verify, but there is ample evidence that brain-traces outlast the stage at which they can give rise to conscious recall. *Re-learning* provides some of the strongest evidence on this point. We may have learned a poem by heart, and forgotten it so completely that we cannot recall a single line. Nevertheless, if we set ourselves to re-learn the poem, we find that we can do it in far less time than would be needed to memorise a poem of the same length that we had never learned before. (An analogous phenomenon—cf. p. 54—is the relative rapidity with which a conditioned response can be re-established after extinction.) Again, memories that are normally quite inaccessible can sometimes be recovered under hypnosis—a fact that will be discussed in Chapter XVIII on the Subconscious Mind.

Blocking

Fading, however, is not the sole cause of forgetting. When we struggle to recall a name or a fact that we know perfectly well, but which has temporarily escaped us, we are concerned with a kind of forgetting different from (say) forgetting what we learned at school about the difference between the gerund and gerundive. In the first case the brain-trace has not faded: the memory is "there" in a sense, but something gets in the way and prevents its emergence.

One of the principal causes of blocking is interference by other, similar memories. We struggle to remember the name "Hetherington" for example, and nothing will come but "Henderson"; or we try to remember the initials of an acquaintance named Forster, and can think of nothing but

"E. M." [1] A similar interference may occur in habit memory, as in changing from tennis to badminton. A possible physiological explanation is that when two very similar brain-patterns are involved, the wrong one may tend to be activated if it has been activated more frequently, more recently, or more intensely, in the past.

When memories have been blocked in this way, it is of little use, as a rule, to try to fight our way through the obstruction. It is better to put the whole matter out of mind, and give the disturbing brain-pattern time to subside. Then the missing fact or name will often, in James's phrase, come strolling back into consciousness when it is least expected.

Retroactive Inhibition

Much light on the whole question of interference has been shed by experiments on what is known as retroactive inhibition. These experiments show that the minimum of forgetting occurs when learning is immediately followed by a period of mental inactivity—preferably by sleep: thus less is forgotten during the night than during the day. Forgetting is at a maximum when learning is immediately followed by some other mental activity, and the more closely the second activity resembles the first, the greater the interference. It has been suggested that the brain-trace gradually "sets," like an impression on a wax surface, and that, if it is allowed to "set" undisturbed, it will be clearer and more lasting than if it is at once overlaid and obscured by other impressions. All this is highly speculative, but it is supported in a striking way by the retroactive effects of certain kinds of shock. Woodworth, for example, describes the case of a young man who struck his head heavily in a fall from a tree, and was knocked unconscious. He soon recovered sufficiently to walk home, in a somewhat dazed condition from which he gradually emerged. But, when he had completely recovered, he remembered nothing of the fall, nor of the walk home, *nor of anything that had happened during the fifteen minutes*

---

[1] On the cover of the writer's telephone directory have been written three numbers: University, 4850: Coal Merchant, 4980: Dr. W., 6790. The similarity of these three numbers caused constant mutual interference.

or so before the fall. A similar phenomenon occurs among patients undergoing Electrical Convulsant Therapy, who are often unable to remember the events just preceding the shock. It would appear that the blow, or the shock, checks a consolidation process. Woodworth suggests that inability to remember the events that occur during high fever, or intoxication, may similarly be due to the fact that abnormal brain conditions have prevented consolidation.

Emotional Causes of Blocking

The causes of blocking are often emotional rather than cognitive. Fear, nervousness or excitement may prevent recall (the actor "drying up" on the first night is a case in point). Some blocking, also, is the effect of repression. Repression will later be discussed at some length, but, for the moment, it may be roughly defined as pushing an unwelcome idea or memory out of consciousness. When this happens, the repressing forces are apt to clamp down, not only on the forbidden idea itself, but on anything that may call it up by association. Thus, when we find ourselves mysteriously unable to recall a fact or a name that we know perfectly well, the cause may be that the fact or name in question is associated with something that we want to forget.

One of Freud's best-known books[1] is devoted almost entirely to the analysis of memory lapses of this kind, and of slips of the tongue and pen, which he explains along similar lines. He accumulates examples, drawn mainly from his own experience, such as forgetting the name of a station through which he frequently passed, because the name (Rosenheim, the home of Rose) suggested the name of a sister with whom he had quarrelled; or forgetting the name of a patient whose case he had diagnosed wrongly. Many of his examples are completely convincing, but, in the writers' view, he goes altogether too far in suggesting that *all* blocking is the result of repression.

---

[1] *The Psychopathology of Everyday Life* (1914). This was republished in Pelican Books in 1938.

The Psychology of Testimony

The study of forgetting links up with the important question of the psychology of testimony. Assuming that a witness is honest, how much reliance, in general, can be placed on his account of what he has seen or heard? A number of facts bearing on this question have already been mentioned. In the chapters on Perception and Attention, for example, it was emphasised that desire, expectation and interest are powerful selective agents, which often determine, and sometimes distort, what we perceive. What is true of perception and attention is true also of memory; we tend to remember things that interest us, and to forget those that do not. A great deal of inadequate and inaccurate reporting is due to these causes alone. But there is yet another source of error, which may be termed retrospective distortion.

Retrospective Distortion

If we happen to be eye-witnesses of some striking event like a car-smash, or if we are told an exciting piece of news at some length, we cannot hope to take in and remember every detail. But as time goes on, the gaps in our memory-record will tend to be closed, or filled. When they are filled, it is not (as a rule) by conscious romancing. But when we have failed to notice some essential link in the chain of events, we tend to imagine what probably happened at this point; and in course of time these false memories become as vivid as the true memories. Also, there is a general tendency (not always completely unconscious) to heighten and dramatise our past experience; in particular, we heighten those aspects that accord with our views and desires. Memories, again, are liable to be subject to a drastic "tidying up" process. What we actually saw or heard may have been a confused and inconsequent jumble, but in a few days' time it has been mentally pulled together: we may have telescoped two or three events into one, provided imaginary links between disconnected episodes, and forgotten other episodes that would not fit into a coherent picture. All of which means that the event as remembered may be very different from the event as it actually occurred.

Many experiments have been made to test the validity of eye-witnesses' reports. Wolters, for example, described how he arranged for two people to burst in during a lecture and create a noisy scene, after which the class were invited to write a detailed account of what had happened. The result may be given in Wolters' own words. "An accurate and full report required just ten essential points. The average number correctly reported was 3·5, and on the average there was one completely false addition. These additions were very various. Incidents which had not occurred, and some which were physically impossible in that room, were reported with complete assurance. Some episodes were seen to occur twice. The noisiest item of all was reported by only one witness out of seventy." [1]

Other experiments have dealt with material presented aurally. A passage may be read aloud to a subject, who attempts to reproduce it after varying intervals of time. Or a passage may be read aloud to *A*, who repeats what he can remember of it to *B*, who repeats it to *C*, and so on, so that we get, in a short space of time, a process in some ways analogous to the spread of a rumour. These experiments are particularly instructive when performed with children. To quote Burt: "If the class is animated by a fairly uniform spirit of literary composition, little by little the divergence between the printed original and the successive reproductions widens, until the final version . . . may eventually emerge unrecognisable. If, on the contrary, the class be inspired with a fairly homogeneous ideal of scientific fidelity, the lack of change will be no less striking." [2] Below is given part of a passage from Ruskin's *The King of the Golden River*, first as it was originally written, secondly as it appeared after it had been subjected to "cumulative reproduction" by a class of sixteen girls aged 12-13, who were evidently animated by a fairly uniform spirit of literary composition.

"On his way out of the town he had to pass the prison, and as he looked in at the windows, whom should he see

[1] *The Evidence of Our Senses* (1933), p. 49.
[2] *Mental and Scholastic Tests* (rev. edit., 1947), pp. 306-7.

but William himself, peeping out of the bars and looking very sad indeed. 'Good morning, brother,' said Tom, 'have you any message for the King of the Golden River?' William ground his teeth with rage and shook the bars with all his strength; but Tom only laughed at him, and advising him to make himself comfortable until he came back again, shouldered his basket, shook the bottle of holy water in William's face until it frothed again, and marched off in the highest spirits in the world."

"One day Dick visited his brother in prison, and his brother said, 'Hullo, my brother, have you brought a pardon from King Charles?' Dick said he had not, and then Tom lost his temper and shook his fist. When Dick saw how rebellious his brother was, he went to a holy man and told his tale to the man. He received a flask of holy wine with instructions to give his brother to drink. After expressing his thanks to the holy man, he again visited his brother, and bade him drink the holy wine; but Tom in another fit of passion dashed the flask against the wall. So Dick turned sadly away, and, as he felt tired, he sat down on the seashore and drank what was left of the foaming wine."

The distorting processes described on p. 164 are here clearly evident. To quote Burt again: "The general tendency is for the incidents to become even more concrete and more dramatic than they are in the original. Unfamiliar phrases and incidents are throughout assimilated to those more familiar to the child; according to Ruskin, Tom shook the bottle of water before William's eyes to taunt him; by the children this is rapidly converted into shaking his fist at him . . . or dashing the bottle to the ground. Similarly, Holy Water, unfamiliar to most Protestant children, becomes transubstantiated into Holy Wine. By the punning process so common in unconscious fantasy-making, the reference in the original to Tom's 'spirits' appears to have partly suggested that he drank the wine . . . Proper names are readily confused, forgotten or misinterpreted: William first becomes 'Dick' and a later hand inverts the two characters; the King of the Golden River becomes King Charles—an intrusion from an historical novel read on the same day . . . Above all, the children's deep-rooted desire to have for every story a happy ending and a simple moral has had free play." [1] (This last fact is more evident when the two passages are quoted in full.)

Rumour

Burt throughout emphasises the point that the distortions that the original story has undergone are in many ways similar to the distortions to which our waking experiences are subjected in dreams (cf. pp. 249-53). This similarity to dreams is even more evident in the spread of rumours, which usually have behind them an emotional "drive" which cannot be reproduced in even the best-organised laboratory experiment. A rumour that was widely current during the First World War went through the following stages:

> When the news of the fall of Antwerp became known, the church bells were rung (*i.e.* in Germany). *Kölnische Zeitung.*

> According to the *Kölnische Zeitung*, the clergy of Antwerp were compelled to ring the church bells when the fortress was taken. *Le Matin.*

> According to what *Le Matin* has heard from Cologne, the Belgian priests who refused to ring the church bells when Antwerp was taken have been driven away from their places. *The Times.*

> According to what *The Times* has heard from Cologne *via* Paris, the unfortunate Belgian priests who refused to ring the church bells when Antwerp was taken have been sentenced to hard labour. *Corriere della Sera.*

> According to information to the *Corriere della Sera* from Cologne *via* London, it is confirmed that the barbaric conquerors of Antwerp punished the unfortunate Belgian priests for their heroic refusal to ring the church bells by hanging them as living clappers to the bells with their heads upside down. *Le Matin.* [2]

This is, of course, an extreme case, and deliberate propaganda motives may have played some part in the distortion.

[1] *Op. cit.*, p. 308.
[2] Quoted by Lord Ponsonby in *Falsehood in Wartime* (1928), p. 161.

But, to a milder degree, the processes it illustrates are constantly occurring. In the Second World War, for example, a provincial town, shortly after a heavy air raid, was buzzing with the rumour that the manager of the chief hotel had been arrested as a spy. The facts behind the rumour were (i) the manager was new to the district, and had a somewhat foreign-sounding name, (ii) he had been away from the town in question on the night of the raid (sure proof that he knew of the raid in advance!), and (iii) a policeman had been seen inquiring for him at the hotel office. Some days later, the manager appeared in court and was fined for a rationing offence!

Many studies of actual rumours have been made, as, for example, in the United States during the Second World War, in Great Britain during parliamentary elections and periods of industrial unrest, and in India after the Darjeeling landslides of 1950. Several conclusions have emerged from these studies—and from numerous experimental studies in the laboratory and in real life, especially those of Allport and Postman.[1] First, rumours tend to arise in conditions where there is "ambiguity" and "motivation"—*i.e.* where people are uncertain about what is happening and yet have an emotional need to form some idea or interpretation of events. Second, during their growth, rumours tend to undergo "levelling" (they become more concise and more easily grasped and told), "sharpening" (they become more dramatic and arresting), and "assimilation"[2] (they are affected by the opinions, present feelings, and persistent attitudes—especially the hopes, fears, anxieties, sympathies, antipathies, and prejudices—of the transmitters). Thirdly, among rumours in real life, where the motivation underlying them is stronger and the individual transmitters' emotional needs and the group's general attitude to the situation are more influential, there is more elaboration and diversification, and less levelling, than among experimental rumours in the laboratory.

[1] Cf. *The Psychology of Rumor* (1947).
[2] "Assimilation" in this context has a different meaning from its meaning on p. 159.

These conclusions have their bearing on all retrospective distortion. They emphasise the important influence on remembering of the situation in which learning and recall take place, and the important influence of emotional factors in determining what is originally attended to and taken in, and what is later recalled and retold.

The Credibility of Witnesses

There has been a tendency to suppose that all false testimony is the result of deliberate lying; but, as will now be obvious, this view is too simple. However strictly a witness may be trying to tell the truth, the whole truth, and nothing but the truth, his account will almost inevitably contain some false statements. Indeed, if a number of eye-witnesses give accounts of the same event that are precisely similar in detail, this is almost certain evidence of collusion. What commonly happens when there is no collusion is that the witnesses will agree on the general outline of what occurred and diverge widely on particular points. All the witnesses of a car-smash, for example, may agree in stating that a lorry struck a car side-on at a certain crossroad, that the lorry was relatively undamaged, but that the car was smashed and the driver taken out unconscious. But when it comes to more detailed information—How fast, approximately, were the two vehicles travelling? Was either, or both, on the wrong side of the road? Did either driver sound his horn, or indicate his intention of turning?—here reports may be so conflicting that it is impossible to form any clear picture of what happened.

The Effect of Leading Questions

Finally, reference must be made to the extent to which false memories can be stimulated by suggestion, and in particular by suggestive or leading questions. The effect of such questions, particularly on children, is still not sufficiently realised. In this connection Wolters described another experiment. "Recently a short film (lasting approximately three minutes) was displayed to about forty schoolgirls. At the end they were asked, among other questions, whether the lamp had been on the table or hanging from the ceiling. The

answers were about equally divided between the two alterna-
tives, but without exception each girl ascribed it to one of the
two positions, though, in fact, there had been neither lamp
nor table.   When the experiment was repeated with adult
subjects they proved less ingenuous.   Nevertheless, in each
group with whom we tried it, someone was found who confidently located the non-existent lamp." [1]

Similar experiments, carried out in Belgium, were described by Muscio.   "Eighteen seven-year-old pupils were
asked the colour of the beard of one of the teachers in their
building; sixteen answered 'black'; two did not answer; the
man had no beard.   Similar results were obtained from older
pupils.   In every case the children fell victims to suggestive
questions.   Twenty-two pupils gave written answers to the
following: 'When you were in line in the yard a man came
up to me, didn't he?   Write his name on your paper.'   No
man had come up; but seven of the twenty-two wrote a name.
The experimenter then continued, 'Was it not Mr. M.?'—to
which seventeen of the twenty-two pupils now answered
instantly, 'Yes.'" [2]

Children, of course, are particularly susceptible to suggestion by adults, but the tendency to return the answer that the
inquirer wants or expects is by no means confined to children
—particularly when the questioner has prestige in the eyes
of the questioned.   Anyone, therefore, who is concerned to
collect accurate information from others, will be wise to
remember that leading questions produce highly misleading
answers.

Transfer of Training

To return to the more formal aspects of memory, a point
of both theoretical and practical interest is how far training
in one form of mental or physical activity is transferred to
other forms.   Belief in such transfer was at one time universal:
it was a common defence of the educational policy which
insisted on all children learning Latin.   Researches carried
out in the early years of this century, however, have shown

[1] *The Evidence of Our Senses* (1933), p. 50.
[2] *Lectures on Industrial Psychology* (1920), p. 19.

that the view is almost entirely mistaken. Transfer occurs in a sense, but not in the sense in which the old educationists had supposed.

Transfer occurs, or appears to occur, only between activities that have elements or methods in common. For example, a boy who has played association football but not hockey will have an advantage in hockey over a boy who has played neither game; for football will have taught him many of the rules and tactics of hockey, and familiarised him with certain techniques, such as dribbling and dodging, that are common to both games. Similarly, a previous knowledge of Latin will help the beginner in Greek by familiarising him with declensions and conjugations, and with personal pronouns implicit in verb-forms, and by acquainting him with the principles of translation and composition. But there is no ground for believing in any more fundamental kind of transfer. It can be quite safely laid down as a principle that the best way to become proficient in any activity, mental or physical, is to practise that activity, and not some other.

The belief that studying Latin has some peculiar effect on proficiency in other subjects is due largely to two facts. First, until recent years there was a marked tendency in schools for the ablest boy to enter the classical side; secondly, as Spearman's researches have made clear, Latin is highly saturated with intelligence, so that the successful study of Latin to an advanced stage is a guarantee of fairly high ability. This has led to the belief that learning Latin develops intelligence; which is rather as though we should argue that the best way to increase one's height is to join the Guards.

Although there is no direct transfer of skill, there may, within limits, be a transfer of *attitude*. The confidence gained by increasing mastery of one subject may lead to a more confident attack upon others, and encouragement of neatness and thoroughness in one branch of work may stimulate neatness and thoroughness in general. The Army's insistence on spit-and-polish has thus a sounder psychological basis than the educationists' insistence on Latin. The extent to which attitudes are transferred, however, seems to depend largely on the extent to which the original training is generalised.

Bagley,[1] for example, quoted by Cattell, described how, when he trained children in precise habits of tidiness in arithmetic, there was practically no spread to geography: but when the *general ideal* of tidiness was explicitly emphasised, considerable transfer took place.

The basic facts about transfer have been admirably summarised by Burt in a report presented to the British Association. "Transfer of improvement occurs only when there are *common usable elements*, shared both by the activity used for the training and also by the activity in which the results of the training reappear. The 'common elements' may be elements of (i) material, (ii) method, (iii) ideal: they are most 'usable' when they are conscious. A common element is more likely to be usable if the learner becomes clearly conscious of its nature and of its general applicability: active or deliberate transfer is far more effective and frequent than passive, automatic, or unintentional transfer. This seems especially true when the common element is an element of method rather than of material, an ideal rather than a piece of information." [2]

Whole and Part Learning

Another point of some practical importance is whether learning is more efficiently carried out by the "part" or the "whole" method. In learning a poem by heart, for example, is it better to begin by learning three or four lines, then three or four more, and so on until the poem is complete? Or should we repeatedly go through the whole poem until it is mastered?

Generally speaking, the "whole" method is the better, for two reasons. First, because on the "part" method the plan of structure of the poem is not fully evident until the end of learning, whereas on the "whole" method the parts are seen from the first in a context which gives them meaning. Second, because on the "part" method the parts tend to stand out as units, and there may be difficulty in linking them together. This is due to the fact that "part" learning usually involves repeating each part over and over several times.

[1] *The Educative Process* (1919).   [2] *Formal Training* (1930).

Thus, associations tend to be formed between the end of each part and the beginning of that same part, instead of between the end of one part and the beginning of the next, as is desirable.

The "whole" method, however, is not invariably to be preferred. The "part" method sometimes gives better results when the learners are young, inexperienced, or lacking in confidence, or when the material to be learned is very unfamiliar or difficult. But, generally speaking, the advantage of the "whole" method is clear. It must, of course, be applied with modification if the poem is very long—no one would set out to learn *Paradise Lost* as a whole. But experiment has shown the "whole" method to be more effective with poems containing up to 240 lines, and longer poems can be divided into "sub-wholes" of suitable length.

It is not only in such activities as learning by heart that the "whole" method is valuable. In studying a chapter of a textbook, it is often a good plan to read rapidly through it and to fix the general outline in the mind, before going back to master the details. The same considerations apply as in learning by heart: facts can be more easily mastered when they fit into a pre-existing framework in our mind.

Spaced Repetition

Many experiments have been carried out on the optimal spacing of learning periods, but since most of these experiments relate to rote learning, the results are not of much practical interest. On general principles, however, there can be no doubt that considerable spacing is desirable in the higher forms of learning. We shall get more value from attending two lectures on psychology weekly over a period of six months, than if the 50-odd hours of instruction were crowded into a week or a fortnight. The intervals give the material time to sink in: we reflect upon it, reformulate it, and relate it to our other knowledge. In the process much of the detail is forgotten, but this is outweighed by the fact that what remains has been mentally digested; it is no longer a mere inert burden on memory, but a functioning part of our mental equipment.

Over-learning

A related point is that, if material is to be permanently remembered, it must usually be "over-learned"; that is, it must be re-learned several times when it begins to be forgotten. Each successive re-learning fixes the material more durably, until a stage finally comes at which there is no appreciable loss of memory with time. Cramming for examinations may achieve its immediate purpose, but if the material is never re-learned, it is very quickly forgotten.

Improvement of Memory

Psychologists are constantly asked whether it is possible to improve a poor memory. The possibilities of improvement are limited, since memory depends largely on innate factors. Assimilation and selectivity of recall are both highly correlated with intelligence, while retention depends mainly on organic conditions which cannot be altered. The position, however, is not quite so hopeless as this statement suggests, for remembering is sometimes handicapped by wrong methods of learning rather than by lack of intelligence or of innate retentiveness, and in such cases a more efficient technique of study may produce marked improvements.

Methods of Study

Advice on improving the memory really resolves itself into advice on methods of learning. Some points of practical importance have already been mentioned, such as over-learning, employing "whole" rather than "part" methods, and giving the material time to sink in. But probably the commonest fault among students is failure to realise that learning is essentially an active process. Too many students sit for hours, passively reading and re-reading notes and textbooks, without ever attempting actively to recall what they have read. The inefficiency of this method has been shown by experiment. Gates,[1] for example, experimented with subjects studying short biographical passages, which they afterwards reproduced. The table shows the proportion of the original material remembered (*a*) when the whole of the

[1] "Recitation as a Factor in Memorising," *Archives of Psychology*, 1917, No. 40.

learning period was devoted to reading and (*b*) when various proportions of the learning period were spent in active recall.

Distribution of learning time			Percentage remembered Immediately	After 4 hours	Retention ratio
All time reading	..	..	35	16	46
One-fifth recall	..	..	37	19	51
Two-fifths recall	..	..	41	25	61
Three-fifths recall	..	..	42	26	62
Four-fifths recall	..	..	42	26	62

In both immediate and delayed memory, the superiority of the active method is obvious. It is notable, too, that the "retention ratio"—obtained by expressing the amount retained for four hours as a percentage of the amount assimilated—is markedly higher on the recall method.

Comparisons of the methods of successful and unsuccessful students confirm that the same principles apply in more advanced forms of learning: for effective memory, some form of active expression is essential. The student, therefore, should read through the material he wants to master with close attention, and should then reproduce the main points aloud, or prepare a written summary (the second method requires more time, but has the advantage of leaving a permanent record): or he may ask himself questions about what he has read, afterwards checking the answers. A short spell of concentrated work of this kind is more effective than a long spell of passive re-reading.

One of the greatest stimulants to active learning is a clearly-defined and not too distant goal. Thus it is always best to start work with some definite aim in view, as, for example, to collect material for an essay, or to clarify one's ideas on a particular point, or to get information relating to a particular question. If we direct our energy to a definite goal, we shall get far better results than if we sit down with merely a vague intention of working for a prescribed period.

Finally, there can be no effective learning without concentration. If the material holds the student's spontaneous interest, concentration presents no great difficulty.[1] But we

[1] In some cases, inability to concentrate is due mainly to anxiety unconnected with the work. The question of anxiety is discussed in Chapter XVII.

are all faced at times with the necessity of "getting up" a topic in which we feel little interest, and concentration in this case demands a repeated effort of will. Many students (particularly those who are studying in their spare time) find such concentration difficult to maintain for long.

To those plagued by this difficulty the best advice that can be given is: it is better to work "all out" for an hour, and then rest and allow the material to sink in, rather than to work for a whole evening at half-pressure. It is a mistake, therefore, for a student to tie himself too rigidly to a timetable. He must, of course, have some sort of a working programme, but if it is too inelastic, it may lead to his sitting doggedly over his books for the prescribed period, though for much of the time he is simply running his eyes over the printed page and taking nothing in.

This practical advice can be summed up in three related precepts: work with concentration; study actively, not passively; always express what you want to remember. Attention to these precepts will not increase our native powers of memory, but it will certainly enable us to make the best of whatever endowments we have.

NOTES ON READING

I. M. L. Hunter, *Memory: Facts and Fallacies* (Pelican Books: 1957), provides a valuable summary of work done in the field of human learning and memory. An important series of laboratory experiments on memory are described in F. C. Bartlett, *Remembering* (Cambridge Univ. Press: 1933). Of the many books that give advice on methods of study, one of the best and most accessible is C. A. Mace, *The Psychology of Study* (Pelican Books: 1962).

CHAPTER XIV

INSTINCT

The South African naturalist Marais has described how he took a young otter from its nest shortly after birth, before its eyes had opened, and induced a bitch to rear it with her litter. The natural home of the otter is, of course, the river bank, and its natural food is fish; but for three years Marais's otter was brought up in unnatural conditions, being fed on birds and other small land animals, and never seeing water except when it was given water in a dish to quench its thirst.

After three years, the otter was taken for the first time to its natural environment, the river bank. In Marais's words, it "just hesitated for a moment or two, then plunged into the water, and within half an hour had caught a crab and a large carp, and devoured them on the rocks." [1]

Lloyd Morgan's Definition of Instinct

The above story well illustrates the distinguishing characteristics of instinctive behaviour. In the classic definition of Lloyd Morgan, such behaviour involves: (i) the performance of complex trains of activity, engaging the whole organism, which (ii) are of biological value to the species, (iii) are similarly performed by all members of the species and (iv) do not have to be learned—they are performed perfectly (or at least adequately)[2] at the first attempt.

This definition was put forward in 1896,[3] but later psychologists have found little in it to modify. It refers to the instinctive behaviour of animals, birds, and insects rather than of

---

[1] *The Soul of the White Ant* (1937), p. 42.
[2] Many instinctive performances improve slightly with practice. An experienced terrier, for example, will have a more finished technique with rats than an inexperienced one. But popular belief exaggerates the amount of learning required for some instinctive activities. Birds, for example, do not really have to learn to fly. The newly-fledged bird flies unskilfully at its first attempts, simply because its nervous and muscular mechanisms are not yet mature. But if young birds are kept in captivity until their strength is fully developed, they will fly perfectly as soon as they are released.
[3] In *Habit and Instinct.*

man; but human instinct differs so widely from that of other members of the animal kingdom that it is almost impossible to frame a definition that applies equally to both. The account that follows will begin with the insects and work upwards to man.

Levels of Instinctive Behaviour

The rôle of instinct becomes less important as we ascend the scale of animal development. Insects, at the lower end of the scale, are governed almost entirely by instinct. They live by routine and learn little from experience. Their fixed patterns of behaviour are adequate to all the normal circumstances of life, but, if the creature is confronted with the unusual, it has little or no power of adaptation. Many insects, for example, starve if their natural food runs out, even though many substitute foods are available. Higher in the scale of development, we find unmodified instinct playing a continually diminishing part, and a larger part played by "adaptiveness," or the power to learn by experience (cf. pp. 149-51).

A typical and well-known example of instinctive activity at the lower level is provided by a species of wasp known as the solitary or mason wasp. This wasp digs an underground tunnel, opening out at the end into a cell in which she lays her eggs. She emerges and finds a grasshopper, which she stings in such a way as to paralyse, but not to kill, it. She then drags the helpless insect into the cell, and leaves it beside the eggs to provide fresh food for the grubs when they hatch. Her last act is to seal up the burrow: this accomplished, she goes away and dies.

Conation and Purpose

At each stage of this complex cycle of activities the wasp's behaviour is precisely adapted to the achievement of a distant goal, yet we must not suppose that the creature itself can foresee that goal. In all reasonable probability, it is simply reacting to present stimuli, both internal and external, by a series of more or less stereotyped activities which are conative, but not purposive.

The distinction between conation and purpose is of some importance. All goal-directed behaviour is said to be conative (from Latin *conari*, to strive), but there is a difference between behaviour that is directed towards immediate goals (as when a baby crawls towards an attractive toy, or pushes away food that he does not want), and behaviour that is directed towards goals that are distant in time or space (as when we book accommodation in February for a holiday in July). Only the second type of behaviour is normally described as purposive. It clearly involves symbolic functioning, whereas the simpler type of conative activity involves nothing more than (to quote Stout) "the perception of a given situation as one that calls for change." [1]

The formula "conation without purpose" probably applies to most forms of purely instinctive behaviour, even among birds and animals. A further example may be quoted in illustration. Most people are familiar with the unpleasing habits of the fledgling cuckoo, which, after being hatched out by foster-parents, proceeds systematically to eject the legitimate fledglings from the nest. This looks like purposive behaviour of a particularly ruthless kind. But, actually, there is no need to assume any conscious purpose or foresight at all. The young cuckoo has a very wide and slightly hollow back, which at one stage of its development is intensely irritable. At this stage, any small object (such as a small stone or a piece of wood) put on the bird's back will cause it to strain and struggle and fling itself about in the nest until the offending object is thrown off. When the irritant is another fledgling, the same procedure takes place.

Many further examples of the same kind could be given. To quote Ogden: "The broody hen sits on her eggs, not through any passion of maternal love, but to allay a local inflammation; and a capon suitably irritated with pepper can be turned into a most devoted foster-mother." [2]

Rigidity of Instinctive Behaviour

But the most convincing proof of the blindness of instinctive behaviour is its rigidity. As will be seen later, this rigidity

[1] Article on Psychology, *Encyc. Brit.*, 14th edition, Vol. 18, p. 683.
[2] *The ABC of Psychology* (1930), p. 98.

has been exaggerated by some writers: even at the lowest level, instinctive behaviour is never wholly inflexible. But there is no doubt that many creatures, even those comparatively high in the scale of development, will at times carry on blindly with a fixed instinctive ritual, although changed external circumstances have made it impossible for these actions to achieve their normal goal.

For example, one species of wasp makes a mud-and-clay nest that is attached to a tree-trunk, and is rendered almost indistinguishable from the bark of the tree by an elaborate outside covering. Hingston[1] describes how one wasp of this species diverged from the normal practice to the extent of making its nest on a white marble mantelpiece in the study of the Archdeacon of Rangoon. For a fortnight the wasp toiled at the external decoration. The outside of the nest was grooved like bark, mottled with coloured clay, and decorated with green and white chalk to resemble lichen. The resemblance to bark was in the end almost perfect; but, of course, the effect in this case was not to camouflage the nest, but to render it highly conspicuous.

In another case, described by Lorenz,[2] a female pigeon was killed by a cat soon after the young had been hatched. The male, as with most species of pigeon, normally took turns with the female in sitting on the nest; and, after her death, he continued to sit out his own shifts, but made no attempt to act as substitute for his mate. At night, when the female was normally on the nest, the male slept as usual on a perch near by. The fledglings, in consequence, perished of cold. Next morning, the male settled down at his usual time on the nestful of corpses, and he continued to brood them at regular intervals for two days.

Examples of this kind could be multiplied, and they suggest that in most cases, if not in all, instinctive behaviour consists only of a series of reactions set off by present stimuli and directed towards immediate goals. Newman's famous lines,

[1] *Problems of Instinct and Intelligence* (1928), p. 75.
[2] *J. Ornithol. Berlin*, 1935, quoted by Russell, E. S., *The Directiveness of Organic Activities* (1946), pp. 103-4.

"I do not ask to see
The distant scene: one step enough for me,"
might well express the animal's viewpoint.

The Chain-Reflex Theory

Many writers, however, would say that the instinctive behaviour of animals is not directed even towards immediate goals, let alone towards distant ones. In other words, they would deny that instinctive behaviour is conative. According to them, it consists simply of chains of linked reflexes—each response becoming in turn the stimulus for the next, so that a whole chain of responses can be set off by a single stimulus.

This view further illustrates the confusion arising from the vague use of the term "reflex." In the strict sense (in which a reflex means an involuntary response that is independent of the higher centres) the statement that instincts are chain-reflexes is obviously false. In the wider sense (in which any response is called a reflex, whether the stimulus is internal or external, and whatever level of the nervous system is involved) the statement is true but unexciting, since it asserts no more than that instinctive behaviour is physiologically determined. Apparently, what the chain-reflex theorists want to assert is something between these two views—namely, that instinctive activity, though it involves cerebral activity, does not involve conation. And this view is quite unplausible. It is one thing to say that the broody hen has no foresight of chickens to come; it is another thing to say that she does not want to sit on eggs.

The chain-reflex theory would be tenable only if instinctive activity involved the repetition of an unvarying series of movements. But, in fact, as Lloyd Morgan long ago pointed out, the outstanding characteristic of such activity is "persistence with varied effort." Even at the lowest level, instinctive behaviour is essentially flexible. The mason wasp, as she drags her paralysed prey to the nest, is not going through a fixed series of movements. She is *transporting the grasshopper*—in other words, she is engaging in conative activity, guided by perception. The actual movements she makes may vary widely in different circumstances—for example, if the grasshopper has to be negotiated up a slope, or round an obstacle. Again, if the grasshopper proves too big to be pulled into the burrow, the wasp will set about enlarging the entrance —a proceeding which involves a complete change in the habitual sequence of movements, and irresistibly suggests the view (so shocking to the chain-reflex theorists) that the wasp *wants* to get the grasshopper into the hole.

In "higher" forms of instinctive behaviour, such as the nest-building of birds, flexibility is still more obvious. The bird must adapt its activity at every stage to the conditions in which it is working—the shape of the fork or hollow in which it has elected to build, the type of building material available, the state of completion of the nest, and so on. It is quite impossible to account for such variable activity in terms of fixed, automatic, stimulus-response connections, however numerous. Indeed, the difficulty about instinctive behaviour at this level is to explain it without reference to long-term purpose. On the face of it, it does not sound plausible to say that the bird has no idea or image of the nest it wants to build, and that it never sees further ahead than the laying of the next twig. Yet, admittedly, there are formidable difficulties in any other view. For if we assume that the bird has some sort of image of what it is aiming at, the question at once arises—in the case of a bird building a nest for the first time—whence was this image derived? Not as might be supposed, from a memory of the parental nest, for if a bird is hatched out in the nest of a different species, it will build its own characteristic nest just the same. The only possible answer is that the image is inherited. This view, or something like it, is held by those who speak of instinct as an ancestral or racial memory. But, though the hypothesis of innate mental images is not quite untenable, it involves acute theoretical difficulties; for the evidence so far available strongly suggests that images and memories—as distinct from behaviour-patterns—are not transmitted by inheritance.

It is impossible to discuss this problem at length, but the point is worth raising, since it is important not to oversimplify the problems of animal behaviour in a reaction from anthropomorphism (cf. p. 138). But whatever may be the truth about long-term purpose, there can be no reasonable doubt that instinctive activity is conative. The essential difference between reflex and instinctive behaviour may be summed up as follows: whereas reflex activity consists simply of the performance of a particular set of movements, instinctive activity always involves *an impulse to alter the perceptual situation in a certain way.* The movements employed to effect this alteration may be to a large extent stereotyped, but they always allow of some degree of variation.

The Physiology of Instinct

The physiology of instinct is still largely an unexplored territory. But there can be little doubt that instinctive behaviour depends, in the last analysis, on innate patterns or circuits of neuronal activity in the brain, which can be set off by relatively simple stimuli. To call these circuits innate does not imply, of course, that they are ready to function at birth; but nothing more than maturation[1] is needed for the necessary synaptic connections to be established.

Fig. 42.

Considerable attention has been paid to the question of the specific stimuli (now generally known as "releasers") that are necessary to evoke instinctive activity. For example, it has long been known that most game-chicks react by crouching to hawks, but not to other birds. K. Lorenz and N. Tinbergen (two of the principal workers in this field) have shown that the crouching reaction can be

[1] "Maturation" involves, of course, reacting to stimuli from the external environment. As Marais's example (p. 177) shows, there can be considerable interference with the environmental stimuli that are natural to a species, without instinctive behaviour being affected. But experimenters have occasionally reared laboratory animals in conditions of such wholly unnatural deprivation that instinctive behaviour-patterns fail to appear. For example, rats were reared in isolation, in cages designed to prevent them from ever picking up and carrying anything. (All food was powdered, and the floor of the cage was of netting, so that faeces dropped down out of reach.) When the breeding season arrived, the rats were given appropriate nesting material, but they did not build nests. Cf. Lehrman, D. S., "A Critique of Konrad Lorenz's Theory of Instinctive Behaviour," *Quart. Rev. Biol.,* 1953, **28**, 337-63.

induced in chicks by a cardboard model of the shape shown (Fig. 42), *provided it is moved from right to left*, when it resembles a short-necked bird of prey. If it is moved from left to right (when it resembles a long-necked waterfowl) it causes no disturbance.

Sometimes the releaser mechanism is highly specific. For example, a male robin attacks and drives away any other robin invading its "territory." The hostile behaviour in this case is evoked simply by the red breast of the rival. A bunch of red feathers dangled from a string is fiercely attacked, while a stuffed robin with the breast dyed brown evokes no reaction.

INSTINCT IN MAN

There has been much controversy on the question of how far, if at all, the concept of instinct can be applied to human behaviour. The chief proponent of the theory of human instinct was William McDougall (1871-1938). In his book *Social Psychology*, first published in 1908, he put forward a definition of instinct which was intended to supplement, though not to supplant, Lloyd Morgan's. The difference between the two was mainly one of emphasis, resulting from the fact that McDougall was thinking primarily of human, and Lloyd Morgan of animal, instinct.

On McDougall's view, instincts are innate tendencies, common to the species, which incline us (i) to attend to, and to be interested in, certain types of object or situation (*cognitive* aspect), (ii) to feel a certain emotion towards these objects (*emotive* aspect), and (iii) to act towards them in a particular way, or at least to experience an impulse to such action (*conative* aspect). He laid particular emphasis on the emotive aspect, which he regarded as fundamental. He held that the simple human emotions, such as fear, hunger, and sexual desire, are inextricably linked with tendencies towards biologically useful types of action.

McDougall also listed, and discussed in detail, what he regarded as the main human instincts. These were: nutrition, curiosity, fear, repulsion, pugnacity, self-assertion, self-abasement, sex, parental instinct, acquisitiveness, gregariousness, and constructiveness.

Criticisms of McDougall's Theory

Social Psychology aroused great popular interest (it went through twenty-one editions in twenty years), but McDougall's views met with considerable criticism, particularly in America. Many psychologists—including some who did not deny that there are instinctive elements in human behaviour—were inclined to jib at McDougall's list of instincts, which they felt savoured too much of the old "faculty" psychology (cf. p. 59). This particular criticism has perhaps been exaggerated: McDougall sometimes used language carelessly, but there is no real ground for saying that he regarded instincts as entities. Another, more justified, criticism was that the tendencies McDougall called instinctive are of widely different types. Such tendencies as self-assertion, for example (which is far from specific, whether in the situations that arouse it, or in the type of activity to which it gives rise), cannot readily be put in the same category as impulses like sex and hunger, which involve specialised physiological mechanisms.

Another objection to instincts is that many of the characteristics of children that used to be regarded as innate have been shown to have been acquired early in life. Again, some social anthropologists claim that their comparative studies of human communities have shown, or at least suggested, that much of the behaviour previously regarded as instinctive—for example, the behaviour involved in aggression and acquisition—is to be attributed to the influence of the institutions, customs, and standards of the group in which the individual is brought up.

Rejoinders may be made to these objections. Thus, the fact that some behaviour-patterns have been mistakenly regarded as innate does not imply that no behaviour is innate. Again, while it is true that in certain communities aggressive behaviour, for example, is discouraged and seldom occurs, this does not mean that the members of such communities have no innate aggressive tendency.

Critics of instinct-theory have also argued that, whether or not the concept of instinct be theoretically valid, it is not, in practice, a particularly useful concept for describing human behaviour, since human beings, once they have passed the stage of infancy, scarcely ever perform a purely instinctive action. In adult human beings, unlike animals, instinct usually does little more than prescribe certain goals, without determining the precise means by which the goals are to be reached. In the lower animals, for example, nearly all the behaviour involved in feeding and rearing the offspring is instinctive. But in the human mother, little more is instinctive than her love for her baby and her desire for its welfare; it is intelligence, not instinct, that leads her to promote its welfare by giving it cod-liver oil.

Moreover, in human instinct, not only the means to the goal, but also the goal itself, is adaptable. We shall see later (pp. 215-17) how some of humanity's highest achievements depend on the redirection of primitive instinctive energy away from its natural goal towards alternative ends that are of greater value.

All these are important considerations, but they do not imply that the concept of human instinct is worthless; and, in fact, there are few psychologists who do not employ it in some form, though many regard the word "instinct" as old-fashioned and prefer some other term, such as "primary drive" or "unlearned motive." Whatever term is used, the essential facts are hardly in dispute. There exist innate tendencies, common to the whole human race (or at least to all members of the same sex), to experience certain fundamental emotions and to pursue certain ends. The means of pursuit may be controlled by training, and elaborated by intelligence, and the goals themselves may be transformed by sublimation. But instinct, however refined and transmuted, is never destroyed. It remains the basic dynamic force in human behaviour.

NOTES ON READING

The relation of instinct to reflex activity on the one hand, and to intelligence on the other, is discussed by McDougall in *An Outline of Psychology* (Methuen: 1923). Other valuable references are N. Tinbergen, *The Study of Instinct* (Oxford Univ. Press: 1951); W. H. Thorpe, *Learning and Instinct in Animals*; and the *Encyclopaedia Britannica* articles on Comparative Psychology by T. C. Schnierla, and Instinct by K. S. Lashley. The interaction of environmental and hereditary forces in animal behaviour is discussed with particular clarity in P. L. Broadhurst, *The Science of Animal Behaviour,* and in Chapter 6 of D. O. Hebb, *A Textbook of Psychology.*

The classical presentation of McDougall's views on human instinct is contained in his *Social Psychology* (Methuen: 23rd revised ed., 1936). Ronald Fletcher, *Instinct in Man* (Allen and Unwin: 1957), is a valuable historical and critical discussion of instinct-theory as applied to human behaviour.

Instinct, edited by R. C. Birney and R. C. Teevan (Insight Books. New York and London, Van Nostrand: 1961) contains a useful selection of readings from books and journals.

CHAPTER XV

SENTIMENTS

As we grow up, our simple instinctive drives become organised into sentiments. To explain the sense in which psychology uses the term "sentiment" it is necessary first to define certain other terms.

Conscious States, Dispositions and Sentiments

The term *conscious state* or *state of consciousness* may be applied to any type of mental experience of which a conscious being is capable. A *disposition* is a tendency to experience a particular type of conscious state in certain circumstances. Fear or anger, for example, are states of consciousness of an emotional kind; timidity or irritability are emotive dispositions.

Dispositions, of course, like instincts, are not to be regarded as entities. To say that someone has a timid disposition is simply a convenient way of saying that he tends to feel fear, and to exhibit fearful behaviour, more strongly, or more often, than most people. Dispositions in psychology are analogous to properties such as elasticity or malleability in physics.

A *sentiment* is *an acquired emotive disposition or organised set of such dispositions directed towards an object*—the term "object" being used in its widest sense. The distinction can best be brought out by examples.

Conscious state	*Disposition*	*Sentiment*
X is frightened	X is timid	X is afraid of cows
X is irritated	X is irritable	X is irritated by untidiness

The terms (i) "acquired," (ii) "emotive," and (iii) "directed," must all be emphasised. (i) Sentiments, unlike the instincts on which they are founded, are not innate. We are born with an instinct of curiosity, but the development of this instinct into a persistent sentiment of inquiring interest in, say, natural history or astronomy, is partly the result of environmental factors. (ii) Not all dispositions are emotive. There are also cognitive dispositions, such as the disposition of being a good mathematician or a fluent linguist; but these are not classed as sentiments. (iii) A sentiment is essentially a directed disposition. It is focused on some "object," so that while John's love for Jean, or his interest in music, or his dislike of gardening, or his admiration for the Queen, are all sentiments, his affectionateness, or timidity, or quick temper, being undirected, are not.

Sentiments range from the purely concrete, such as affection or dislike for a particular person, through the semi-abstract, such as interest in the theatre, or admiration for the Navy, to the purely abstract, such as hatred of injustice, or admiration for courage. Concrete sentiments may be further classified as *particular* and *general*—the former being directed towards some particular person, thing, animal, etc. (*e.g.* John loves his dog), and the latter towards a group or class (*e.g.* John loves dogs).

A single sentiment may give rise to a variety of emotions. If, for example, *A* loves *B*, this will cause *A* to feel pleased when *B* is successful, grieved when *B* is thwarted or unhappy, and anxious when *B* is in danger. A sentiment, therefore, may perhaps best be described, not as a single emotive disposition, but as an organised set of such dispositions directed towards an object.

Complex Emotions and Sentiments

Much of the richness and complexity of our emotional life depends on sentiment-formation. Many complex emotions (as distinct from the simple emotions, such as fear, anger and curiosity, which are directly linked with instincts) cannot be experienced until sentiments have been formed. Such an emotion as shame, for example, can be experienced only by one who has formed sentiments towards moral principles, in the light of which he sees his own conduct as unworthy. Similarly, jealousy is possible only when a sentiment of affection has been formed—and so on.

Sentiments and Character

Sentiments are, in McDougall's phrase, the chief organisers of our affective and conative life. Without permanent sentiments, we should be at the mercy of every transient and momentary impulse. But the existence of firmly-established interests and attachments and loyalties often leads us to resist the immediate promptings of instinct for the sake of more permanent satisfactions.

Individual differences in character derive largely from the sentiments: at the instinctive level we are all very much alike. The growth of personality consists, to a considerable extent, in the growth of the dominant sentiments. Every adult has a variety of sentiments, but usually there is one, or a small number, of powerful dominant sentiments, which form, as it were, a nucleus round which the minor sentiments are organised. In one the dominant sentiment may be personal ambition; in another, love of home and family; in another, devotion to scientific research; in another, desire for social justice; in another, love of sport and country life—and the list could be prolonged indefinitely. When we know what a man's dominant sentiments are, we know a great deal about his character. As Cattell says, "When it is known what things a man reveres, what things he scorns, loves, hates, and admires, his conduct has become to some extent predictable." [1]

Sentiments and Moral Development

Sentiments, as already emphasised, are not innate. The infant is not born with any sentiments, but he rapidly acquires concrete sentiments towards his mother, father, brothers and sisters, and other persons in his environment. When this stage is reached, his conduct is no longer determined simply by the pursuit of pleasure and the avoidance of pain. To a certain limited extent he can be influenced, like a dog, through his affections.

But at this stage—again, like a dog—the infant has still no genuine moral sense. He has notions of right and wrong,

[1] *General Psychology* (1941), p. 163.

which sometimes triumph in action over his immediate instinctive urges. But these notions are not founded on moral principle. "Right," to the young child, is simply what pleases grown-ups, and "wrong" is what makes them angry. No moral standards can exist in an individual until abstract sentiments have been formed.

The moral code of an adult, in so far as it is not purely conventional, depends mainly on the abstract sentiments developed in childhood and youth. A moral sentiment that develops comparatively early, and is almost universal in some form, is *self-respect*, or, as it is called by McDougall, the self-regarding sentiment. It may seem paradoxical to class this as an abstract sentiment, but it is abstract in the sense that it is directed to the individual's ideal of himself—to himself as he would like to be, rather than to himself as he actually is. Self-respect must not be confused with complacency or self-satisfaction. These are undesirable tendencies, but self-respect is held by many to be the basis of morality, since it implies the presence of an ideal standard by which the individual's actions are judged.

What other abstract sentiments the child develops will depend largely on circumstances, and particularly on the adults with whom he comes in contact. Studies of the origin and growth of abstract (and semi-abstract) sentiments have brought out the important fact that they very commonly originate in concrete sentiments—particularly in sentiments towards persons.[1] When a child develops an admiration for an adult, or even for a character in history or fiction, he is liable to take over any abstract sentiment that the object of his admiration displays. Moral sentiments, in short, are formed by personal example and influence far more than by explicit moral teaching. There is much truth in the statement that "morals are caught, not taught."

To a more limited extent, it is also true that concrete sentiments may arise from abstract ones. A person who has a strong sentiment of attachment to, say, Roman Catholicism or Communism, will be predisposed to form favourable concrete sentiments towards persons who share his views.

[1] Cf. Phillips, M., *The Education of the Emotions* (1937).

Concrete Symbols for Abstract Sentiments

Abstract sentiments, even at their strongest, are usually less powerful spurs to action than concrete sentiments. Most people find it easier to make sacrifices for a person than for a principle. For this reason, abstract sentiments are often reinforced by concrete symbols. National flags and anthems, uniforms, school and regimental colours, and even the rites and ceremonies of religion, are all concrete symbols of this type. They fulfil an important function in strengthening ties and loyalties that might otherwise prove too frail.

When some concrete object symbolises a revered principle or institution, intense emotions may become centred on the symbol itself. The suggestion that Scottish regiments should discontinue the wearing of the kilt aroused a grief and indignation that were perfectly genuine; and a British subject may experience a startling surge of feeling when he unexpectedly encounters the Union Jack on a holiday abroad.

McDougall on the Sentiments

By way of summary and conclusion, we may cite a well-known passage from McDougall.

> "The growth of the sentiments is of the utmost importance for the character and conduct of individuals and of societies; it is the organisation of the affective and conative life. In the absence of sentiments our emotional life would be a mere chaos, without order, consistency, or continuity of any kind; and all our social relations and conduct, being based on the emotions and their impulses, would be correspondingly chaotic, unpredictable and unstable. It is only through the systematic organisation of the emotional dispositions in sentiments that the volitional control of the immediate promptings of the emotions is rendered possible. Again, our judgments of value and of merit are rooted in our sentiments; and our moral principles have the same source, for they are formed by our judgments of moral value." [1]

NOTES ON READING

The standard references on the sentiments are W. McDougall, *Social Psychology*, and A. F. Shand, *The Foundations of Character* (Macmillan: 2nd revised ed., 1920).

[1] *Social Psychology* (23rd ed., 1936), pp. 159-60.

CHAPTER XVI

PERSONALITY

As we have seen, an individual's character or personality[1] consists of his sentiments and other emotive and conative dispositions, and in these respects, as in abilities and knowledge, one individual differs from another. Indeed personality has been defined as "the characteristics that lead people of similar intelligence and knowledge, when placed in similar circumstances, to react in different ways."[2]

THE STRUCTURE AND GROWTH OF PERSONALITY

Many attempts have been made to divide personality into types, or to discover basic factors of personality in terms of which individuals may be described and differentiated. One of the first was that of Hippocrates, who held that there were four main types of personality, the sanguine, the phlegmatic, the choleric and the melancholic, and that the type to which an individual belonged depended on whether the predominant fluid in his body was blood, phlegm, yellow bile, or black bile. Other views of this kind have been put forward in the course of history. Thus physiognomists and phrenologists tried to relate differences in personality to differences in the contours of the face or skull. But these speculations belong to the pre-scientific stage of psychology.

Jung's Types

Among contemporary studies of personality types, or of basic personality factors, four may be specially mentioned.

First, Jung (1875-1961) divided personality into two main types, the extravert and the introvert, according as the individual's basic orientation is outward or inward. The extravert

---

[1] Although in ordinary usage there was, and perhaps still is, some distinction between "character" and "personality," in contemporary psychology the two terms are practically synonymous, and since "personality" is, if anything, the more comprehensive term, it is usually preferred. The term "character" tends to be employed only when the individual's dispositions are being ethically evaluated or his moral sentiments are being stressed.

[2] Cf. Wallon, H., *La Vie Mentale*.

"gives his fundamental interest to the outer and objective world and attributes an all-important and essential value to it." For the introvert, on the other hand, "the objective world suffers a sort of depreciation or want of consideration, for the sake of the exaltation of the individual himself." Each main type has four sub-types, according as thinking, feeling, sensation, or intuition is the predominant way in which the individual functions. The "thinking" extravert is a thinker concerned with objective facts, like the experimental scientist. The "thinking" introvert is exemplified by philosophers and other theorists of the more abstract and doctrinaire sort, who are less concerned with the world as it is than with deducing from first principles what it "must" be like. The "feeling" extravert is sociable, impulsive, emotional, and an easy mixer. The "feeling" introvert has deep, strong feelings that he cannot readily express. The "sensation" extravert takes a direct, practical pleasure in sensory experience and needs constant stimulation from outside to ward off boredom. The "sensation" introvert seeks in sensory experience for opportunities of aesthetic and other forms of discrimination. The "intuitive" extravert tends to act, sometimes very successfully, on "leads" and "hunches," but is often unstable and over-confident. The "intuitive" introvert also tends to leap to conclusions, but these relate not so much to the world of action as to the world of thought.

Jung's classification was based on personal observation and clinical experience, but recent work, involving the exploration and appraisal of personality by tests and other objective techniques, has confirmed its main assertion that, although most people are intermediate types or "ambiverts," some are distinguishable as extraverts and others as introverts. The eight sub-types, however, though obviously corresponding with the facts to some extent, have not yet been similarly confirmed.

Kretschmer's Types

A second system of typology is that of Kretschmer (1888-1964), a psychiatrist who began by observing that, among the insane, schizophrenics, who are withdrawn into themselves and almost completely out of touch with reality, tend to be tall, slight of build, long-limbed, and oval-faced; whereas manic-depressives, who are more in contact with their environment, but subject to alternating moods of excitement and depression, tend to be short, plump, and round or shield-faced. He then extended his observations beyond the mental hospital, and found similar correspondences outside. Normal individuals who resembled schizophrenics or manic-depressives in physique tended to possess, though to a less marked and non-morbid degree, the corresponding type of personality.

Kretschmer finally produced a complete classification of mental and physical types. The short, plump physique, called *pyknic*, is associated with a clearly-defined personality-type, which is known as *cyclothyme, cycloid,* or *cyclophrene* according as the individual is normal, maladjusted, or insane. The tall, slight physique, called *asthenic* or *leptosome*, is similarly associated with a personality type known as *schizothyme, schizoid,* or *schizophrene*.[1]

The person of cyclothymic temperament swings easily between elation and depression; he expresses emotion freely, and is sociable, impulsive, realistic, self-indulgent, and tolerant. The schizothyme is more stable in mood; he has difficulty in expressing emotion, and is self-sufficient, cautious, idealistic, intolerant, and austere. It is not difficult to find examples of these types in public life; Sir Winston Churchill, for example, was a typical cyclothyme, and Sir Stafford Cripps was a typical schizothyme.

The maladjusted cyclothyme, or cycloid, is usually over-emotional and irresponsible; the maladjusted schizothyme, or schizoid, may be a fanatical doctrinaire, or he may live an intense, self-centred life in a world of his own, and appear outwardly apathetic and cold.

Kretschmer's classification accords strongly with common opinion, as expressed in folk-lore and cartoons. With striking

---

[1] There is a third physical type, the *athletic,* tall like the asthenic but broader and more muscular. Kretschmer originally regarded the athletic body-type as intermediate between pyknic and asthenic, but he later came to regard it as a type of its own. The person of athletic physique tends to be of schizothyme temperament, but less so than the asthenic.

regularity, the jovial, "good-fellow" type is depicted as stout and burly (cf. John Bull), and the austere, puritanical type as long and lean (cf. Mrs Grundy). In literature, Don Quixote is a classic example of the schizothyme and Sancho Panza of the cyclothyme; and it is noticeable that in book illustrations the two are nearly always depicted as, respectively, asthenic and pyknic in physique.

Some of the details of Kretschmer's typology have been criticised; in particular, Eysenck claims to have shown that schizophrenia and manic-depressive insanity are not just extreme forms of schizothymia and cyclothymia, but involve a different "dimension" of personality (cf. p. 199). On the whole, however, later investigations have confirmed Kretschmer's main hypothesis, that the cyclothyme-schizothyme dimension (which, of course, has much in common with Jung's distinction between extravert and introvert) is a basic factor in personality and is paralleled by the pyknic-asthenic dimension in physique.

Sheldon's Types

A third contemporary theory of types of personality, which has much in common with Kretschmer's, is that of Sheldon. Sheldon caused four thousand young men to be photographed, naked, from the front, back, and side positions, and arranged the photographs in series, to see whether definite physical types were apparent. There were no clear-cut, discontinuous types, but there were three obvious "dimensions of variation," the extreme cases in each dimension resembling Kretschmer's pyknics, athletics, and leptosomes. These extreme types were called by Sheldon *endomorphs* (round and soft, with a predominant digestive system), *mesomorphs* (wide-shouldered and hard, with a predominant muscular system), and *ectomorphs* (delicately formed and linear, with a predominant nervous system).

In Sheldon's system, an individual is rated on a seven-point scale in respect of each of these three dimensions. Thus the extreme endomorph has a rating of 711; the extreme mesomorph, of 171; the extreme ectomorph, of 117. Such extreme cases, however, are rare. Many individuals get a rating near the average, which is around 444, but in most people one of the three components predominates, so that it is common for ratings to include the figure 5 in one of the three places, but no figure higher than 4 or 3 in the other two. A person's physical rating is known as his *somatotype*.

When this system of somatotyping had been devised, Sheldon made an intensive study of thirty-three young men, to determine whether the different physical types were associated with different types of personality. Each student was given twenty or more analytic interviews, and observed closely in a variety of situations over a period of a year; and, in the light of this procedure, he was rated on a seven-point scale in respect of various personality traits. The intercorrelations between the traits were studied and three fairly well-defined "clusters" of traits emerged; each cluster containing some seven or eight traits, and each being associated with a different type of physique. A further experiment, involving one hundred subjects, made it possible to add more traits to each cluster; and Sheldon finally produced three lists of twenty traits, defining three different personality tendencies, which are called *viscerotonic*, *somatotonic*, and *cerebrotonic*, and which are associated, respectively, with the endomorphic, mesomorphic, and ectomorphic types of physique. An individual is rated on a seven-point scale in respect of each tendency, the result being his Index of Temperament (IT), which usually fairly closely resembles his somatotype.

Among the traits defining the three types of temperament are:

Viscerotonic. Is relaxed in posture and movement; likes physical comfort; likes ceremony, ritual, overt expressions of "good form"; dislikes being alone; has an even, tranquil disposition; is tolerant; is greedy for affection and approval; is well-informed about people and "knows who to go to for what"; expresses emotion freely; needs people when he is troubled.

Somatotonic. Is unhesitating and aggressive in posture and movement; likes adventure and excitement; is energetic; likes to dominate people and situations; is insensitive to others' feelings; has a direct manner; is physically courageous; is competitive and aggressive; is extraverted and objective; needs action when he is troubled.

Cerebrotonic. Is tight and restrained in posture and movement; "trips over himself" and is easily embarrassed; loves privacy; is alert, attentive, often apprehensive; hides his feelings and keeps his emotions under restraint; shrinks from social contacts, especially new ones; lacks poise, confidence and self-possession; resists habits and routine; has a youthful, intent manner; needs solitude when he is troubled.

In the full list of sixty traits, every trait correlates positively (to the extent of not less than ·6) with the other traits in the same cluster, and negatively (to the extent of not less than − ·3) with the traits in the other two clusters. Most of the positive correlations are considerably higher than ·6; and the correlations between physical type and temperament are in the neighbourhood of ·8.

Sheldon claims that these correlations have been confirmed by further experiments involving large numbers of subjects. But the correlations are so much higher than those usually found in this type of investigation as to raise doubts of their genuineness. Some critics have suggested that Sheldon's mathematics are faulty; but, apart from this possibility, his work is open to a fundamental criticism, namely that, at all events in the later experiments, the personality ratings were made by people who were familiar with Sheldon's typology. As was emphasised in Chapter VIII on Sensation and Perception, we are always more ready to notice what we expect or are looking for; and an interviewer confronted by a student of markedly endomorphic physique is likely to perceive small signs of relaxation, tolerance, sociability, and the like, which in a student of different physique he might fail to notice. What we need are independent estimates of temperament and physical type; and until such estimates, with the correlations based on them, are forthcoming, Sheldon's detailed conclusions must be held "not proven."

Eysenck's "Dimensions"

A different approach to the study of personality is that of the factor analysts. These psychologists do not attempt to classify personalities into types. They employ tests, inventories and other strictly objective methods of personality assessment, and analyse the results by the same sort of statistical techniques as have been applied by Spearman and others to the results of intelligence tests (cf. pp. 127-8). Spearman found, it will be remembered, that various "factors"—g, verbal ability, numerical ability, etc.—entered in varying degrees into the performance of different intellectual tasks. There is now strong evidence for the existence of various factors in the field of personality.

Opinions differ on whether these factors correspond to actual, basic, personality-qualities, or whether they are merely abstract categories for classifying the results of personality tests—in which case they may not correspond to any easily recognisable personality-characteristics, any more than the mathematical constructs which physicists employ need correspond to actual physical existents. But even if personality factors are no more than mathematical constructs, they, like the physicists' constructs, are of undoubted value; they enable us to map out the sphere of personality more economically, so that we can see which traits go together, which are independent of one another, and how traits vary in the weight and width of their influence on behaviour.

Eysenck is one of the leading British investigators in this field. He and his co-workers have applied objective personality tests to large numbers of subjects, and they claim to have shown, by statistical analysis of the results, that there are three basic factors or "dimensions" of personality. These are introversion-extraversion, neuroticism (tendency to neurosis), and psychoticism (tendency to psychosis). On Eysenck's view, these are genuine personality traits, not mere mathematical constructs. Between the three factors or dimensions there is no correlation, either positive or negative, so that knowledge of an individual's position in one dimension tells us nothing about his position in either of the others. (On the Eysenckian system, every individual is to be considered as located at a particular point in each of the three dimensions.) On this view, abnormal individuals (*i.e.* those who would ordinarily be described as neurotic or psychotic) differ from normal individuals only in degree, not in kind; they possess to a more marked extent, characteristics which, in some degree, are possessed by everyone.

In addition to the basic factors, which are wide in scope, Eysenck's researches point to the existence of other, less general factors, which underlie our behaviour in special situations. Among these narrower factors are conservatism-radicalism, simplicity-complexity, and toughmindedness-tendermindedness.

Eysenck and his school are intolerant of all methods of studying personality that do not involve objective tests and rigorous statistical analysis. They regard as quite unsatisfactory all descriptions and assessments of personality that are based merely on clinical observation or everyday experience, unchecked by experiment. Others think that this attitude is too rigid. They hold that the psychologist who depends on insight rather than on factor analysis has still an indispensable contribution to make, both to psychotherapy and to the advance of psychological knowledge. There are signs that the conflict between these two schools of thought is becoming a major issue in psychology. But perhaps a compromise will be reached on the basis that, while "intuition" and "insight," whether in clinical work or in ordinary life, must be allowed to provide hypotheses about personality, these hypotheses can be validated only by objective techniques.

Personality and Physiological Processes

Although there is still much to be discovered about the relations between temperament and body-type, it is clear, as we saw in earlier chapters, that an individual's personality is linked with the physiological condition of his body. For example, if a man begins to suffer from thyroid deficiency, he becomes slow, lethargic, and unable to concentrate. Moreover, distressing changes in personality may arise from disease or injury of the brain (as in Alzheimer's or in Pick's disease, in which atrophy of the brain is accompanied by presenile dementia), and changes of a different and welcome kind can be produced by therapeutic "interference" with a disordered brain, as in electrical convulsant therapy and prefrontal leucotomy.

Two other pieces of evidence also illustrate the interconnection between our body and our personality. There is the observed influence of drugs on personality, as when mescaline or lysergic acid induces such changes in a normal person that he temporarily undergoes an experimental psychosis and may during this time closely resemble a schizophrenic. This reinforces much other evidence that links biochemical factors with personality. Again, there is the fact that certain differences in personality are correlated with differences in the electrical activity of the brain, as recorded by the electroencephalograph. For example, as stated on p. 46, some of the brain-rhythms of adults who are markedly aggressive and lacking in self-control often resemble those of young children more than of normal adults. In short, the old tag "a healthy mind in a healthy body" is more than games-master's maxim. It expresses the fundamental fact that, if an individual is to have a normal personality, his endocrine and nervous systems, and many other parts of his body, must function normally.

Obviously, a person's physical make-up may also affect his personality by affecting his activities and social contacts—as when an athletic physique helps a young man to become a world-touring tennis champion, or a crippled condition keeps a child in an invalid's chair. Moreover, our bodily condition has indirect as well as direct effects on our personality. As Adler pointed out, people who are physically handicapped often strive either to overcome or to compensate for their inferiority, and sometimes (like Demosthenes with his stammer) they become famous in the very field of their initial weakness. Adler also pointed out that some people are affected in the opposite way; their inferiority leads them to retreat into self-pity and resentment. Adler's views derived from his clinical experience and his observation of children. But they have been supported by many subsequent investigations, which have shown that a physical defect rarely leaves the personality of its possessor unaffected, and usually produces effects of the sort that Adler described.

Hereditary Factors

Besides studying the structure of personality, psychology is also concerned with the factors that influence its growth. Among these, some are constitutional and inborn, and others environmental. Extreme environmentalists deny, or at least disregard, the existence of hereditary factors, but usually their attitude (like the opposite attitude of extreme hereditarians) derives less from a study of the facts than from some basic political or philosophical assumption. Actually, there is clear evidence that individuals start life with structural differences in their nervous systems and other bodily organs, and that these differences, which entail functional differences, affect the growth and organisation of their personality.

Several investigations indicate the influence of hereditary factors. Thus it was found that, among the relatives of 691 schizophrenics who all had twin brothers or sisters, the incidence of schizophrenia was as follows: step-brothers and sisters, 1·8 per cent.; marriage partners, 2·1 per cent.; half-brothers and sisters, 7 per cent.; parents, 9·2 per cent.; full brothers and sisters, 14·3 per cent.; non-identical (dizygotic) twins, 14·7 per cent.; and identical (monozygotic) twins, 85·8 per cent.[1] It is true that the identical twins of patients who had been brought up apart from their twins, had a smaller incidence (77·6 per cent.) than those who had been brought up with them (91·5 per cent.), and this shows that environment exerts some influence even in this psychosis. But the fact that the incidence among identical twins is more than five times as high as among non-identical twins is strong evidence of the presence of a hereditary factor. Again, another investigation, also involving identical and non-identical twins, led to the conclusion that, among normal people, an individual's emotional stability is a matter much more of heredity than of environment.

That hereditary factors influence personality is also shown by the results of systematic observation of young children. Among new-born babies there are differences in general

[1] Kallman, F. J., "The Genetic Theory of Schizophrenia," *Amer. J. Psychiat.*, 1946, **106**, 309-22. Reprinted in Kluckhohn, C., and Murray, H. A., *Personality in Nature, Society and Culture* (Cape: 1949).

activity or "motility," and in emotional expressiveness, which persist from month to month. These dispositions are rudimentary or nuclear qualities of personality, which play an important rôle in determining the modes of adjustment that the individual develops later.

The Influence of Culture-Pattern

Among the environmental influences that affect personality, one of the most important is the culture-pattern—the values, expectations, customs, and institutions of the community in which the individual grows up. Evidence of the importance of this factor has come mostly from social anthropologists, who have studied the way different culture-patterns encourage the development of different attitudes and dispositions. Thus Mead has shown that, in New Guinea, different primitive communities favour quite different types of personality, and that they actually produce these types of personality by their different methods of bringing up children, by the different rôles they assign to the two sexes, and by the different emphasis they lay on competition and aggression. For instance, among the Arapesh, children are gently nurtured; men and women are expected to have much the same affectionate temperament; and peaceful co-operation is preferred to competition and aggression. Among the Mundugumor, on the other hand, children are subjected to a hardening process, especially by their fathers; men and women are both expected to have a strong, forceful temperament; and competition and aggression are encouraged and rewarded. The result is that, among the Arapesh, people who are aggressive and self-assertive are very rare, whereas they represent the standard personality among the Mundugumor.

There are also cultural differences between developed communities—as between the Americans and ourselves. In comparison with people in Britain, Americans set less store by authority and tradition; they are easier mixers and more experimental and pragmatic; and, as children and adolescents, they are more assertive and more in evidence. All these differences in personality are influenced by our different culture-patterns, working through the home, the school, and the various institutions and agencies by which attitudes are formed.

Again, social psychologists and sociologists have shown that, in complex communities, a powerful influence is exerted on an individual's personality by the particular regional, ethnic or occupational sub-group in which he is brought up. Our aspirations and anxieties, our political attitudes, and many other components of our personality, are all affected by the socio-economic conditions in which we live. In the United States, there are important cultural differences between the South and the North, between the East and the Middle West, and between the right and wrong sides of the tracks in the same town. Similarly, in Britain, the percentage of electors who vote Conservative is much higher in South Kensington than in South Shields; the percentage of readers of *News of the World* is much greater among the lower income groups than among the higher; there are differences in outlook between miners in Derbyshire and farmers in Norfolk (and between miners in Derbyshire and miners in Glamorgan); and, as Sprott has put it, even when Dyke Street and Gladstone Road are in the same town and contain householders of the same economic status, they often differ widely in their standards and attitudes, including those that affect the incidence of delinquency.[1]

The Influence of Rôle and Status

Our rôle and status also affect our personality, and many psychologists, especially in America, are studying these influences. We have all seen how people, when they move from one rôle to another, or acquire a different social status, tend to develop new attitudes and patterns of behaviour. They often, as we say, "grow into their new rôle," and undergo some change of personality in the process. Some psychologists are particularly interested in the contrast between an individual's "basic" personality, and his various "rôle" or "status" personalities which are generated by the different expectations (in himself and in other people) that he tries to satisfy in different sets of circumstances. Among these investigators, some stress

[1] Sprott, W. J. H., "Delinquescent Worlds," *The Listener*, 53, 1014.

the way in which social rôles promote persistence of sets of dispositions, and so consistency of personality. Others emphasise the fact that the changes in our rôle or status that occur when we move from one social group to another, inevitably "make chameleons of us all."

The latter include the field theorists, who have brought into social psychology and the study of personality some of the basic principles of the *Gestalt* psychologists; in particular the principle, first developed in the study of perception, that the nature of any part is affected by the nature of the whole in which it is included, and by its relation to other parts. This unexceptionable principle has underlain many recent studies of personality. By moderate field-theorists, it is expressed in the form that "the behaviour of a person is due to the distribution of forces in the social situation as a whole rather than to supposedly intrinsic properties of the individual." [1] By extremists, it is exaggerated to become "the 'individual' is a myth—a person is a set of social relationships." [2]

The Influence of the Family

Of all the social groups that influence the growth of personality, the most important is undoubtedly the family. The Freudians were the first to explore in detail the influence of the family on an individual's development, but the Adlerians and the Jungians, and indeed all clinical and other psychologists, also emphasise its importance. Many hold that the Freudians, at all events in their early days, underestimated the influence of social factors outside the home; but it would be admitted even by these critics that, where very young children are concerned, the influence of other groups is exerted almost entirely through the family. These other groups affect the infant by the way they affect his parents and his older brothers and sisters.

There are differences about many matters among the Freudians, the Adlerians, and the Jungians, but they all

[1] Cohen, J., "Analysis of Psychological 'Fields'," *Science News*, **13**, 146.
[2] Montagu, M. F. A., "The Origin and Nature of Social Life and the Biological Basis of Co-operation," *Horizon*, 1949, 393.

stress the importance of infancy as a formative period in the development of personality. The Freudians are particularly interested in the lasting effect on our motives of our conscious and unconscious reactions to our parents during our earliest years. They hold that the situations that cause trouble in adult life are those that revive the unresolved conflicts of childhood. The Adlerians are less exclusively concerned than the Freudians with the child's reactions to his parents: they emphasise, also, the importance of his reactions to other members of the family, in particular to brothers and sisters. In the Adlerian view, it is primarily through the child's efforts to achieve a sense of adequacy in his interactions with parents, siblings, and the physical environment that he forms his "style of life"—his habitual, though not consciously for-mulated, way of feeling and acting and dealing with difficul-ties. They hold that the origin of an adult's "style of life" is to be found in the way in which, as a child, he habitually sought to achieve a sense of adequacy, whether by a direct frontal attack on his difficulties, or by an attempt to assert himself in some alternative way, or by a retreat into phantasy or psychogenic illness. The Jungians attach much less import-ance to the individual's past than to his present, but they still consider it important to disentangle his previous history right back to infancy, since, in their view, childhood experiences and environment are important in determining which of the individual's potentialities are actualised, and which remain dormant.

Maternal Deprivation

Recent research has also suggested that lack of affection in infancy may have an important and lasting effect on the development of personality. Infants need far more than to be kept warm, clean, and well-fed. They have a profound need for affection, and for the stimulation and security pro-vided by the presence of benevolent adults. If they are brought up in large, impersonal institutions where, although their physical needs are amply cared for, they are left alone for long periods during the day, and seldom fondled, talked to, or played with, their personality may be greatly damaged

—the damage commonly taking the form of an incapacity to form affectionate and trusting relationships with others. In the words of Dr. John Bowlby, who has been prominently associated with work in this field: "What is believed to be essential for mental health is that the infant and young child should experience a warm, intimate, and continuous relationship with his mother (or permanent mother-substitute— one person who steadily 'mothers' him) in which both find satisfaction and enjoyment." [1]

This conclusion has already greatly affected the attitude of public authorities towards the care of homeless children. The tendency to-day is to bring up such children, where possible, not in institutions, but in foster-homes which provide, as far as possible, the atmosphere of a normal family. In the institutions themselves, also, attempts are being made to create small familial groups where something of this atmosphere is reproduced.

THE ASSESSMENT OF PERSONALITY

Many psychologists are now concerned to develop means of assessing personality. Some of them hold that only "holistic" methods—methods that seek to assess the individual as a whole—are appropriate. They claim that, if we try to assess separate qualities, or traits, or factors, of an individual, we are not judging him as a unique and integrated whole, and are not in contact with his "organised structure," which is his essential characteristic. There is considerable evidence, however, that although in ordinary life (and in some forms of clinical work) the individual's total personality is frequently appraised, this approach to assessment is so subjective and unreliable that, to quote Vernon, "a few really reliable objective measurements of people provide better predictions of educational and vocational success than do subjective generalisations about their personalities as wholes." Consequently, while some psychologists are developing methods of assessing "total personality," others are developing objective methods of measuring the chief dimensions of personality and the more important of our interests and social attitudes.

[1] *Child Care and the Growth of Love* (Pelican Books, 1953), p. 11.

Apart from observation of an individual's behaviour over a long period, and the physical signs of personality already discussed, other ways of assessing personality that are now being closely studied are the interview, projection techniques, questionnaires and inventories, and group situations.

The Interview

In its conventional form the interview has low reliability: *i.e.* it yields markedly divergent ratings of the same people, especially in respect of their fitness for a particular post or for a particular course of training. The correlations between different interviewers interviewing the same people is rarely more than ·5 or ·6, which, as Vernon says, means that "if two schoolmasters independently interviewed 100 candidates for a grammar school, and each picked the twenty best in his opinion, they would agree on nine of their choices only and disagree on eleven." [1]   The ordinary interviewer also has low validity. It is subject to bias, and to what is called the "halo effect," which is the tendency in an interviewer to allow his impression of one aspect of an individual's personality to distort his judgments of the others.

There is evidence, however, that the reliability and validity of the interview as a means of assessing personality are increased if the interview is carefully planned, if the interviewer has acquired skill as the result of training, if he confines himself to qualities which cannot be better assessed by other methods, and if he then treats his interview as one test in a set of tests, all of whose results must be combined. This was shown by a group of psychologists responsible for the selection of officers in the American Army. They decided that the interview should be given a specific and unique purpose—that of assessing the candidates' "social interaction," or ability to deal with people. When this was done, there was a sharp rise in its reliability and in its validity as a selection instrument.

Critical comments in the validity of the interview as a means of assessing personality do not imply criticism of its value in such fields as the diagnosis and treatment of mental

[1] *Personality Tests and Assessments* (1953), p. 24.

illness, and educational and vocational guidance. The interview is indispensable in psychotherapy and in all situations where one person is seeking to make contact with another, to learn about his present and past outlook and behaviour, and to assist him in a process of self-discovery and adjustment.

Projection Techniques

Projection techniques provide the individual with a means whereby he may unwittingly express some of the dominant features of his personality. These tests all have two characteristics in common: the subjects are presented with an "unstructured" or ambiguous situation, which is the same for all of them but may elicit many different reactions; and the subjects are induced to reveal themselves without being aware that they are doing so. Thus in the Rorschach test there are ten standard inkblots, each of which yields many different responses from different subjects in answer to the question, "What could that be?" or "What do you see?". These responses are scored in a prescribed way, and, although there is much dispute (and too little experimental evidence) about the reliability and validity of the test, it does seem able, in skilled hands, to help in the differential diagnosis of mental patients, if not in predictions about normal people.

The same may be said of a second projection technique that is in common use—the Thematic Apperception Test, or TAT. In this test the subject is shown a standard series of pictures in a definite sequence, and, as each picture is shown, the tester says, "Tell me what events have led up to the present occurrence, what the character (or characters) in the picture is (are) thinking, and what the outcome will be." When the subject has provided a "theme" for each picture, the themes are analysed as projections of his inner fantasies. Often one theme recurs many times in a subject's interpretation of the pictures: it may involve such things as a desire for affection or recognition, or for escape from a predicament, or a preoccupation with death or propriety or security.

There are many other projective tests besides these two, and in practice more than one test is often employed. Pending their scientific validation, all the tests are treated less as measures of personality than as special channels of observation that help the interviewer to learn more about the person being studied.

Questionnaires and Inventories

In standardised questionnaires and inventories, which are often referred to as "pencil-and-paper" tests, the subject is asked questions about his dispositions or behaviour, or invited to rate himself in one or more respects. Some of the tests are designed to assess factors such as extraversion-introversion, ascendance-submission, emotional stability, hypochondriasis, masculinity-femininity, or anxiety. Other tests concentrate on attitudes and interests. In well-constructed tests the items are all objectively scored by reference to norms that have been experimentally established, and the value of each item depends, not on its face-value, but on its correlation with an external criterion. Thus, in Allport's test of ascendance-submission—the tendency to be dominating or submissive in face-to-face relationships with other people—the value of each possible answer to each item was calculated by comparing the answers of people who had been rated by their associates as ascendant with those of people who had been rated as submissive. For this reason, tests of this kind are often referred to as "objective" measures. What is meant is that an individual gets the same score whoever marks the test—his score does not depend on the subjective interpretation of the tester.

These tests are now widely used, and much is known about the way they should be constructed to make their items effective and acceptable to the subjects. However, they have many serious weaknesses. First, their validity is affected by the attitude of the subjects, who may deliberately set out to show themselves in a favourable light. This is often not a serious objection to the use of such tests in research or guidance, especially when the subjects are university students, who are usually willing to co-operate; but it undermines their value in vocational selection, and in other situations where there may be some inducement to fake the results. Some tests, however, are so constructed that the faking of answers can to some extent be detected and allowed for.

Secondly, if a test allows the testee to omit answers, to answer by a question mark, or to give various grades of response, the results of the test will be affected by the extent to which an individual is cautious or non-committal. Again, some tests try to provide corrective checks, while others use forced-choice items in an attempt to eliminate this weakness. But in many existing tests it is an important source of error.

Except in the United States, the weaknesses of these tests have long prevented them from being widely used in clinical work or in educational and vocational selection. Recently, however, closer study of the tests has had two notable effects. It has led Americans to use them more cautiously, and it has shown psychologists elsewhere that some of the tests (like the Minnesota Multiphasic Personality Inventory) are much more valid than others, and that there are ways in which the weaknesses of tests of this kind can be greatly diminished.

Group Situations

During the Second World War, British and American psychologists developed techniques in which candidates for commissions were given tasks that afforded opportunities of observing how each of them behaved in a small group. Sometimes the group was given a task such as moving a heavy and cumbersome object over streams, walls, and other obstacles, and was left to work out its own solution; sometimes the group engaged in discussion of a general topic or of some imaginary military problem that it was called upon to solve. In either case the behaviour of the candidates was observed, and the observers made ratings of each candidate's personality as a whole—noticing which candidates behaved merely as passengers, which sought to dominate the rest or to indulge in self-display, and which seemed to come to the fore by acting in the group's interests rather than their own.

Since the war these "group observational procedures" have become common in selecting candidates in industry, in the Civil Service, in teacher-training, in the ministry, and in many other spheres. This has been due to their great acceptability and to the natural supposition that we can make a better assessment of a person if we see him in a social situation, where he is doing or discussing things with several other people, than if we merely see him by himself in a conventional interview. But the high value that is sometimes claimed for these procedures has not yet been scientifically established. They have not been shown to be markedly superior to the conventional interview. Since they yield subjective interpretations of behaviour, they are extremely dependent on the observers' skill, impartiality, and freedom from crotchets; and, since they involve complex social situations, candidates are sometimes apt to approach them with the definite intention of playing a part and showing a particular type of personality.

Attempts to assess personality are also made in other group situations. In some, each member of a group is asked to choose the person in the group he likes best, the person with whom he would prefer to live, or the person with whom he would prefer to work. In others, the group is observed, either continuously or at intervals, over a period, and attempts are made to reduce the subjectivity of assessments by systematically recording the individuals' actions—especially those that involve some form of social contact—under various specified heads and calculating the relative incidence of each type. These methods, however, though promising, are subject to various difficulties that have not yet been wholly removed.

Conclusion

Besides the ways of assessing personality that have been discussed, there are many others—for example, the analysis of such expressive movements as walking, writing, speaking, etc. However, in spite of all that is being done, and of the increasing recognition that tests of personality are not impracticable (although the same tests are not all equally suited to selection, experimentation, and diagnosis or guidance), we must not suppose that the assessment of personality has reached the same level of precision as the assessment of abilities or attainments. As Vernon has put it: "the testing or assessment of human personality is fraught with so many difficulties—it is more complex indeed than any other problem in individual psychology—that even the application of the highest psychological skill and technical accomplishment cannot be expected to bring about rapid success." [1]

NOTES ON READING

A standard reference work on personality is C. S. Hall and G. Lindzey, *Theories of Personality* (New York and London, John Wiley: 1957). The typologies of Jung, Kretschmer and Sheldon are fully described in C. G. Jung, *Psychological Types* (Kegan Paul: 1923); E. Kretschmer, *Physique and Character* (Kegan Paul: 1925); and in two books by W. H. Sheldon, *The Varieties of Human Physique* (New York, Harper: 1940) and *The Varieties of Human Temperament* (New York, Harper: 1942). An account of some of the main theories of personality, and of Eysenck's factorial studies, is given in H. J. Eysenck, *The Structure of Human Personality* (Methuen: 1953).

Highly readable non-technical accounts of the nature and assessment of personality will be found in two Pelican books by H. J. Eysenck—*Sense and Nonsense in Psychology* (1958) and *Fact and Fiction in Psychology* (1965). At a more specialised level, the assessment of personality is dealt with in H. J. Eysenck, *The Scientific Study of Personality* (Kegan Paul: 1952), P. E. Vernon, *Personality Assessment* (Methuen: 1964), Anne Anastasi, *Psychological Testing*, and Lee J. Cronback, *Essentials of Psychological Testing*.

[1] *Op. cit.,* p. 206.

CHAPTER XVII

CONFLICT AND THE MENTAL MECHANISMS

Mental conflict is inevitable. Even animals feel the pull of incompatible instinctive impulses, such as fear and hunger, or fear and pugnacity; and in human beings, with their more complex organisation of sentiments, the possibilities of conflict are far greater.

Conflict in human beings occurs at many levels. There may be a direct clash of instincts, such as is constantly seen in animals. Or the conflict may lie between an instinct and a sentiment, as between fear and self-respect, or between sex desire and moral principle. Or two sentiments may conflict: family affection, for example, may conflict with affection for a friend or fiancé, or loyalty to a person with loyalty to an ideal. A similar situation arises when a powerful impulse is frustrated by circumstance, as when a woman with a strong maternal impulse is unable to have children, or a sociable person is forced into work of a solitary kind.

The effects of mental conflict are always disturbing. Anxiety, emotional tension, irritability and depression are among the commoner symptoms. Another effect may be a kind of paralysis of action: the sufferer cannot follow either of the conflicting tendencies effectively, because of the opposing pull of the other. Sometimes this paralysis spreads beyond the area of the original conflict, so that there is a loss of initiative and energy in all departments of life.

In some cases, mental conflict can be solved by purely rational means, either by altering the circumstances that produced it, or by some form of compromise between the conflicting tendencies. The sociable individual who finds solitary work distasteful may be able to change his job; or, by joining various clubs, he may to some extent satisfy his social impulses in his leisure. But straightforward solutions of this kind are not always possible, and, even when they are, the person concerned cannot always make the adjustment himself. Sometimes, however, a well-timed mental "shove" from a sympathetic friend will overcome the paralysis produced by conflict, and help the sufferer to take the obvious steps to solve his problem.

Where a conflict cannot be solved at the rational level, the mind makes use of various methods of evading it or of making it less painful. These methods were first distinguished by Freud (1856-1939), who referred to them as the "mechanisms" of the mind. The most important of these mechanisms are sublimation and repression.

RE-DIRECTION AND SUBLIMATION

Where an impulse conflicts with internal or with external forces, and cannot be directly satisfied, it can often find a substitute satisfaction by being re-directed into an alternative outlet. The pugnacious impulse, for example, may be re-directed into fighting for a cause, unsatisfied maternal impulse may find expression in work for child welfare, or the sex impulse may be re-directed into intellectual activity or artistic creation. In all of these examples the alternative outlet is a desirable one, but this is not always the case. The maternal impulse, for example, may find expression in pampering a lap-dog. But where the unsatisfied impulses are re-directed into valuable activities, the process is called *sublimation*.

Sublimation is the best possible way of dealing with mental conflict and frustration. Its function goes far beyond that of solving the individual's problems. Civilisation, art, science, and all the highest achievements of humanity depend, in the last resort, on the energy derived from the re-direction of powerful instinctive impulses. Without such re-direction we should still be leading lives that were, in Hobbes's phrase "nasty, brutish, and short."

Sublimation and Civilisation

Freud has asserted that the price of civilisation is the denial of instinct, and the statement is true in a double sense: not only in the obvious sense that instincts cannot be freely indulged in a civilised society, but in the more fundamental sense that civilisation could not have arisen without the motive-power derived from instinctive energy that has been dammed up and then re-directed.

To quote Freud himself on this important subject:

> "We believe that civilisation has been built up . . . by sacrifices in gratification of the primitive impulses, and that it is to a large extent for ever being re-created as each individual . . . repeats the sacrifice of his instinctive pleasures for the common good. The sexual are among the most important of the instinctive forces thus utilised: they are in this way sublimated, that is to say, their energy is turned aside from its sexual goal and diverted towards other ends, no longer sexual and socially more valuable."[1]

In the light of this quotation, it is difficult to understand the common view that Freud was an immoral and subversive writer who advocated the unrestricted indulgence of all our impulses, particularly the sexual!

Freud's conclusions on sublimation receive strong support from the work of the Cambridge anthropologist, Unwin.[2] Unwin has studied various primitive communities, and produced evidence which suggests that the level of cultural development attained is connected with the amount of sexual restraint. All savage communities regard marriage as more or less binding; but many allow complete sexual freedom before marriage, and such communities, though they are often happy and free from neurosis, tend to be culturally undeveloped. Some of Unwin's criteria of culture may be questioned, but his general findings strongly confirm those of Freud. If the promptings of instinct are always and immediately followed, there is no reservoir of energy available for "higher" pursuits.

Thus Freud regards the control of instinctive impulses as an essential means to the attainment of more civilised satisfactions. Far from being subversive, his views might be held to provide a sounder basis for morality than the codes which

---

[1] *Introductory Lectures on Psychoanalysis* (1922), p. 17.
[2] *Sexual Regulation and Human Behaviour* (1933) and *Sex and Culture* (1934).

preach abstinence as an end in itself. But these considerations lie outside our present scope.

Re-direction in Children

The successful handling of children depends to a large extent on encouraging re-direction rather than repression. Considerable tact, self-restraint and patience are required, for children cannot consciously re-direct their impulses for themselves. Adults must try, as unobtrusively as possible, to provide alternative outlets and to steer inconvenient impulses into harmless channels, such as playing football instead of smashing windows. Though this is doubtless a counsel of perfection, the aim should be never to forbid a child to do anything without providing an alternative. In putting forward the alternative, incidentally, it is sound diplomacy not to present it as a *faute de mieux,* but to suggest that you expect the child to regard it as an improvement on his original intention.

REPRESSION AND SUPPRESSION

When an impulse cannot be successfully sublimated, it may undergo repression. Repression is a wholly undesirable way of evading mental conflict. To understand its nature, we must clearly distinguish it from suppression or self-control, with which it is very often confused.

We suppress an impulse when we decide, consciously and deliberately, to deny it expression. This is in no way harmful: indeed, if we did not all constantly practise suppression, we should revert to the law of the jungle. When we control our impatience with a child's constant questions, suppress a desire to yawn or to fidget, keep an appointment that we should greatly like to break, refrain from jumping a queue, or laugh politely at a story we have heard three times before, we are practising suppression; and the process, though not enjoyable, is harmless to the individual concerned, and essential to the smooth running of society.

The essential fact about *suppression* is that we are aware of experiencing the impulse, although we deny it an outlet and refuse to allow it to dominate our conscious thoughts.

In *repression*, on the other hand, we deal with an unwelcome tendency by refusing to admit its existence. When we feel an impulse that shocks our self-respect, we may disown it and attempt to banish it from consciousness. If the attempt succeeds, as it frequently does, the disowned impulse becomes literally unconscious, in the sense that it is inaccessible to introspection. Nevertheless, it continues to exist, and to produce effects. Repression may be applied to impulses and emotions (including anxieties, which will be discussed separately); to sentiments, such as hatred or jealousy; or to memories. A repressed sentiment is known as a *complex*.

Repression and Guilt-Feeling

It must be emphasised that we do not repress the memory of an experience because the experience itself was unpleasant. Many experiences that were acutely unpleasant to live through may be quite pleasant to dwell on in retrospect. (*Forsan et haec olim meminisse juvabit.*) But none of us gets pleasure from remembering experiences that were humiliating—occasions when we made fools of ourselves, behaved badly, or tried to impress and failed. This is the sort of memory we tend to repress; together with memories of experiences which, though pleasant at the time, cause shame in retrospect. Similarly, we repress impulses and desires, not because we know that they cannot be satisfied, but because we are ashamed of feeling them. In more technical language, repression always involves guilt-feeling—the latter term being used by Freud to cover any feelings of shame, self-reproach, or personal inadequacy. As will appear in connection with the subconscious mind, the standards by which we condemn our own impulses are often quite irrational: but the guilt-feeling is no less acute on this account.

A second point that must be emphasised is that repression is not an "all or none" process. Often it is only partially effective, and the disowned impulse lurks, so to speak, on the outer fringes of consciousness. From this region it can be brought back into full consciousness by a strong effort of will, if the person is willing to make it. But usually this is the last thing he desires to do.

Harmful Effects of Repression

Repression has many harmful effects.   In the first place the repressed impulse does not remain inactive.   It is constantly struggling to re-enter consciousness, so that there is a continual battle between the repressed impulse and the repressing forces (called by Freud the *censor*) that are striving to hold it down. This involves a constant drain on nervous energy, for few things are more exhausting than conflict.   Chronic fatigue for which there is no adequate physiological cause is one of the commonest symptoms of repression.

Secondly, though the repressed tendency can seldom re-enter consciousness directly, it exerts many indirect effects: some of them harmless (such as dreams, which will be discussed later), others decidedly harmful.   It may make matters clearer to begin with an illustration.

If a man has a brother who is better-looking, more popular, and more successful than himself, he would not be human if he did not at times feel jealous.   If he admits to himself that he is liable to jealous feelings, but resolves not to show them, and, if possible, not to come into direct competition with his brother, he will be dealing with a difficult situation in the best possible way.   But he is more likely to repress his jealousy; and then one, or both, of two results may follow.   He may develop a somewhat extravagantly cordial and demonstrative manner towards his brother: or he may do him some injury (such an injury, for example, as might follow from forgetting to post an important letter, or "inadvertently" letting slip some fact to his brother's discredit), which he sincerely believes to be accidental, but which in fact is motivated by his unconscious jealousy.

Reaction Formations

This example illustrates two of the commonest effects of repression.   First, reaction-formations, where the tendency opposite to that which has been repressed appears in consciousness in an exaggerated form.   In the example given, repressed hostility appeared as over-friendliness, but it may also happen that repressed love appears as hostility, as with Benedick and Beatrice in the first acts of *Much Ado*.

One of the commonest reaction-formations is excessive prudery, which nearly always indicates strong repressed sex interests. Those Victorians who, for modesty's sake, used to drape the legs of their tables and pianos, were clearly capable of deriving indelicate suggestions from the most unlikely sources. Another common reaction-formation is boastfulness, and an excessive concern with personal prestige. The boastful and touchy individual, who will never admit ignorance or confess himself wrong, is nearly always compensating for a repressed sense of inadequacy. If he were really confident of his own merits and status, he would not be so concerned lest others should under-rate them. The point is well illustrated in a remark by Oscar Wilde of a friend: "I can't understand that fellow So-and-so—always worrying about whether he's put at the head of the table at dinner-parties. These things don't worry me—I always think that where I am *is* the head of the table!"

Indirect Expression of Repressed Tendencies

A second effect of repression is exemplified by the "accidental" injury, which was in fact motivated by unconscious jealousy. If a repressed impulse can find expression *in a form in which it is unrecognisable by the person concerned*, it frequently does so.

Once again, the sex impulse provides the clearest examples. The announcement of an "outspoken" sermon denouncing sexual laxity will bring many to church who are not often present, and who would be indignant if they were told their true motive for attending. A marked interest in scandals of a sexual kind; a preoccupation with nudity ("for purely aesthetic reasons"); a gloating interest in whippings and beatings;[1] these—and other symptoms too numerous and recondite to discuss—are all disguised manifestations of repressed sex interest.

[1] The Rev. Francis Kilvert, in his *Diary*, unconsciously provides many examples of this.

PHANTASY

Phantasy, or day-dreaming, is another mechanism that is almost universal. At all times, but particularly when we are anxious, frustrated or unhappy, we are liable to retreat from the real world into the more manageable and more exciting world of phantasy. The day-dreams in which we indulge may be comparatively realistic; or they may be only slightly less fantastic than night dreams, and we "come round" with a start to realise that we have been mentally riding a Grand National winner, or discovering the perfect defence against hydrogen-bombs.

Phantasy is not undesirable *per se*: indeed, the more realistic type of day-dream may provide a valuable spur to action. The office-boy who dreams of becoming a partner and works hard to that end, may live to find his dream fulfilled. But phantasy may be dangerous if it grows so absorbing as to become a substitute for action. The office-boy's day-dream will be a brake, not a spur, to advancement, if he becomes so absorbed in it that he forgets to stamp the letters.

Day-dreaming, in short, is like alcohol—consoling and stimulating in moderation, but harmful in excess. Like most of the other mechanisms described in this chapter, it can be seen in its most advanced form among psychotic[1] patients, for whom, in many cases, the distinction between phantasy and reality has ceased to exist.

IDENTIFICATION

Identification is closely allied to phantasy. When some impulse in ourselves is frustrated, we often gain a measure of satisfaction by identifying ourselves in imagination with someone (either an existing person or a character in history or fiction) who seems to us to possess the qualities that we long for or the opportunities that we lack.

Identification is particularly evident among children. The games of dramatic make-believe in which young children

[1] For the distinction between "psychotic" and "neurotic," see footnote, p. 44.

delight, derive much of their attraction from the fact that the players identify themselves with parents, teachers, military commanders, engine-drivers, and others who seem to them to enjoy an enviable degree of power and freedom. But identification is by no means confined to children. Most of us have at times felt a peculiar affinity with some character of whom we have heard or read, and the types with whom we have at various times identified ourselves may provide a revealing index of our interests and scale of values. A youth may see himself as Dan Dare, or John Osborne, or Shelley; a young woman may identify herself with Audrey Hepburn, or with Florence Nightingale, or with the captain of the England Hockey XI. The appeal of "pop fiction", and of many boys' and girls' weeklies,[1] depends largely on the opportunities they provide for identification. The teen-age factory girl absorbed in a "paper-back" with a title like *From Hoxton to Hollywood* has bought a ready-made day-dream which will release her for a time from the frustrations and monotony of real life.

The psychotic sometimes carry identification to the point of actually believing themselves to *be* the admired person. Every mental hospital has its quota of kings and queens, Napoleons and Joans of Arc.

The characters with whom we identify ourselves are not always remote or imaginary. Hart,[2] for example, quotes the case of a patient who threw himself with extraordinary zest into a lawsuit that an acquaintance was bringing against his wife. On his own showing, his motives were affection for his friend, and concern for abstract justice. Investigation revealed, however, that the alleged friendship was of only a few weeks' standing, and that the justice of the case was all on the other side. The real cause of the patient's interest in the lawsuit was that he was himself engaged in a bitter quarrel with his wife, and he had identified himself with his acquaintance, in whom he saw his own position reflected.

[1] It is a popular device to provide the famous detective or inventor with a boy assistant (cf. Sexton Blake's Tinker) with whom the young readers find it particularly easy to identify themselves. Cf. George Orwell on "Boys' Weeklies" in *Critical Essays* (1946).

[2] *The Psychology of Insanity* (1930), pp. 160-1.

It is common for parents to identify themselves with their children, and to attempt, through the children, to satisfy their own thwarted ambitions.   This is a somewhat dangerous tendency, as it may cause children to be forced into activities for which they are unfitted.   A father, for example, may have longed to be a doctor, but have been unable to afford the training; and he is determined that his son shall have the career he himself has missed.   If the son has the ability and the desire to become a doctor, all may be well.   But too often in such cases the son's abilities and inclinations are not considered: he has been destined for the medical profession from his cradle, and there is no more to be said.   Many false starts and failures, and much unnecessary misery, have been caused by this form of identification.

PROJECTION

When some tendency in ourselves arouses guilt-feeling, we very commonly project it, and become inordinately critical in others of the impulse that we are trying to repress in ourselves. The man who is always complaining of other people's conceit, or snobbishness, or meanness, usually has a tendency towards these foibles himself.

This mechanism is now widely recognised: but there is another form of projection, not so generally understood, where what is projected is not the unwelcome impulse, but the moral sentiment which condemns it.   Those who suffer from this form of projection are constantly on the defensive against imaginary criticisms;   they are always taking offence, and seeing veiled slights and innuendoes where none are intended. In pathological cases, this form of projection may lead to hallucinations, in which the patient "hears" voices denouncing him, and "sees" fingers pointed at him in accusation.

RATIONALISATION

Rationalisation may be defined as hunting for arguments to justify us in doing what we want to do, or believing what we want to believe: and, having found the arguments, specious or otherwise, convincing ourselves that they were the real motives that led to our belief or action.

This technique is often employed to avert a conflict between an impulse and a moral sentiment. By a more or less elaborate process of casuistry, we convince ourselves that, though what we have done, or intend to do, might *seem* inconsistent with our principles, there are circumstances in this particular case which make it allowable. We get off the bus without paying, and tell ourselves that, as we had to stand all the way, the Company is not really entitled to demand a fare. The workman pilfers from his factory and argues that "the firm owes it to him." But it is impossible to resist quoting James in this context:

> "How many excuses does the drunkard find when each new temptation comes. It is a new brand of liquor, which the interests of intellectual culture in such matters oblige him to taste; moreover, it is poured out and it is a sin to waste it; also, others are drinking and it would be churlishness to refuse. Or it is but to enable him to sleep, or just to get through this job of work; or it is not really drinking, it is because he feels so cold; or it is Christmas Day; or it is a means of stimulating him to make a more powerful resolution in favour of abstinence than any he has hitherto made; or it is just this once, and once doesn't count, etc., etc., *ad libitum*." [1]

There is a certain type of insanity in which the patient cannot perform the simplest action, such as blowing his nose, without producing a string of elaborate reasons for doing so. Rationalisation is also constantly employed by the insane in order to bridge the gap between their primary delusions and reality. A paranoiac,[2] for example, may believe that he is being slowly poisoned by his family. If he is assured by a doctor that he shows no symptoms of poisoning, and that in fact he is suffering from a common type of delusion, he will probably form a secondary delusion that he is the victim of a widespread plot in which the doctor is also involved.

[1] *Textbook of Psychology* (1892), p. 453.
[2] Paranoia—a form of neurosis characterised by chronic suspicion.

DISSOCIATION

Conflict is sometimes solved by dissociation, where the conflicting tendencies are satisfied alternately, but are never allowed to enter consciousness together. A mild form of dissociation may be seen in those who keep incompatible beliefs or standards in logic-tight compartments of the mind. The incongruous beliefs never come into contact, and so the person is untroubled by a sense of inconsistency. Some people, for example, contrive to be both Christians and Marxists, though belief in dialectical materialism is logically quite incompatible with belief in theism, absolute values, or personal immortality. Again, many people have one moral code for business and another for private life : or one standard of manners within the family and another outside. But once more it is in the mental hospital that the logic-tight compart-ment is seen in its full perfection. The insane do not always need a bridge of rationalisation between their delusions and reality. Often, as Hart remarks, "the 'Queen of the World' will contentedly carry out her daily task of scrubbing the ward floor, and the omnipotent millionaire will beg plaintively for a small gift of tobacco"[1]—quite undisturbed by the incongruity between their pretensions and their acts.

Somnambulisms

In its more advanced forms, dissociation is responsible for some of the strangest phenomena in psychology. Sometimes there is an apparent splitting of consciousness, so that two separate activities or trains of thought can be carried on independently and simultaneously. Automatic writing is a phenomenon of this type. Some neurotic patients, while carrying on a conversation with one person, can at the same time be induced to write answers to questions whispered in their ear by another person. In such cases, the patient is quite unaware of what his hand is writing, and the sentences written may even contain information that he is not consciously aware of possessing.

[1] *The Psychology of Insanity* (1930), p. 33.

Some writers regard dissociation as a variant, or a more advanced form, of repression; others treat it as an entirely separate mechanism. This question is still *sub judice*, but there is no doubt that one form of dissociation resembles repression in its early stages, in that it involves the banishment from normal consciousness of some painful idea or system of memories. But the banished system does not, as in repression, find conscious expression in disguised and distorted forms. It breaks through periodically in an undisguised form, and re-occupies the entire field of consciousness, to the exclusion of normal life.

A famous case of dissociation was described by the French psychologist, Janet. One of his patients, a young woman called Irène, had nursed her mother through her last illness in peculiarly distressing circumstances. After her mother's death, Irène appeared to remember nothing of the tragic events that preceded it; she discussed her mother without emotion, and was reproached by her relatives for callousness. From time to time, however, she would pass suddenly into trance-like states (known technically as somnambulisms) in which she would re-enact with intense emotion the scene of her mother's death. While in this state, Irène was quite unconscious of her actual surroundings; but, when the trance ended, as suddenly as it had begun, she would resume normal existence without realising that it had been interrupted.

Fugues

Another type of dissociation occurs when a person who has been suffering intolerable strain in his work or private life is found wandering far from his normal surroundings, completely lost, and unable to remember who he is, or any facts about his past life. Such dissociated states are known as *fugues*. Occasionally, though rarely, the patient does not merely lose his "true" identity during a fugue, but develops a complete secondary personality, which is apparently well-integrated, and capable of adjusting itself normally to the new environment. Such was the famous case of the Rev. Ansel Bourne, first described by James. In January, 1887, this man drew a large sum of money from a bank in Providence, U.S.A., and boarded a tramcar. He was not heard of again for two months. In March of the same year, in Norristown, Pennsylvania, some 200 miles away, "a man calling himself A. J. Brown, who had rented a small shop six weeks previously, stocked it with stationery, confectionery, fruit and small articles, and carried on his quiet trade without seeming to anyone unnatural or eccentric, woke up in a fright and called in the people of the house to tell him where he was. He said that his name was Ansel Bourne, that he was entirely ignorant of Norristown, that he knew nothing of shopkeeping, and that the last thing he remembered—it seemed only yesterday— was drawing the money from the bank, etc., in Providence. He would not believe that two months had elapsed."[1]

Multiple Personality

There have been other recorded cases of dual or multiple personality, the best known being probably that of Miss Beauchamp, described by Morton Prince.[2] Miss Beauchamp, an hysterical patient who was undergoing treatment that involved hypnosis, developed, during this treatment, two separate, and markedly different, personalities, which took charge alternately, and had no common memories, except of the period of Miss Beauchamp's life before the splitting took place. These personalities were designated B1 and B4: and there was also a third mischievous and irresponsible personality known as Sally, which sometimes held the field completely, but which also appeared capable of existing co-consciously when either B1 or B4 was in possession. No sweeping conclusions can be based on Miss Beauchamp, however, since there is little doubt that in her case the dissociation was largely the result of hypnosis. It is extremely rare for a secondary personality, which is apparently normal and well-integrated, to appear spontaneously, though such cases have undoubtedly occurred.

[1] *Principles of Psychology* (1890), Vol. I, p. 391.
[2] *The Dissociation of a Personality* (1906).

CONVERSION HYSTERIA

One of the most important developments of recent years has been the increasing realisation of the extent to which physical illness may depend on psychological causes, such as stress and emotional conflict. Illnesses due largely, or primarily, to such causes are known as *psychosomatic* (from Greek *psyche*, mind and *soma*, body).

In describing a disease as psychosomatic we are not, of course, renouncing the brain-dependence hypothesis, and denying that the cause is ultimately entirely physical. But psychomatic disorders are due in large part, not to such causes as infection or organic lesion, but to processes in the brain, the autonomic nervous system, and the ductless glands.[1] Examples have been given in Chapter V.

In the present context, however, we are concerned only with that sub-class of psychosomatic disorders known as *conversion hysterias*. The distinguishing feature of conversion hysteria is that it is subconsciously motivated: the illness is not merely a result of emotional conflict, but provides a means (though an unsatisfactory one) of resolving or evading it. The term "conversion hysteria" (not to be confused with conversion in the religious sense) is used to denote the conversion of a mental conflict into a physical symptom.[2]

This does not mean, however, that the conversion hysteric is a malingerer: there is still much misunderstanding on this point. He is, in fact, ill, and his condition differs from organic illness only in its cause. It is a complete mistake to think that the conversion hysteric is not genuinely ill, or that he does not really feel pain. Pain is no less painful for being due to emotional rather than to organic causes.

It is true that in one sense the conversion hysteric *wants* to be ill. But he wants to be ill only in the sense in which we "want" to stand in a cinema queue—*i.e.* as an undesired

---

[1] This does not imply that all illnesses involving the ductless glands are psychosomatic.

[2] Terminology in this field is not completely standardised, and some writers use "conversion hysteria" and "psychosomatic illness" as synonyms. But in the present discussion "conversion hysteria" will be used exclusively to mean a subconsciously motivated psychosomatic illness.

means to a desired end. And even in this sense, the desire is usually quite unconscious. At the conscious level, the patient makes great efforts to get well, often undergoing one form of unsuccessful physical treatment after another. The fact that our conscious and unconscious desires may conflict will be explained more fully in Chapter XVIII.

Causes of Conversion Hysteria

Among the commonest causes of conversion hysteria is the *desire to escape* from a situation that has become intolerable to the patient. A man, for example, may feel that his work is beyond him and long to retire; but he is still far from retiring age, and a premature resignation would straiten his means and would also be a confession of failure. In these circumstances, he may develop a timely illness, which will allow him to retire without discredit, and which will also excuse any recent loss of efficiency. In such cases, the nature of the illness developed may be specifically related to the work from which it provides an escape. A teacher or clergyman, for example, may develop speech difficulties, a draughtsman hysterical blindness, or a surgeon a tremor of the hands. It must again be emphasised that, consciously, the patient has no idea of the true cause of his illness. Usually at first he makes great efforts to get well, believing, quite sincerely, that his difficulties are due mainly to ill-health, whereas, in fact, his ill-health is due mainly to his difficulties.

Another common cause of conversion hysteria is *desire for sympathy and attention*. This form is common in children: it is particularly likely to occur in a child who has been "dethroned" by the birth of a new baby, who is jealous of the greater attention shown to other members of the family, or who feels, however irrationally, that he is unloved or neglected. The writer recalls, for example, being asked whether asthma was infectious. The inquirer had two sons, of whom the elder had for some time been asthmatic, and had been the object of considerable solicitude on that account. Recently the younger boy had also had several attacks, which always came on a few hours after those of his elder brother.

Yet another cause is *desire for power*. This motive is closely allied to the preceding one, and they are often found together. A widowed mother, for example, may use illness as a means of preventing her daughter from leaving home; or a neglected wife, or a henpecked husband, may unconsciously seek through illness to exact the attention, and the deference to their wishes, that they cannot otherwise obtain.

Relevance of Past Medical History

As has already been mentioned, the nature of a particular psychosomatic illness is often determined by the nature of the situation from which it provides an escape. Where no factor of this kind is operating, it may be largely a matter of chance what particular form a conversion hysteria will take. But if there is some pre-existing physical weakness, this often determines the unconscious choice of symptoms. If, for example, a patient with poor eyesight becomes ill through emotional causes, he is rather more likely to develop acute headaches or disturbances of vision than some other condition (such as heart trouble) for which his past medical history provides no excuse. Again, if a limb has been broken or injured in childhood, this is the limb most likely to be affected by hysterical paralysis. This fact is in some ways unfortunate, since it makes it more difficult to convince the patient that the real cause of his illness is emotional: he is apt to reiterate that "his doctor told him" that his symptoms were all due to his short sight, or to his injury in childhood.

Treatment of Conversion Hysteria

The only permanent cure for conversion hysteria is to resolve the conflict that produced it. With children this is often a comparatively simple matter, but with adults it may require a long process of analysis. It is not enough, unfortunately, simply to convince the patient that his illness is unconsciously motivated, though this is often the first step. The unconscious conflict must be brought out into the open and resolved by rational means; and this may involve prolonged investigation of the patient's personal history. As will be explained more fully in Chapter XIX, the origin, or predisposing cause, of most neuroses goes back to early life.

In addition to psychological treatment, direct treatment of symptoms by the ordinary methods of the physician may be necessary, but such physical treatment is never enough in itself. It may produce marked temporary improvement (as may also such methods as "faith healing" and suggestion under hypnosis); but if the underlying conflict is not resolved, another symptom will sooner or later take the place of the one that has been "cured."

NOTES ON READING

A book by Bernard Hart with the somewhat misleading title, *The Psychology of Insanity* (Cambridge Univ. Press: 1912; fifth, paperback, edition, with an historical introduction, 1956), provides a good introduction to the study of conflict and the mental mechanisms, though it is out of date on one or two points, particularly in its view of the nature of the repressing forces. A more comprehensive book, dealing fully with psychosomatic illness, is *An Introduction to Psychological Medicine*, by R. G. Gordon, N. G. Harris, and J. R. Rees (Oxford Univ. Press: 1936). Further titles are given in the *Notes on Reading* for Chapter XIX.

CHAPTER XVIII

ANXIETY AND GUILT-FEELING

The discussion on repression in the last chapter was confined mainly to the repression of desires and impulses. The effects of repressed anxiety have still to be considered.

Most "normal" anxiety is due simply to circumstance. We may be worried about the international situation, about illness, about money, about approaching examinations, and so forth. Such anxieties are unpleasant while they last, but usually they disappear with their cause and leave no permanent ill-effects. The really dangerous forms of anxiety are those that involve guilt-feeling.

Displacement of Repressed Anxiety

Anxieties that we are unwilling to admit, even to ourselves, may be repressed, just as other tendencies are repressed. In such cases the anxiety is usually displaced; the person ceases to worry consciously about the real cause of trouble, but develops an obsessive anxiety about something else—usually something about which he has no objective ground at all for concern. Fear of poverty, fear of insanity, and fear of illness (particularly certain forms of illness, such as venereal disease and cancer) are among the commonest forms that such displaced anxiety may take. Or, instead of being obsessed by one persistent anxiety, the person may suffer from a succession of worries about matters, trivial in themselves, to which he attaches excessive importance. He has a different worry every day or week, but there is always something. Many of us know people who lie sleepless, because they have posted two letters, and cannot feel sure that they did not put them in the wrong envelopes; or because they fear that something they said may have been misinterpreted, and have caused offence; or because they cannot quite remember if they locked the office safe; or for a thousand-and-one similar reasons. In such cases, as in cases where displacement gives rise to one persistent anxiety, the sufferer often knows quite well that his worry is groundless, but the knowledge makes little difference to his state of mind.

When anxiety becomes so acute as to be incapacitating, the condition is known as an *anxiety-state* or as *anxiety-neurosis*.[1] Such states often continue even after the original cause of anxiety has disappeared.

Thus, when a person continually feels anxiety for which there is no adequate objective justification, two things are fairly certain. First, the real cause of his anxiety is not what he is temporarily worrying about, but something more fundamental, which has been repressed. Secondly, the repressed anxiety contains an element of guilt-feeling. Worries of which we are in no way ashamed may produce much strain and unhappiness, but they seldom or never give rise to anxiety-states. Striking confirmation of this fact was provided during the Blitzkrieg on London in the Second World War. There can seldom have been a time when the objective grounds for anxiety were greater, yet the incidence of anxiety-states was actually reduced. Nervous exhaustion, due to prolonged strain and sleeplessness, sometimes made it impossible for a time for the person to carry on, but these cases were not neurotic: nothing more than rest was needed to restore them to normal. Pathological anxiety-states were not, of course, unknown during the air-raids, but where they occurred they were due less to fear of death or injury than to fear of being afraid; the sufferers feared that in a crisis their nerve might give way, and they might disgrace themselves, and endanger others. Behind nearly every "nervous breakdown" is a fear of falling short of one's own standards.

It is a paradoxical fact that the people most subject to guilt-feeling, and so to anxiety, are usually the people who, objectively, have least to feel guilty about. The sufferer from anxiety-neurosis is usually a highly conscientious person with strong moral sentiments. He is constantly falling short of his own standards, but this is not because his behaviour is worse than other people's but because his standards are higher.

[1] What is popularly known as a "nervous breakdown" is usually an acute anxiety-state.

He has usually been morally over-driven in childhood (cf. p. 244). He is the type whose friends say of him that he expects too much of himself, that he drives himself too hard, and that he cannot relax. In a person of this type, neurotic symptoms nearly always take the form of anxiety, whereas the simpler person, with less exacting standards, is more prone to conversion hysteria.

Symptoms of Repressed Anxiety

Repressed anxiety may give rise to various symptoms of a neurotic kind. Among the more familiar of these are phobias, compulsive or obsessive actions, and *sentiments d'incomplétude*.

Phobias are irrational fears. Reference has already been made to the groundless fears—*e.g.* of insanity, disease and financial ruin—that often result from displaced anxiety. These would be quite natural objects of fear if the patient had any real reason to believe himself threatened by them. But in the more typical phobias, the object or situation that is feared is in no sense dangerous, though it arouses an inexplicable dread in the patient. Freud gives a list of some of the commoner phobias—remarking that "they sound like the ten plagues of Egypt, except that there are far more than ten of them." They include darkness, open air, open spaces, cats, spiders, caterpillars, mice, thunder, blood, enclosed places, crowds, isolation, crossing bridges, and travelling by land or sea.[1] A mild aversion from some of these objects or situations is not abnormal, but an acute dread of something recognised to be harmless is an almost certain indication of repressed anxiety.

It is widely believed that many phobias are the result of childhood experiences that have been repressed. If a child is terrified by a dog, for example, or by being shut up in a dark cupboard, he may repress all memory of the experience, but may retain a neurotic dread of dogs, or of confined spaces, for the rest of his life. This is true in a sense; but, where such cases are investigated, it is usually found that the childhood experience was more than simply terrifying. It also

[1] *Introductory Lecture on Psychoanalysis* (1922), p. 332.

involved an element of guilt-feeling; otherwise it would not have been repressed. If a child has an alarming encounter with an angry dog, he may develop a strong conditioned fear of dogs which will last for some time. But such fears are not neurotic, and they do not persist indefinitely. Later contacts with harmless and friendly dogs will gradually reassure the child, or he may be deliberately and more rapidly deconditioned by the sort of technique described on p. 57. If a neurotic dread of dogs persists into adult life, we can be reasonably sure that some guilt-feeling attached to the original experience. The child may have been taunted for cowardice, and have experienced a peculiarly unpleasant combination of self-reproach, humiliation and rage. Or he may, in an inarticulate fashion, have regarded the hostile dog as sent to punish him for his own hostile feelings towards his brother or some other member of the family. Mere physical fear, however intense, is not enough in itself to produce a lasting phobia; there must be an element of self-condemnation as well. When Scott wrote in *Marmion*:

> "Thus oft it haps, that when within
> They shrink at sense of secret sin
> A feather daunts the brave."

he showed a remarkably clear insight into the cause of neurotic fears.

Compulsive or obsessive actions are another symptom of anxiety. These are rituals which the person feels obliged to perform, although he can give no reason for them. Constant hand-washing is a well-known form of compulsive action, of which the symbolic significance is obvious. Milder forms include stepping over the cracks in the pavement, or touching every post in a fence as we walk past; but these are much too widespread to be regarded as pathological.

A *sentiment d'incomplétude* is an obsessive fear of having left something undone. Many people suffer mildly from this obsession when they are worried: it may lead them, for example, to get out of bed three or four times to make sure that the front door is locked, that no lights have been left burning, or that they have not forgotten to put the cat out.

In extreme cases, the obsession may become so serious as to make the victim unfit for normal employment, since he can do nothing without going back three or four times to make sure that he has done it properly. The alleged tendency of murderers to revisit the scene of their crime may perhaps be partly due to a *sentiment d'incomplétude.*

NOTES ON READING

R. G. Gordon, N. G. Harris, and J. R. Rees, *An Introduction to Psychological Medicine,* may again be recommended. For further references, see *Notes on Reading* for Chapter XIX.

CHAPTER XIX

THE SUBCONSCIOUS MIND

Frequent reference has been made in preceding chapters to unconscious (or, more accurately, subconscious)[1] desires and motives. Recognition of the importance of such motives has revolutionised modern psychology, and the history, and the implications, of this discovery must now be considered in more detail.

Hypnosis

The existence of subconscious mental processes was first clearly revealed by hypnosis. Hypnosis is a technique for inducing trance-like states in which suggestibility is greatly heightened, and the activity of the censor, or repressing forces, is reduced.[2] It was first practised extensively about the year 1880 by the French psychologists, Janet and Charcot, and among the more striking phenomena they produced were the following:

(i) *Post-Hypnotic Suggestion.* A subject is hypnotised, and is told that after a precise time-interval—say fifty-five minutes —he is to carry out some series of actions, such as going upstairs and fetching his hat, putting it in the centre of the table and walking round it three times. When he is awakened from the hypnotic trance he remembers nothing of these instructions. Nevertheless, when the prescribed time is up, he will carry out the programme in every detail. If he is asked why he is behaving in this curious fashion, he will usually produce some highly ingenious rationalisation which he sincerely believes to be the true cause of his actions. He

---

[1] In this chapter, the terms "unconscious" and "subconscious" will be used interchangeably; but "subconscious" is preferred, as being less liable to create linguistic difficulties.

[2] For a fuller discussion of hypnosis see H. J. Eysenck, *Sense and Nonsense in Psychology* (1957).

may say, for example, that he had noticed that morning that a friend's hat was asymmetrical, so had resolved to make a careful inspection of his own.

(ii) *Removal of Symptoms by Suggestion.*   Many neurotic symptoms can be removed, temporarily at least, by suggestion under hypnosis.   For example, if a patient with an hysterical paralysis is hypnotised and told that he can move the paralysed limb, he is frequently able to do so.

(iii) *Recovery of Buried Memories.*   Many neurotic symptoms are due to past experiences of a shocking and terrifying kind, which have now been forgotten.   Under hypnosis, the patient may live through the shocking experience again, and this, for reasons which will later be discussed, is often sufficient to remove the neurotic symptom.

These discoveries were the beginning of explorations that have opened up a new continent of the mind.   There was, of course, nothing fundamentally revolutionary in the concept of subconscious memory, for it had long been realised that brain-traces outlast the stage at which they can give rise to conscious recall (cf. p. 161).   The new facts revealed by hypnosis were: (i) the extent to which forgetting is caused by inhibition rather than by fading, and (ii) the extent to which memory-traces, though blocked from consciousness, may yet remain active and affect behaviour. A third fact, more clearly revealed by later investigators, is (iii) that inhibition may be applied to emotions, desires and sentiments, as well as to memories.   The work of Freud and others has now made it clear that the greater part of our mental activity is subconscious, and that our conscious thought and behaviour are continually influenced by dispositions and processes of which we are normally unaware.

Objections to the Term "Unconscious"

We must here refer briefly to the criticism, which is still sometimes made by philosophers, that terms like "subconscious" (or, still more, "unconscious") desire or memory are self-contradictory.   Memory and desire, it is argued, are by definition states of consciousness, so that a subconscious (or unconscious) desire is as inconceivable as an unfelt pain or a silent noise.

The *terms* "subconscious memory," etc., are, perhaps, ill-chosen: some term like "quasi-memory" or "latent memory" might cause less misunderstanding. But, whatever term is employed, the fact it denotes is now beyond dispute. To confine the discussion to memory, it is undeniable (i) that a person's behaviour and emotions may be profoundly affected by some past experience that he cannot normally recall, and (ii) that in such cases, memory of the experience can often be restored by special techniques such as hypnosis. To say that the person has an unconscious, or subconscious, memory of the past experience is a convenient way of expressing these facts, but the phrase is admittedly somewhat unfortunate: it recalls the term "soldiers' unmarried wives," which was coined by the Ministry of Pensions at the beginning of the Second World War. Still, the latter term, however philologically regrettable, was in fact quite unambiguous in its reference: none of those who criticised the phrase supposed that by so doing they were casting doubt on the existence of the persons to whom it referred. Similarly, the philosophers who object to such terms as "subconscious mind" are not thereby destroying the foundations of modern dynamic psychology. In the discussion that follows, we shall continue to use the disputed terms when it is convenient to do so; since these terms, however anomalous, are now part of the standard psychological vocabulary.

Our Knowledge of "Unconscious" States

One of the most difficult facts to grasp about unconscious states is that they really *are* unconscious, in the sense that they are inaccessible to ordinary introspection. How, then, it may naturally be asked, can we claim to know anything about such states? The answer to this question can perhaps best be conveyed by analogy. The mind may be compared with a large circular hall, filled with a great variety of objects, and lit by one small and heavily-shaded electric-light bulb in the centre. Just under the bulb there is a pool of light in which everything can be seen clearly. Further out there is a half-lit area in which the shapes of objects can be dimly perceived; further out still, there is complete darkness. Any knowledge we have of the contents of the outer spaces of the hall must be gained otherwise than by sight—by touch, by inference from what we can see in the central areas, or by some other means. Similarly, what knowledge we have of the deeper layers of the unconscious mind must be gained by other means than introspection—by inference from behaviour, or by indirect methods such as psycho-analysis and the analysis of dreams.

Origin and Nature of the Subconscious Mind

The subconscious mind is a product of repression. In the infant there is apparently no dualism of conscious and subconscious, but the process of repression begins as soon as he realises that certain of his actions and feelings evoke disapproval in adults. Forbidden impulses are then often pushed out of consciousness, and form the nucleus of the subconscious mind, to which many unwanted impulses are thenceforward consigned. It was originally supposed that the main difference between the conscious and subconscious levels of the mind lay in their contents, and in the fact that the subconscious layers were inaccessible to introspection. But it soon became clear that not only the contents but the processes of the subconscious differ fundamentally from those of the conscious mind.

Infantile Nature of the Subconscious Mind

The subconscious mind, whose foundations are firmly laid in infancy, remains essentially infantile throughout life. Now, the outstanding characteristic of the baby is a primitive and ruthless egoism: he blindly pursues his own instinctive satisfaction, regardless of the claims, the comfort, or the convenience, of anyone else. Other people are important to him just in so far as they minister to his welfare. The subconscious mind retains this outlook throughout life. There is profound truth in the old French saying, *Grattez l'adulte et vous trouverez l'enfant.*

The ends desired by the adult subconscious mind differ somewhat from those desired by the baby, though the difference is not so great as might at first be imagined. The baby desires, above all else, food, warmth, physical comfort, and the attention of adults. The subconscious mind of the adult is chiefly concerned with satisfaction of the sex, self-assertive and aggressive impulses—these being the instincts that are most strongly repressed in adult life. But the subconscious mind pursues its ends in the same ruthless and intemperate fashion as the baby. It is as unhampered as the infant by moral scruples, or by consideration for others, and it is as incapable as the infant of seeing things in proportion, or of weighing present against future satisfaction. To quote Ernest Jones, the main attribute of the subconscious mind is "a never-ceasing demand for immediate gratification of various desires of a distinctly lowly order, and literally at any cost."[1] The word "literally" here is (for once) to be taken literally. A person's subconscious mind will pay any price, either in his own suffering or in that of others, for immediate instinctive satisfaction.

It is unnecessary to be shocked by this fact. The ruthlessness of the subconscious, like that of the young child, is due to incomprehension rather than wickedness. For example· a small boy lived a few miles outside a large town, which was often visited by bombers during the Second World War. Air-raids to him were a thrilling and delightful spectacle, and, when they became less frequent, his disappointment was great. No reasonable person would be shocked by this attitude. Air-raids meant death and mutilation and bereavement, but this was a fact that the child was too young to grasp. He might know it intellectually, but emotionally it meant nothing to him. Just the same naïve ruthlessness is to be found in the unconscious mind, for which nothing that is not directly conducive to the prompt satisfaction of instinct has interest or meaning.

The subconscious mind is not only amoral; it is also supremely irrational. It has no more idea than the baby of

[1] *Papers on Psycho-Analysis* (1923), p. 3.

counting the cost of anything it wants, and it will purchase immediate satisfaction with its own suffering almost as readily as with that of others. Its attitude towards pain resembles that of the savage, to whom loss of "face" is far more abhorrent than physical suffering. This helps to explain a fact that is sometimes found puzzling: namely, that conversion hysteria so often takes physically painful forms. One would expect, for example, that where illness is due primarily to the desire to evade an unwelcome responsibility, the victim would select some complaint (such as a mild degree of heart-strain) which gives the minimum of pain and discomfort. And this does sometimes happen; but neurotics in the situation described also frequently suffer from asthma, neuralgia, stomach cramps, migraine, or other conditions far more painful and incapacitating than the unconscious goal of their illness requires.

Ego, Superego, and Id

In his earlier formulations, Freud, to whom most of our knowledge of the subconscious mind is due, regarded the mind as divided into two main levels, the conscious and the unconscious; and he regarded the censor, or repressing forces, as part of the conscious mind. For the sake of simplicity, this point of view has been tacitly assumed in the preceding chapters. But as Freud's clinical work continued, it became clear that his original formulation was too simple. If all the repressing forces were part of the conscious mind, they would presumably be under conscious control, and once a patient had been enlightened about the evils of repression, he would be able to cease repressing, and to bring buried memories and feelings back into consciousness, by an act of will. But in fact he could seldom do anything of the kind. He had no more control over many of the repressing forces than over the tendencies that had been repressed.

It also became evident that the morality of the censor was more childish and less enlightened than that of the conscious mind. When, by various techniques, a repressed impulse had been brought back into consciousness, it often turned out to be shocking only by nursery standards: in the conscious mind of the adult it evoked no disapproval whatever.

These facts led Freud to revise his original dualism of conscious and unconscious. He now postulated a threefold division, into elements which he called the Ego, the Superego, and the Id. The Ego is the conscious mind—the civilised, rational layer, which is the only part of which we normally have much knowledge. The Id is infantile, amoral, non-rational, and almost wholly unconscious. The new character in the drama is the Superego. Like the Id, the Superego is mainly unconscious; but, unlike the Id, it is a moralist of the most fanatical and intolerant kind. The Superego takes the place of the censor in Freud's earlier formulations. It is the Superego that is responsible for repression: and repression, it is now realised, is not always carried out in the light of civilised moral principles, but more often in the light (or darkness) of a crude and irrational morality that has been retained from the nursery.

The Superego

The Superego, in fact, like the Id, is an unconscious survival of infancy. It embodies the first crude moral notions of childhood—formed when "right" and "wrong" were, to the child, still quite arbitrary and non-rational conceptions. The young child sees no reason for the prohibitions imposed on him by adults. He learns that certain actions are called naughty, just as he learns that certain animals are called cows. And, as there are no degrees of cow-hood, so, to begin with, there are no degrees of naughtiness: a thing is either naughty or it is not. Tolerance, sense of proportion, ability to distinguish between mild and serious misdeeds—all these are later developments.

Thus the Superego is a relic of the first, pre-rational stage of moral development. But other factors are also involved in its formation. It contains a large element of what is techni-cally known as "introjected aggression." A young child inevitably has feelings of anger and aggression towards his parents when they thwart his impulses, but, when sentiments of affection have been formed towards the parents, the aggressive impulses are felt to be wrong and dangerous,[1] and are repressed. Aggression, however, is one of the most difficult impulses to control. If it cannot be expressed directly, it is often displaced—it is a commonplace that the clerk who has been "dressed down" by his employer will often vent his feelings on the office-boy. If no external outlet is available, the aggression may turn inwards on to the individual himself, and give rise to various forms of irrational self-torment. This is what happens in the case of the baby. His repressed rage and hostility are introjected, and form the basis of the self-punishing and self-thwarting tendencies, and the irrational feelings of guilt, which spoil so many lives.

The most troublesome Superegos tend to be found, not among those who have been harshly brought up, in the sense of being controlled by a strict external discipline, but among those who in childhood have been subjected to too much moral pressure. It is far better for parents to spank a child and have done with it, than to make him feel that his conduct has grieved them beyond measure, and that they no longer love him as they did. A child who feels fundamentally secure in his parents' affection suffers no harm from an occasional spanking. But the child who does not feel confident that he is loved and wanted, and who is constantly made to feel that he is falling short of his parents' standards, is the potential adult neurotic: for it is in childhood, when the Ego is weak, that the seeds of neurosis are sown.

This is an over-simplified account of an obscure and highly important topic, but limitation of space prevents a fuller treatment. The Superego may be described as a sort of unconscious conscience, whose harsh and irrational standards often conflict with the comparatively reasonable and enlightened demands of the conscious conscience, which comprises our moral sentiments. The Superego often causes us to feel

---

[1] An important fact revealed by child analysis is that young children regard their aggressive impulses as dangerous to others. At this age they do not distinguish clearly between feelings and actions, and aggressive impulses are thought to be capable of injuring the person at whom they are directed. A similar attitude is found among savages, who often believe that they can destroy or injure enemies by a strong enough effort of will.

twinges of guilt when we are doing something which our conscious conscience does not condemn—such as playing golf on Sunday, having breakfast in bed when we are not ill, or reading about the sex impulse in a textbook of biology or psychology. In extreme cases, the Superego may induce the type of fanaticism which condemns all natural pleasures, simply because they are pleasant; an attitude which is a relic of the childish feeling that what you don't like is always good for you, and what you want to do is usually wrong.

But the chief menace of the Superego to happiness lies in its power to make us feel guilty about our desires and feelings. This is quite irrational: anti-social and uncivilised impulses are part of our instinctive heritage, and it is unnecessary to feel guilty about their existence, provided that we control their expression in our behaviour, and do not allow them to dominate our conscious thought. The Id, as has already been sufficiently emphasised, is completely self-centred and ruthless. If a man due for promotion falls ill, those below him on the list will be led by their Egos to wish him a speedy recovery; but the reaction of the Id will inevitably be, "Hooray —hope he dies!" From time to time, impulses of this "Iddish" kind make a fleeting appearance in consciousness, often to the shame and horror of the person concerned. But, to quote Churton Collins, "We are no more responsible for the evil thoughts that pass through our minds than a scarecrow for the birds which fly over the seed-plot he has to guard; the sole responsibility in each case is to prevent them from settling."[1] The Superego, however, like the infant, draws little distinction between feeling and actions: both are condemned and punished with equal severity.

The conscious and civilised Ego has to attempt to mediate between conflicting claims. It has to adjust to external reality, and at the same time attempt to give a measure of satisfaction both to the Superego, with its harsh repressive morality, and to the Id, with its insatiable demands for instinctive pleasure. It is not surprising that the attempt sometimes fails, and the individual becomes neurotic.

[1] Aphorisms in *The English Review*, April, 1914.

Freudian Treatment of Neurosis

It is a cardinal point of Freud's theory that the origin of every neurotic symptom goes back to early childhood. Some immediate circumstance usually precipitates the neurosis, but the mature Ego of the adult can stand an immense amount of strain and suffering without breaking down. The conflicts which lead to breakdown are those which link up with, and revive, conflicts of early life that the childish Ego was too weak to resolve.

Thus treatment of neurosis along Freudian lines always involves disinterring from the subconscious some unresolved conflict of childhood.[1] The relief obtained in this way is often immense: for, when the true nature of the early conflict is revealed, the irrationality of the guilt-feeling it aroused often becomes obvious, and the childish terrors dissolve in the daylight of rational consciousness.

Freud's Attitude towards the Intellect

As will now be evident, Freud has never held the view so often attributed to him, that man is completely dominated by irrational and primitive instincts. Certainly we are less rational than we like to suppose. But we are not wholly irrational; and the chief aim of psychotherapy is to increase the area of rational consciousness, or, in Freud's words, to increase the power of the Ego and to decrease that of the Id and Superego. Freud would have utterly rejected the view, so enthusiastically proclaimed by some of his less balanced admirers, that the way to achieve mental health is to repudiate the claims of reason and civilisation, and to plunge into the "dark stream" of the unconscious. But on this subject we may let Freud speak for himself.

> "We may insist as much as we like that human intellect is weak in comparison with human instincts, and be right in doing so. But nevertheless there is something peculiar

---

[1] This is the orthodox Freudian treatment. But it takes a great deal of time, and is clearly not always practicable. Many neurotic conditions can be satisfactorily treated by resolving the immediate conflict, if the patient thereafter can avoid the type of situation in which he is liable to break down.

about this weakness. The voice of the intellect is a soft one, but it does not rest until it has gained a hearing. Ultimately, after endlessly repeated rebuffs, it succeeds. This is one of the few points in which we may be optimistic about the future of mankind ... The primacy of the intellect certainly lies in the far, far, but still probably not infinite, distance." [1]

NOTES ON READING

Among the best introductions to Freudian theory are Ernest Jones, *What is Psychoanalysis* (Allen and Unwin: 1949), and the articles on Psychoanalysis in the *Encyclopaedia Britannica* by Freud and others, and in *Chambers's Encyclopaedia* by Ernest Jones. There is a useful chapter on Psychoanalysis and Related Schools in R. S. Woodworth and M. R. Sheehan *Contemporary Schools of Psychology*. J. A. C. Brown, *Freud and the Post-Freudians* (Pelican Books: 1961) can also be recommended.

The student is advised to begin his reading of Freud with the selection from his writings published in the Pelican series under the title *Two Short Accounts of Psychoanalysis,* and to continue with *Introductory Lectures on Psychoanalysis* (Allen and Unwin: 1922). *New Introductory Lectures on Psychoanalysis* (Hogarth Press: 1933) is more advanced and less comprehensive, and is not suitable as an introduction to the subject.

Ernest Jones's monumental three-volume biography of Freud (Hogarth Press: 1953, 1955, 1957) is now available in shortened form in the Pelican series under the title *The Life and Work of Sigmund Freud*.

[1] *The Future of an Illusion* (1943), p. 93.

CHAPTER XX

DREAMS

Dreams have been described as "the royal road to the interpretation of the unconscious." They provide one of the commonest outlets for tendencies that are repressed or unsatisfied in waking life.

Two objections are commonly made to this statement: first, that many dreams are caused by nothing more mysterious than indigestion; and, secondly, that some dreams are unpleasant or terrifying, and so can hardly be held to satisfy impulses, whether repressed or not. The answer to the second difficulty involves an understanding of the dream mechanisms, and must be deferred until later, but the first point can be answered briefly. It is undoubtedly true that indigestion (or any other physical discomfort) can, simply by making us sleep less soundly, cause us to dream more vividly than we normally do. But it does not determine *what* we dream; and it is the content of the dream, and not the fact of dreaming, that is significant.

The Dream as Guardian of Sleep

Freud has described the dream as "the guardian of sleep." Sleep is threatened by disturbances of two kinds: outside disturbances, such as noises, and inner disturbances, such as anxiety or mental conflict. The dream often deals successfully with outside noises by weaving them into its texture. The alarm clock goes off, for example, and we dream that we are watching a house on fire, and hearing the shrill bell of the approaching fire-engine; and sometimes, if the bell is not too insistent, we may thus be able to sleep on undisturbed.

If the disturbance is of the second kind, the position is more complex. If the conflict, or frustration, is one of which we are perfectly conscious, the unsatisfied impulse often finds a simple fulfilment in a dream. The starving man will dream of a good dinner, or the separated lovers dream of reunion. Dreams of this straightforward wish-fulfilment type show clearly their affinity with day-dreams. They are particularly common among children. The child who has been forbidden to go to the circus will go there in his dreams: the child kept short of sweets will dream he has been turned loose in a confectioner's shop: the child who collects birds' eggs may dream that he has found an immense nest, containing dozens of eggs, all different and all rare.

More often, however, particularly with adults, the impulse seeking fulfilment is one that is not merely unsatisfied, but repressed. Such impulses cannot be directly expressed, even in dreams. But in dreams, as in hypnosis, the vigilance of the Superego is relaxed: and, to use Freud's metaphor, when the watchman drowses, the prisoners may slip past in disguise. The interpretation of a dream involves the progressive stripping off of these disguises, until the identity of the fugitive is revealed.

The Dream-Work

At this point some technical terms must be introduced. The *manifest content* of a dream is the series of images, visual and other, that constitute the dream as it is dreamt. The *latent content* comprises the ideas and impulses of which the dream is a disguised expression. The *dream-work* is the process by which the latent content is transformed into the manifest content. The dream-work follows certain principles, or mechanisms, of which the most important are Symbolisation, Dramatisation, Condensation and Displacement.

Symbolisation

Few of the elements in dreams can be taken at their face value; almost everything is a symbol of something else. The symbolism employed in dreaming is closely analogous to that used, for example, in political cartoons. In cartoons during the Second World War, Germany was sometimes symbolised as a wolf or a gorilla, Britain as a lion, and France as a maiden in distress. Events, also, were symbolised by historical or other familiar episodes to which they were in some way analogous: the Nazi Fifth Column by the Trojan horse, for example, or Italy's invasion of France after Germany had rendered her helpless by a jackal devouring the remains of the tiger's "kill."

Some dream-symbols are common currency. Kings and queens, for example, usually stand for the dreamer's father and mother, and small animals may represent brothers and sisters. The wide currency of certain symbols is evident from the fact that some dreams are almost universal—such as the dream of falling, the dream of flying, and the dream of appearing in public inadequately clad. As these certainly do not represent common waking experiences, their frequent appearance in dreams strongly suggests that they provide symbolic expression for impulses that are widely felt and frequently repressed.

Besides these universal symbols, everyone has also a private symbolism, which may vary from day to day, and which has meaning for him alone. This fact greatly complicates the interpretation of dreams, since it means that we cannot, so to speak, turn up the meaning of any particular symbol in a code-book. Often the meaning reveals itself only after long exploration of the dreamer's emotional state, and his past and recent history.

It may be mentioned in parenthesis that many folk-legends and fairy-tales present wish-fulfilling phantasies under a symbolism very like that of dreams. In children's stories, as in dreams, kings and queens are usually father-and-mother symbols; and the small but dauntless hero (Jack the Giant-Killer) is the child himself. The cruel stepmother, the prince in disguise, the talking animals, and other familiar features of fairy-tales, all indirectly symbolise feelings and attitudes that are common among young children.

Dramatisation

Dramatisation is allied to symbolism, in that conflicts and tensions in the mind of the dreamer are externalised and made more vivid. An attack of conscience, for example, may be represented as an attack by physical enemies, or confronting a difficulty as scaling a precipice.

The following dream, quoted by Gordon,[1] provides a good illustration of both symbolism and dramatisation. The dreamer, a young man who was over-dependent emotionally on his mother, had become interested in a young woman, and was in a state of acute indecision about proposing marriage. He dreamed that he was sitting on a high fence (itself no bad symbol of his attitude), and that the girl in whom he was interested was standing below and urging him to jump down. He made several half-hearted attempts, but always baulked at the last; then he discovered, not wholly to his regret, that it was no use jumping, because he was firmly fastened to the fence by his tiepin. The symbolic significance of the tiepin was revealed by his answer to a question by the psychiatrist, "Oh, it's a safety pin. Mother gave it to me!" Thus the dream was a clear symbolic expression of his reluctance to break away from his mother, and to renounce the comfortable sense of safety that was bound up with his life at home.

Condensation

A single dream-symbol will often stand for two or more ideas, events or persons. This mechanism again can be seen in cartoons, where (for example) the artist may convey his opinion of some prominent political figure by blending his features with those of a sheep or a bulldog. In dreams, condensation works both ways: a single symbol may stand for two or more objects, and a single object may be represented by two or more symbols. The fact that there is not, so to speak, a one-one relationship between object and symbol adds immensely to the difficulties of dream-interpretation. It means, also, that a dream may be susceptible of different interpretations, so that, if two people explain a dream differently, it does not necessarily follow that one of them is wrong; if the interpretations are not totally incompatible, both may be correct as far as they go, though neither is complete.

A good example of condensation is provided by one of Freud's own dreams, in which a professional colleague, who, in fact, was clean-shaven, was endowed in the dream with a long yellow beard which in real life belonged to Freud's uncle.

[1] *An Introduction to Psychological Medicine* (1936), p. 163.

The uncle in question was regarded by all his relations as stupid: so, by identifying him in the dream with his colleague, Freud was symbolically expressing a low opinion of the latter's intelligence.[1]

Displacement

Displacement has two different, but related, aspects, both of which serve to disguise the dream's true meaning. First, *Displacement of Affect*: the feeling that we have in real life towards one person or object may be displaced in the dream on to another. For example, we may fall asleep feeling resentful towards *A*, and dream that we are fighting or injuring *B*, towards whom in real life we feel no resentment whatever. In such cases, *A* sometimes appears in the dream in a minor rôle: he has been displaced, so to speak, from the lead, and given a walking-on part. If we ask why *B*, rather than another, should have been chosen to stand for *A*, the answer usually lies in some resemblance to *A* (often quite trivial) in appearance, manner or circumstances, or even in the sound of his name.

The second aspect is *Displacement of Emphasis*. The most important element in the manifest content of a dream is not always the most important in the latent content. Often the clue to the interpretation of a dream lies in some apparently minor or trivial incident.

Regression and Secondary Elaboration

Two further tendencies must be briefly mentioned, though they do not fall into quite the same category as the mechanisms just discussed. In dreaming, there is *regression* to childhood, in the sense that the events and characters of dreams resemble those of children's stories rather than the more prosaic happenings of adult waking life. *Secondary elaboration* occurs after waking. In the interval between dreaming a dream and relating or writing it down, the dream is usually tidied up and made more coherent and logical. For this

---

[1] See *The Interpretation of Dreams* (3rd edition, 1932), pp. 142-7. The dream, and the interpretation, involve many more factors than are here discussed.

reason, a dream recorded immediately on waking is usually much more absurd than one that is recorded some time later.

As was mentioned on p. 167, many of the dream-mechanisms can be clearly seen at work in waking life, in the transformation of our past memories, and particularly in the progressive distortion that a rumour undergoes as it passes from mouth to mouth.

Dreams as Wish-Fulfilments

Freud's statements on the dream-mechanisms are now widely accepted, but there is still considerable scepticism about other parts of his theory—in particular, his view that all dreams are wish-fulfilments, direct or disguised. This view has been criticised by Hadfield,[1] and scornfully dismissed by Eysenck.[2] It is not, however, as absurd as it appears at first sight. Freud did not say that the central element in every dream is a wish-fulfilment—that if we dream we are going to be hanged, for example, it means that we unconsciously want to be hanged. What he asserted could perhaps be better expressed by saying that every dream *contains a wish.* In his view, every dream, when fully analysed, will be found to contain some element that is a wish-fulfilment, or at least an attempted wish-fulfilment; and he maintained that this element provides the chief clue to the dream's latent content, though, through displacement of emphasis, it may play quite a minor part in the dream as dreamt.

Freud gave many convincing examples of dreams, which, though superficially unpleasant, clearly reveal themselves as wish-fulfilments when the circumstances of the dreamer are taken into account. One of these may be quoted. A young doctor newly embarked in practice had been making out his income-tax return. His income for the past year had been small—a fact that he was rather reluctant to disclose, even to the revenue authorities. That night he dreamed that an acquaintance came from a meeting of the tax-commission, and told him that, while all the other returns had passed unquestioned, the commissioners had refused to believe that the

[1] In *Dreams and Nightmares* (1954).
[2] In *Sense and Nonsense in Psychology* (1957).

doctor's income was as low as he had stated, and he was therefore to be punished with a heavy fine. Thus the dream is a thinly-disguised fulfilment of the wish to be known as a physician with a large income.[1]

Another convincing example is provided by a young man's dream that he looked in the mirror and was surprised to see that his hair, which was dark, had turned a pale straw-colour. This dream, he maintained on waking, was certainly not a wish-fulfilment, for he greatly disliked fair hair in men. The dreamer was in love with a young woman, who did not return his affection, but preferred someone else—who had straw-coloured hair. Thus the dream was a disguised expression of the dreamer's wish to put himself in the place of his rival.

The dream of the young man and the tiepin (p. 251) might also be quoted in this connection. On the surface it is hardly a pleasant dream, but when its meaning is understood, its wish-fulfilling function is obvious.[2]

Thus a strong case can be made for Freud's apparently paradoxical theory. But the question has still to be answered why, if dreams are wish-fulfilments, they are not always and wholly pleasant. To this question Freud gave various answers, none of which wholly satisfied his critics. One answer was that, when the "wish" is repressed, the fulfilment has always to be smuggled, so to speak, past the Superego, and there is no more effective way of concealing a wish-fulfilment than by including it in a dream of which the affective tone is predominantly unpleasant—as a smuggler might attempt to get brandy through the Customs in a bottle labelled "Cascara."

Another suggested answer—first expressed in a footnote added to *The Interpretation of Dreams* in 1930—was that some dreams are the work of the Superego rather than of the Id, and express a subconscious desire for self-punishment.

---

[1] *Op. cit.*, p. 161.
[2] It is noticeable in all the examples quoted that the repressed "wish," once revealed, is not shocking to the Ego. It is at most—to use an expressive phrase—a trifle shy-making. Eysenck criticises Freud's theory on this ground also, but he takes insufficient account of the fact that repression is the work of the Superego, and that the standards of the Superego are far harsher and less tolerant than those of the conscious mind.

But there would have been no need for these ingenuities if Freud had adopted what would seem to be the obvious view, that dreams sometimes express fears, repressed or conscious, as well as wishes. Freud admitted this, by implication, many times—as when he described and analysed a dream of his own, which, as he recognised, was primarily an expression of his anxiety for the safety of his son, fighting in the 1914-18 War.[1] But in discussing such cases, Freud was always mainly concerned to argue that, though the dream was based on the sleeper's anxieties, it was none the less fulfilling its function as "guardian of sleep" by disguising the anxieties under a cloak of symbolism, and by steering the sleeper's thoughts, as far as possible, away from the worst aspects of his problem in the direction of solution and reassurance. (Where this attempt fails, we get the acute anxiety-dream, which will be discussed later.) Watt,[2] arguing along similar lines later, suggested that the guiding *motif* of every dream could be expressed by the phrase "it would be all right if . . ." In the young man's dream of the fence and the tiepin, for example, the unconscious soliloquy might run somewhat as follows: "I'm more or less committed to X . . . there's no doubt she expects me to propose . . . but I don't want to decide . . . it would be all right if I didn't *have* to decide . . . if there were some reason that made it impossible for me to leave home"— and so on.

Even the familiar dream of appearing unclad in public may be interpreted as a wish-fulfilment along these lines. It is highly probable (though Freud gave a different interpretation) that this dream symbolises doing, or saying, "the wrong thing." (A friend of the writer's had an interesting variant, in which she attended a fashionable wedding in her best clothes, but carrying with her a large cabbage wrapped in newspaper.)[3] Now it seems the general experience that, though in the dream we ourselves are covered with confusion, no one else takes the least notice of our unconventional toilette. May not the

---

[1] *Op. cit.*, pp. 515-16.
[2] In *The Common Sense of Dreams* (1929).
[3] A convinced Freudian would no doubt find further symbolic significance in the cabbage.

dream, then, be a symbolic way of saying, "That was a shocking *faux-pas* I made to-day. But it would be all right if nobody noticed"?

Again, many people who have been to a University dream periodically that they have to sit their final examination again. Freud asserted (though perhaps on inadequate evidence) that this dream is experienced only by those who, in fact, passed their examination. It is thus a symbolic way of saying, "I feel very anxious about this coming ordeal. But I was anxious about the examination too, and I passed that. It will be all right if this is like the examination."

The Anxiety-Dream

In some cases, however, the mechanisms fail. The waking anxieties, repressed or conscious, are too strong and insistent for the dream-work to deal with them, and they force their way into the sleeper's thoughts and produce an acute anxiety-dream, or nightmare, from which he usually wakens in a panic. To call dreams of this type wish-fulfilments (as Freud insisted on doing)[1] is to strain language to breaking-point; but they may at least be described as attempted wish-fulfilments, in which the dream has done its best, but failed.

NOTES ON READING

A section of the *Introductory Lectures on Psychoanalysis* is devoted to dream-interpretation, but Freud's *magnum opus* on this subject is *The Interpretation of Dreams* (Allen and Unwin: 3rd revised ed., 1937). *On Dreams* (Hogarth Press: 1952) is a resumé of this book for the general reader, originally written by Freud a year after the publication of the larger work.

J. A. Hadfield, *Dreams and Nightmares* (Pelican Books: 1954), is a valuable exposition and discussion, written from a theoretical standpoint somewhat different from Freud's.

[1] Freud put forward two alternative explanations of anxiety-dreams. The first is approximately as stated above. The second is, that anxiety-dreams occur when some repressed wish is on the point of gaining undisguised expression, and the Superego, unable at this stage to change the course of the dream, "sounds the alarm" and wakes the sleeper. Many besides the writers find this part of Freud's theory unplausible.

CHAPTER XXI

APPLIED PSYCHOLOGY

Psychologists are concerned, not only to extend psychological knowledge, but also to apply this knowledge to the practical problems of life. As in most other sciences, pure and applied psychology reinforce one another. Sometimes a discovery that results from pure research has a direct bearing on the solution of some practical problem, and sometimes an attack on a practical problem yields a discovery that enriches psychological theory. Thus research into the nature and distribution of human abilities contributed to the development of mental tests, which are now profitably employed for many purposes; and conversely, the use of mental tests for these practical purposes (especially for personnel selection in the Services in the Second World War) has contributed to our knowledge of the nature and distribution of human abilities. Here, as in many other fields, there has been a relation of mutual improvement between theory and practice.

The field for applied psychology is extensive. In domestic, occupational and social life,—indeed, wherever human relationships are concerned—a knowledge of the springs of human action, and of the conditions of mental health, can be of practical value. Apart from these general applications, however, there are three clearly-defined branches of applied psychology, namely (i) educational psychology, (ii) medical psychology, and (iii) occupational (or, as it is often called, industrial) psychology.

Educational Psychology

The task of educational psychology is to conduct research in the educational field, and to provide teachers, and all concerned in education, with the psychological knowledge that is relevant to their work. The main subdivisions of educational psychology comprise: (i) Study of the nature and growth of human abilities, and of the means by which individual differences may be assessed. Information about the intellectual, temperamental and physical differences among children is of the utmost importance, both to teachers and to educational administrators engaged in planning the organisation of schools and curricula. Such knowledge is now the more necessary since it has become a statutory duty to provide every child with the type of education suited to his "age, ability, and aptitude." (ii) The physiological factors that affect educability. Since a pupil's thought and behaviour, in school as elsewhere, are affected by the sensory, neural, motor, and endocrinological processes going on in his body, it is useful for teachers to have some knowledge of physiological psychology, and particularly of the ways in which the development of intellect and character is helped and hindered by physiological conditions. (iii) The factors that influence attention, learning, memory, reasoning, creative thought and sensibility. Teachers should know how attention may be most readily caught and retained; how learning may be facilitated; how memory may be improved; how reasoning and constructive thought may be stimulated and trained; and how taste may be developed. They should also know something of the special psychological factors involved in the teaching and learning of reading, spelling, handwriting, arithmetic, and other special school subjects. (iv) The factors, conscious and unconscious, which underlie the growth and formation of personality and character. (v) The nature, causes, and treatment of the intellectual, emotional, and behavioural defects and disorders by which some children are handicapped. Teachers, of course, are not expected to be psychotherapists in any technical sense, but they should have some knowledge and understanding of handicapped and "difficult" children, of the causes to which their difficulties are due, and of the ways in which these difficulties should be treated, or, better still, prevented.

Moreover, as is made plain in the section on Clinical Psychology, many educational psychologists are employed in the child guidance service. The function of child guidance centres and clinics is to provide appropriate special treatment for handicapped backward or maladjusted children —children who present some disorder or defect of thought or behaviour which unaided common sense cannot explain and the normal methods of correction cannot remove.

Clearly, educational psychology covers a large field, and it is therefore not surprising that, in addition to comprehensive textbooks on the whole subject, there is a steady stream of books and articles on one or other of its particular aspects. Thus there are books and articles that deal with the pre-school child, or the adolescent, or the backward child, or the problem child; and others that deal with attention, or learning, or mental tests, or children's emotional and social development, or some other special topic. All this literature bears witness to widespread and vigorous activity in conducting investigations in the educational field, and in applying psychological findings to educational problems.

Clinical Psychology

Clinical psychologists are employed in child guidance centres or clinics, mental hospitals, psychiatric clinics, neurosis units, rehabilitation units, general hospitals, and other institutions concerned with the diagnosis and treatment of mentally ill or mentally handicapped persons. Many of those employed in child guidance centres or clinics are employed by Local Education Authorities, and are sometimes classified as educational psychologists. Nearly all the other clinical psychologists are employed in the National Health Service, although a few are on the staffs of Universities or of such bodies as the Medical Research Council.

Often clinical psychologists work under the direction of psychiatrists. At other times—especially in child guidance services provided by Local Education Authorities in Scotland —the position of the psychiatrist is that of a consultant, to whom (as to the speech therapist) only some of the children being treated by the clinical psychologists are referred.

A few clinical psychologists devote their whole time to research, and many who are not full-time research workers are often called on to help in the design and carrying-out of investigations in the clinical field. But the great majority of clinical psychologists spend most of their time in direct contact with patients, either children or adults, and their main activities are those of diagnosis, assessment, treatment,[1] and rehabilitation. In diagnosis and assessment, they employ tests, questionnaires, projective techniques, and other means of assessing a patient's intellect and personality. In treatment, even when they are not carrying it out themselves but are assisting a psychiatrist, they provide objective appraisals of the changes taking place during the course of treatment, and, in their interviews with patients, they help them to gain a better understanding of themselves and of their capacities and limitations. Similarly, in the rehabilitation of patients, whether mentally or physically handicapped, they are able to help by recommending occupations which will make the most of the patient's capacities, and the least demand on his intellectual or emotional weaknesses.

Clinical psychologists also often take part in courses on psychology for medical and other University students, and in courses on aspects of clinical psychology relevant to the work of the medical and nursing staffs of hospitals.

Medical Psychology

The medical psychologist, or psychiatrist, or specialist in psychological medicine, is a doctor concerned with the diagnosis and treatment of mental illness. At first, medical psychologists tended to confine their attention to the psychoses —the various forms of insanity. Now, however, they devote more of their efforts to the psychoneuroses—the various illnesses, due to psychological causes, that arise in people who are in no sense insane.

Psychoneurotic illness, which is often called simply "neurosis," is more common than is usually supposed. Investigation of over 3,000 industrial workers in thirteen factories showed that, in the previous six months, 10 per cent. had suffered from definite and disabling neurotic illness, and

[1] The part played in treatment varies considerably from one clinic to another. In some cases—particularly, as has been said, in child guidance services provided by Education Authorities in Scotland—clinical psychologists are themselves responsible for the treatment that the service provides. In other cases the treatment they give is under the general direction of a psychiatrist, while in others they play no direct part in treatment, but are concerned only with diagnosis, assessment, and/or rehabilitation.

a further 20 per cent. from minor forms of neurosis.[1] Twenty-five years ago, people suffering from some form of neurotic illness were reluctant to seek advice, since they felt that by so doing they would proclaim themselves weak-willed or even mad. Recently, however, and especially since the Second World War, when medical psychology achieved striking results in the treatment of psychoneurotic casualties, there has been a change of attitude. To-day, many general hospitals have psychiatric wards, and the "trick-cyclist," to use the army nickname, has become a comparatively familiar figure.

Like other medical men, psychiatrists are becoming increasingly interested in the prevention, as well as the cure, of illness. More and more, their researches, like those of clinical psychologists, are being directed to the discovery and maintenance of the conditions that conduce to mental health.

Occupational Psychology

The occupational psychologist—or the industrial psychologist, as he used more often to be called—is concerned with the application of psychological facts and principles to the practical problems of occupational life, especially those that arise in industry. The problems with which he deals fall under three main heads: (i) vocational psychology—ensuring that, so far as possible, individuals are engaged in work for which they are suited by temperament and capacity, (ii) the improvement of conditions and methods of work, and (iii) market research and advertising.

The vocational psychologist has a double task; that of choosing the right job for a particular man (vocational guidance), and the right man for a particular job (vocational selection). In vocational guidance, the psychologist examines the individual and recommends the types of work in which he is most likely to be successful and happy. In vocational selection, the psychologist studies a particular occupation and devises a selection procedure which will ensure that the most suitable applicants are engaged. In Great Britain, the National Institute of Industrial Psychology has for many

[1] See Russell Fraser, "The Incidence of Neurosis among Factory Workers," *Industr. Health Res. Bd. Report*, No. 90, 1947.

years been concerned with vocational psychology. Individuals seeking advice on the choice of a career can consult the Institute in the same way as they consult a medical specialist; and industrial and commercial firms who wish to improve their methods of selecting workers can call in the Institute to devise a suitable selection procedure. For occupations above the unskilled manual level, this procedure usually involves taking account of the applicant's intelligence, special aptitudes, attainments, interests, temperamental traits and physical condition, and assessing these various factors by tests, by study of the applicant's previous experience and history, and by a planned and skilful interview. Once the selection procedure has been established, it can often be applied by personnel managers or other members of the firm's staff; but in some cases the psychologist has not only to devise the selection procedure, but to co-operate in carrying it out. Always, of course, it is necessary to know, not only what qualities an applicant possesses, but also what qualities are demanded by the post for which he is being considered. The aim of the psychological technique in vocational selection is to present a picture of each applicant in the round, showing his merits and defects in relation to the work that he wishes to do. In the Second World War, the procedures employed by the Army, Navy and Air Force in selecting recruits were based largely on the experience of the National Institute of Industrial Psychology. Since then, procedures making use of the psychological technique have been adopted by the Civil Service Commission for the selection of applicants for its various branches. They have also been adopted by many industrial and other organisations, and by some of the special agencies which undertake the selection of managers (or of other employees) for industrial clients.

In connection with conditions and methods of work, the psychologist is concerned, first, with the effect of environmental conditions on mental and physical efficiency, and he studies, among other things, the different kinds of lighting and ventilation that are required in different kinds of work. This activity now occupies less of the occupational psychologist's time than it did, because architects and lighting and ventilating engineers, under the influence of occupational psychology, are now devoting much more attention to these factors. Secondly, he investigates the best way of doing various jobs—the movements that save unnecessary effort and secure the maximal result in chocolate-packing, lathe-turning, or whatever it may be. This involves the lay-out of workshops and offices, and the supply of materials and arrangement of work, which must be such as to promote an easy, direct and uninterrupted flow of production; it also involves the design of tools, machines and instrument-panels, which are not always adapted to the psychophysical characteristics of the human beings who have to use them; and it includes the training of the workers in the methods that systematic study shows to be best for their various tasks. This study, which was initiated by occupational psychologists some fifty years ago, is now commonly called "methods study" or "work study," and the present emphasis on productivity has led to its becoming a prominent and rapidly developing branch of industrial activity. Thirdly, the psychologist can give useful advice, based on factual investigations, about the optimal working hours in different types of occupation, and the best distribution of periods of work and rest. Fourthly, he is concerned with the psychological factors in industrial sickness and accidents. Fifthly, he addresses himself to the motives and social relations that have such an important effect on satisfaction and efficiency at work. This is not merely a matter of financial incentives, vital though these are in all kinds of employment. It includes, too, what it is now customary to call "human relations"—the factors that make for good relations between managers (including foremen) and workers, among the workers themselves, and among the managers, who, of course, have to co-operate not only with one another but with the various specialists, who are becoming more numerous every year. The study of human relations in industry is now occupying much more of the occupational psychologist's time and attention than it did. More employers now recognise the bearing of good human relations on work; more, too, now regard industry as owing a duty to the producers as well as the consumers of its products—the duty of giving them, as far as possible, the satisfactions at work that human beings need; and there is now more ascertained knowledge about these satisfactions and about the foundations on which good human relations rest.

The problems of distribution with which the psychologist is concerned are advertising and market research. In advertising, he lays bare the psychological factors that cause an advertisement to catch attention and to secure a favourable response. In market research, he deals with the various techniques—opinion-surveys, attitude-surveys, behaviour-studies, etc.—whereby the beliefs, preferences, motives and behaviour of consumers may be assessed. It was from market research that the systematic study of public opinion in general originally developed. Surveys of opinions and attitudes on political and social questions were first developed by psychologists—such as Dr. Gallup, who was formerly engaged in investigating public preferences regarding newspaper and magazine features. Such sampling surveys of public opinion represent one of the most important recent developments in applied psychology, since they make it possible to obtain, with a minimum of expense and disorganisation, information which nothing but a national plebiscite could previously have supplied. For keeping a democratic Government in touch with the changing views and feelings of the electorate, such surveys are indispensable.

Psychology, like all other sciences, can be misapplied—as in the disturbingly successful techniques of "brain-washing" and political and religious indoctrination. But, rightly used, psychology can make an immense contribution to human happiness: and for this reason, applied psychology is justly regarded as one of the most important of the social sciences.

NOTES ON READING

A general survey of the field of Applied Psychology is given in H. J. Eysenck, *Uses and Abuses of Psychology*. In Educational Psychology, two outstanding textbooks are R. Lovell, *Educational Psychology and Children* (Univ. of London Press: 1958), and Lee J. Cronbach, *Educational*

Psychology (New York, Harcourt Brace: 2nd ed., 1963). In Medical Psychology, D. Stafford-Clark, *Psychiatry To-day* (Pelican Books: 1952) and Peter Hays, *New Horizons in Psychiatry* (Pelican Books: 1964) may be recommended. In Industrial Psychology, J. Munro Fraser, *Industrial Psychology* (Pergamon Press: 1962) gives a compact account of the field, which is described in more detail in H. C. Smith, *Psychology of Industrial Behaviour* (McGraw-Hill: 1955) and, with special reference to the social aspect, in J. A. C. Brown, *The Social Psychology of Industry* (Pelican Books: 1954).

INDEX

References in the Notes on Reading are not included in the Index.

PRINTED IN GREAT BRITAIN BY UNIVERSITY TUTORIAL PRESS LTD
FOXTON, NEAR CAMBRIDGE